PROPHETIC BOOT CAMP

Book 4 – The Prophetic Field Guide Series

Second Edition

COLETTE TOACH

www.ami-bookshop.com

Prophetic Boot Camp
Book 4 – Prophetic Field Guide Series
Second Edition

ISBN-10: 1626640076
ISBN-13: 978-1-62664-007-8

Copyright © 2016 by Apostolic Movement International, LLC
All rights reserved
5663 Balboa Ave #416,
San Diego,
California 92111,
United States of America

1st Printing August 2015
2nd Edition April 2016

Published by **Apostolic Movement International, LLC**
E-mail Address: admin@ami-bookshop.com
Web Address: www.ami-bookshop.com

All rights reserved under International Copyright Law.
Contents may not be reproduced in whole or in part in any form without the express written consent of the publisher.

Unless specified, all Scripture references taken from the New King James Version®. Copyright © 1982 by Thomas Nelson. Used by permission. All rights reserved.

Contents

Chapter 01 – Prophetic Preparation 10
    Defining Prophetic Preparation..............................10
    Childhood 12
    Adolescence 14
    Adulthood...17
    Understanding Prophetic Preparation 19

Chapter 02 – The Death Process 24
    The Purpose of the Fire 26
    The Three Crosses – A Prophetic Death 28
    The Death Process..30
    1. Death Process Begins in the Soul 32
    2. Death Process and the Body...............................43
    Not Destroyed… 50

Chapter 03 – Die Already: Your Secret Passage Through the Cross..54
    The Road to the Cross 55
    The Leg Breaking Experience.................................58
    What Death to the Flesh Feels Like 63

Chapter 04 – Templates and Triggers in the Training Process 68
    Templates, Templates Everywhere!.......................71
    My Hiding Place 74
    Sinful Templates 78

Chapter 05 – How Templates are Exposed 82
   Pressure Causing You to "Erupt" 83
   Identifying Triggers 84
   Transforming Templates: Step by Step 87
   Why the Lord Does It 91

Chapter 06 – Ministering Inner Healing 98
   Inner Healing is a Five Step Process 99
   Step 1 – Wait for Them to Ask for Help 101
   Step 2 – Identifying the Source 103
   Step 3 – Dealing With Sin 112
   Step 4 – Speaking Healing 116
   Step 5 - Counsel 117
   Conclusion 118

Chapter 07 – Resurrection is a Choice 122
   Victory Over Death 122
   Resurrection is a Choice 122
   Strength of Sin is the Law 126
   When Do You Resurrect? 131
   Flesh Dies, Spirit Moves In 132
   How Do You Resurrect? 134
   Arise and Use Your Weapons! 135
   Don't Just Resurrect - Do More 138
   Resurrection is a Choice 140
   It is in the Mind 144

- Go Heal My People 149
- Chapter 08 – The Categories of the Prophet 156
  - Category 1: Sons of the Prophets 161
  - Category 2: Elisha – The Leader of Prophets 166
  - Category 3: Elijah – Appointer of Kings. Trainer of Prophets 171
  - Understanding the Transition 176
  - Moving Through the Categories 177
  - Determine Your Place 178
- Chapter 09 – Prophetic Training Phase 1: Cherith 182
  - Prophetic Training – Elijah's Story 182
  - Your Next Season 185
  - Making the Transition 185
  - Clear Signs of Cherith: 202
- Chapter 10 – Prophetic Training Phase 2: Zarephath 204
  - Welcome to Zarephath 205
  - Why Zarephath is Needed 207
  - Transition Into Zarephath 209
  - Signs that This Phase is Ending 222
  - Clear Signs of Zarephath: 224
- Chapter 11 – Prophetic Training Phase 3: Carmel 226
  - 1. Resurrection of a Vision 227
  - 2. Ministry Opportunities Open Up 229
  - The Purpose of Training 231

- 3. You Face the Final Test 231
- 4. Placed in Prophetic Office 234
- Becoming Like a Hot Coal 236
- Clear Signs of Carmel: 237
- Prophetic Training Pointers 238
- Recapping Preparation vs. Training 240
- Training is Easier With a Mentor 242
- Assessing Where You Are At 244
- Jesus – The Reflection in the Mirror 244

Chapter 12 – The Training of Elisha 248
- How Elisha's Training Differs 249
- There is No Such Thing as a Perfect Mentor 251
- What You Should Look for in a Mentor 253
- Do Not Overlook This Benefit 256

Chapter 13 – Mentorship: The Double Portion 270
- The Signs That You Are Ready 274
- Mentorship Guidelines 101 278
- Step Into the Clearing… 281

About the Author 283

Recommendations by the Author 285
- Prophetic Warfare 285
- Prophetic Counter Insurgence 286
- I'm Not Crazy - I'm a Prophet 286
- Prophetic Anointing 287

The Way of Dreams & Visions Book with Symbol Dictionary Kit 287

A.M.I. Prophetic School 288

Contact Information 289

Chapter 01

Prophetic Preparation

Chapter 01 – Prophetic Preparation

> *Galatians 1:14 And I advanced in Judaism beyond many of my contemporaries in my own nation, being more exceedingly zealous for the traditions of my fathers.*
> *15 But when it pleased God, who separated me from my mother's womb and called me through His grace,*

Every step that you have taken in life, has brought you to the place where you stand today. Perhaps you have considered the roads that you have travelled, a random series of events. Circumstances filled with personal decisions, interruptions and rivers of events that carried you against your will.

The truth is, regardless of the roads you have traveled, this passage has followed you since the day you were conceived in your mother's womb:

> *Romans 8:28 And we know that all things work together for good to those who love God, to those who are the called according to His purpose.*

Defining Prophetic Preparation

There is a reason why you have always been so different from everyone else. From the time you were born and made your first step into the world, you were likely the child that stepped amiss, and found themselves flat on their face.

You did not fail because of lack of trying. In fact, you are one that was passionate about trying! You put your heart into what came your way, but still managed to step amiss!

Today, you are going to be brought to a new realization - one that will guide you through the various valleys of your life to pinpoint how the Lord has been gearing you for something great, all your life. The scraped knees, endless tears, and misunderstandings are about to come into focus as you realize that you are not crazy. Rather, you have simply been in the throes of prophetic preparation.

Imagine if you will, a baby with a prophetic call being born into this world. A baby that is innocent and unaware that one day he would carry the mantle of the most High God. I am reminded of John the Baptist, and wonder to myself if he could feel the buzz around his birth.

From the name God gave him, to the entire circumstance surrounding his birth, there was no doubt that this child was different. Even his relatives said, "What manner of child is this… ?" He was destined to live a life that did not mirror those around him.

Instead of waxing strong in the arms of those he cared for, his days were found in the wilderness. It was here that he discovered who he was, and came to understand the purpose that was placed on his life.

In the same way, from the time you were born, your calling was announced in the spirit. In your case though, it was not just your immediate family that started to notice the difference. The enemy also heard the call, and he sought, from that day, to try and deter you from it.

It is almost ironic that the Lord used everything that the enemy threw at you to bring you to this point today! No matter how many hard times the enemy brought your way, the Lord managed to direct your path.

> **KEY PRINCIPLE**
> The truth is, you have been conditioned for this call from birth. It started from as far back as you can remember!

CHILDHOOD

The preparation for your call started right from childhood. The prophet is one that lives in a fantasy world. I was no different. I escaped to my "alternate reality" to try to avoid the pressures that were put on me through life.

Growing up poor, rejection from my peers stung and ingrained in me a strong poverty mentality. I always felt inferior and insecure. When I did finally open my mouth to say something, I, more often than not, said the wrong thing and that just invited more rejection.

I felt very much like the ugly duckling that all the "prettier" ducks made fun of. So I did what anyone would do... I pretended. I tried to hide my poverty. I tried to be something I was not - all along wondering why God made me this way.

I struggled with Him, and wondered what I had done to be born into my family. As if the pressures could not get any worse, I was the pastor's daughter. Pressure, poverty, and a double portion of "always putting my foot in it," did not make me popular.

THE PROPHETIC CHILD

So the prophetic child is one that hides into their fantasy world. I hid my nose in book after book that took me to far off places. I lay on the grass, stared into the sky, and imagined a life that was anything but the one I had.

Today, I thank the Lord for the rejection I faced back then. It positioned me! It took me by the hand and led me that much closer to the realm of the spirit. Only later, would I learn how essential thinking in pictures was for a prophet. Right there in my childhood, the Lord was beginning to shape my character.

He was forging something in me that I would need later on.

Adolescence

As if being a prophetic child is agony enough, adolescence comes on you with its own share of pressures. Every teenager faces the pressure of rejection from peers. For the prophet, this is even truer. You struggle to just be normal and fit into what everyone else thinks.

There is just a little problem with that. You see things in black and white. No matter how hard you tried to adapt and "blend in," you stood out like a very black speck on a very white wall. While everyone went in one direction, you went in the other.

Everyone was trying to march in time, and you were the one tripping up the entire squadron! It's not like you intended to be that way. You did not intend to open your mouth and say exactly what you thought.

You did not intend to bring offense. If you were naïve, do not feel bad, because I think I outranked you on that one! I really thought that people would appreciate it so much if I told them what their problems were.

I figured that if I could point out why they kept experiencing hard times in life, they would clamor for my wisdom. I am pretty sure that you know where I am going with this. It turns out that people did not want to hear what their problems were! They certainly did not want to hear that it was their fault that they kept failing in life.

I did not get it. Why did the Lord open my eyes to see everything that was wrong, only to feel like my mouth was kept shut when I tried to express it? I felt like I was living the saying, "You are damned if you do, and damned if you don't." I felt like there was no answer for making friends.

There were certainly none that understood me, and when I finally found one, either they found a better friend, or I ended up offending them. I was not exactly a catch.

From there, romantic relationships took the focus of my life. I thought to myself, "Finally! Perhaps I can find someone who will love me as I am."

Rejection. Disappointment. More bad experiences. You would not be the first prophet to experience abuse and rejection in your relationships. To be used and thrown out. It leaves you asking yourself, "What is wrong with me? Why can't I find someone that loves me?"

THE GENTLE CALL TO JESUS

It is in this moment, that you feel the drawing of the Lord Jesus. While other arms pushed you away, you found His tender touch as a blanket surrounding you. At times, you did not understand. In hindsight, you see how much the Lord was running after you. You see how He protected you even when you did not realize it.

Yet it was because of the deep yearning inside your heart, that you drew closer to Jesus. You hungered for the unconditional love that He had for you. You craved the healing that He held in the palm of His hand. More than anything, you sought after a place of rest where you could put aside your striving, and your need to perform.

ALL THINGS WORK FOR GOOD

Child of God, don't you realize that in your deepest rejection, Jesus was calling you unto Himself? In all of this, He was preparing you for the call on your life. He was giving you a heart of compassion.

How could you ever identify with those that are bruised, if you had never taken that beating? How could you ever identify with the broken-hearted, if you had not had your own cut in two?

Yes, many times it was the hand of the enemy bringing these circumstances against you, but in each one, Jesus stepped in and pulled you out.

Haven't you ever asked yourself why others who faced what you did, turned to the things of the world, but you turned to Jesus? You look at brothers, sisters, parents and those around you, and you say, "They have so much more than me. Why don't they have the same fire for God that I do?"

It is because God called you from your mother's womb! I love what Paul says in 1 Galatians 1:15, "... and called [me] by his grace."

> **KEY PRINCIPLE**
>
> You are different because God called you by His grace. He put you in the family He did, and allowed you to face the situations you did, to create in you the very character of a prophet!

You are different because God called you by His grace. He put you in the family He did, and allowed you to face the situations you did, to create in you the very character of a prophet!

You would have learned in the *Prophetic Essentials* book what a prophet looks like. Consider that no matter where you go in the world, we all have the same heart. It is the grace given to us! The very grace that led us through each circumstance, drew out of us the nature we needed to serve the Lord in this manner.

ADULTHOOD

As you emerged into adulthood, your character was just about formed and you carried with you baggage that was both good and bad. Regardless of what you did though, rejection seemed to follow. You took your passion with you into the church. Surely there, you would finally find your place.

Perhaps it is there that others would identify with your fire for God. To be fair, it is likely that you charred a few well-meaning pastors along the way. However, you even found rejection there. You were either too loud or too soft.

You were too abrasive, or you were not a "team player." From church, to the workplace, to your personal relationships, rejection followed.

There was only one thing that remained constant in your life – the presence of the Lord Jesus. Sure, you had your moments of running away. There were times when the heat was so much you tried to escape it. Each time though, you felt like Jeremiah who said,

> *Jeremiah 20: Then I said, "I will not make mention of Him, nor speak anymore in His name.* ***But His word was in my heart like a burning fire shut up in my bones…"***

This grace continued to work in you. It put you in place. It led you into circumstances you would never have gone willingly. With each situation you faced though, the Holy Spirit was always at work. He was preparing you. He was giving you a heart to love, a mind to understand, and a spirit that was broken.

It is only when you grasp this concept will you appreciate the treasure that the Lord Jesus has forged in you. It is in the ashes of your life that the Church will find its beauty.

Rejection and humiliation followed you just like it followed Christ. Once you grasp the truth that you were meant to be set apart, you are ready to begin your training.

UNDERSTANDING PROPHETIC PREPARATION

However, before your prophetic boot camp can begin, you must get prepared. The preparation of the prophet separates him unto God. It forges certain character traits inside of you that you will need later on.

It gives you a heart for the broken. It gives you compassion for the needy. You cannot live in poverty and not be moved by someone who has no food or clothing.

You cannot live through abuse and rejection without your heart going out to someone who is scorned. The Lord forged in you, the heart of a protector and a healer. That is why you are different.

You were always different. You will always be different. This is not a hindrance in your life - this is what defines you!

And so prophetic preparation positions you. Later on in the book, I am going to lay it out very clearly how this falls into line with the various stages of training that you will also go through.

> **KEY PRINCIPLE**
>
> Prophetic preparation is also the longest part of your journey. It is what "puts you into place" so that the Lord can begin using you.

In my experience, it can take anywhere up to 40 years for you to finally "get it" and to surrender to the Lord's will on your life. Fortunately, John the Baptist did not take that long – and you do not need to take that long either.

All you need to do is… surrender.

PROPHETIC PREPARATION – THE WILDERNESS

So before you even start operating in your ministry, the Holy Spirit will send you off to the wilderness, just like He did with John the Baptist.

It is here that you will learn to buffet your flesh. You will come to terms with what you are, and what you are not. You will also finally embrace this calling on your life.

In fact, until you come to peace about your past and your present, there is no future in ministry for you. While you continue to fight the hand of God, and complain about all the hills you have had to climb, you will never move forward.

Preparation puts the kind of pressure on you, that brings you to a point of readiness – a point where you can say, "Speak Lord, your servant is listening."

CHAPTER 02

THE DEATH PROCESS

Chapter 02 – The Death Process

> *Galatians 2:20 I have been crucified with Christ; it is no longer I who live, but Christ lives in me; and the life which I now live in the flesh I live by faith in the Son of God, who loved me and gave Himself for me.*

I had no idea just how heavy a bar of gold was! My family and I attended a gold refining workshop in South Africa where they explained and demonstrated the process for us. Time and time again the same gold was put into a scalding hot furnace.

The furnace was so hot that the workers had to wear protective clothing from head to toe. Just watching them reminded me of the story of the Hebrew children who were put into the furnace for not bowing down to the idol.

When you looked into the furnace, everything glowed. The gold, as well as its container and the instruments that were used, all shone with the intense heat. It was fascinating to learn that this was not a one-time process either. Before the refining could even begin, the gold that was taken from the earth, had to be crushed.

From there it was melted in the heat. A chemical is added to help the separation process along. As I watched, I understood Peter very well in this famous scripture:

> *1 Peter 1:6 In this you greatly rejoice, though now for a little while, if need be, you have been grieved by various trials,*
> *7 that the genuineness of your faith, being much more precious than gold that perishes, though it is tested by fire, may be found to praise, honor, and glory at the revelation of Jesus Christ:*

It would interest you to know that not all gold is created equal! In fact, depending on how pure the gold needs to be, determines how many times it must be melted and refined. Peter, more than anyone, understood this process well.

He expressed how the temptations and pressures that come at us from the world is the fire that tries us. We often overlook this essential little piece of information. When you, as a prophet, are going through trials, you often think that God is doing this to you.

Sure enough, God has led you to this place of being tested, but it is not God that does the testing. It is the pressure of the world, and the pressure of those coming on you from without, that will bring the most heat into your life.

Perhaps it is because we think that we are so good at hearing God that He has to allow us to face pressures from the world around us. How often do you say to the Lord, "Lord I will do whatever you ask," only to leave that time of prayer and get into a conflict with someone?

In that moment, the fire comes on you. Instead of submitting to that fire, you say to the person instead, "Hey! What do you think you are doing? I am not going to stand here and take this fire!"

So as you embrace the call on your life, you stand in the ranks of those that have gone before you - men and women of God, who all lined up for a turn in the fire. It is only when you learn to identify and then submit to it though, that the gold can shine!

THE PURPOSE OF THE FIRE

Make no mistake – there is gold of great quality inside of you. The Word tells us that we have this treasure in earthen vessels. Unfortunately though, those earthen vessels have a habit of hindering the gold from shining.

> **KEY PRINCIPLE**
>
> Although you have faced preparation that has led you to this point, there is a lot more that you have picked up along the way that is hindering your gold from shining.

And so the Lord starts the crushing process, preparing you for the separation of flesh and spirit.

It is this sorting process that equips you for the prophetic calling on your life. So – congratulations! You finally got to the point where you have accepted the call of God on your life. Now the journey really begins!

Now the Lord will begin to strip from you the things that do not reflect the image of Christ. In years to come, you will be used of God to heal, change, equip and unify the church. Each time you stand up to be used, it is the gold of your faith that they should see, and not the dross that besets you along each step of your road.

THE REFINING PROCESS

This is a good place to mention that every believer is called to this process. We should all reflect the image of Christ. I share in *The Crucified Life* that every believer is called to walk in victory, by laying down their lives for Christ.

Each one of us is called upon to identify with the crucifixion of Christ, as well as His resurrection. I would daresay that this is what you began to learn in your preparation process. You began to learn that your life is not your own. You have come to realize that it is only when you surrender, and let God have His way that you start to experience real life!

This is only the start for the prophet though. The believer is called to yield the old man up to the cross. As a prophet, both old and new must be surrendered to Christ.

You may have learned in preparation that you need to give up "all things unrighteous," but you are about to learn that as a prophet, God will ask even the righteous aspects of your character to be brought to the cross!

THE THREE CROSSES – A PROPHETIC DEATH

We look at Golgotha and what do we see there? We see three crosses standing up for all to see: a thief who was repentant, a thief who was unrepentant, and then finally we have Jesus who had no sin at all.

This is what the price of your calling looks like. God will call the sinner in you that is unrepentant to the cross. He will call the sinner in you that is repentant to the cross. He will call the righteousness in you to the cross as well.

Why the need for such intensity? What is wrong with the righteous aspects of your character? Do you remember what you learned in the *Prophetic Anointing* book? There I taught you that because you are called, you also receive the anointing. I taught you that the problem was not with the anointing, but rather the vessel you are. To walk in greater power, you needed to become a greater vessel.

In other words, you needed to become a vessel of honor! To become such a vessel is going to require change. There are parts of your character that are hindering you from being the kind of person that walks in the anointing that God has put inside of you.

RIGHTEOUS CHARACTER TRAITS

Let us take Ezekiel for example. God asks him to cook his food over dung. Ezekiel was a righteous man. He is offended by what God told him – and so he should! It was laid out in the law very clearly how to walk in righteousness. To obey this instruction, he would have to go against the law.

Was God calling Ezekiel to give up sin in his life? Not at all, God called upon him to give up the very conviction that defined him as a man.

God said to Peter in a vision, where unclean animals are lowered on a cloth, "Peter, rise and eat!" Peter was offended. Peter was a righteous man and he said, "Lord I have never disobeyed your law!" The Lord was calling Peter to let go of his strict moral code, because He had a greater plan in play.

The Lord had to be greater than Ezekiel's conviction and Peter's righteousness. He had to be God of all. The same holds true for you. There are moral codes and ethics in your life that are not surrendered to the Lord. There are character traits that are standing in the way of you being the kind of vessel that God needs to send to a certain kind of person.

In fact, Paul had it the toughest of all. Raised as a Pharisee and perfect in every letter of the law – God sent him to the gentiles. His upbringing equipped him with a mindset to understand the Word, but it also forged in him a conviction that cut across what God wanted to do in his life. His convictions led him to persecute the church. That conviction had to come to the cross.

So on his way to Damascus, he got a good first-time experience of the cross. From there, it snowballed. He was stripped of his position and family. He was stripped of his arrogance and firm doctrinal beliefs.

In fact, he was so stripped that he tells us in the passage below that there was only one piece of gold he needed – Jesus!

> *Philippians 3:13 Brethren, I do not count myself to have apprehended; but one thing I do, forgetting those things which are behind and reaching forward to those things which are ahead.*
> *14 I press toward the goal for the prize of the upward call of God in Christ Jesus*

THE DEATH PROCESS

So what does this death process look like? This is what Apostle Paul depicts beautifully in this passage:

> *2 Corinthians 4:7 But we have this treasure in earthen vessels, that the excellence of the power may be of God and not of us.*
> *8 We are hard- pressed on every side, yet not crushed; we are perplexed, but not in despair;*
> *9 persecuted, but not forsaken; struck down, but not destroyed -*
> *10 always carrying about in the body the dying*

of the Lord Jesus, that the life of Jesus also may be manifested in our body.
11 For we who live are always delivered to death for Jesus' sake, that the life of Jesus also may be manifested in our mortal flesh.
12 So then death is working in us, but life in you.

> **KEY PRINCIPLE**
>
> The stripping process will begin in your soul. Your soul is the seat of your mind, emotions, and will.

There is a good reason for this. As you learned in the *Prophetic Functions* book, the soul is the control tower! It dictates where your spirit or your flesh will dominate.

As a prophet, you must learn to allow your spirit to dominate so that you can hear God. Without the realm of the spirit, you are dead in the water. This is, after all, where all the gold lies. Remember how I shared about the refining process?

Well what the Holy Spirit does, is take you through a process to get rid of the dross. The gold is already inside of you. Now all he needs to do is sort through everything in your spirit, soul, and body so that it can begin to shine.

1. Death Process Begins in the Soul

The process begins with the soul, because from here, you will have the liberty to sense in the spirit what else needs to go.

Mind

> *2 Corinthians 4:8 ... we are perplexed, but not in despair;*

So, I was the shortest and skinniest in my class. This did not make me a candidate for aggressive sports like hockey or netball (a girl's sport a lot like American Basketball.) Add to that the fact I felt horrified every time I accidentally stepped on someone, that did not give me the competitive edge I needed.

So I veered in the other direction, and leaned on what I did have – my intellect and also my creativity. I was quick with my tongue and I could get good marks if I wanted to, so it was not long before I was leaning on my ability to figure things out.

It is funny I guess, how quickly we turn a natural ability into a "gift from God" – especially when it becomes our boast. Because I found that it was the only thing I was good at, I leaned on my ability to "figure things out."

Imagine the shocking reality I faced when this became one of the first things that the Lord started putting a block on. Suddenly things I could figure out without a second thought became difficult. He sent me disciples whose problems I could not solve.

He led me into ministry opportunities where I could not find the answers. It did not take me long to realize that I was no different to Paul in the passage above – I was perplexed!

So what happened to my "great gift from God"? As it turned out, it was not a spiritual gift at all, but just a strength of my soul I was leaning on. This is a frustrating part of the process for the prophet.

It seems that you just keep making the wrong decisions. What you thought you knew, suddenly does not work. Then to top it off, the Lord will tell you to do something that does not make sense at all.

He will tell you to submit to a fleshly leader. He will tell you that you have to "die" and "surrender" in a situation, when you are perfectly in the right. You will be called to offer up the "other cheek" even when you did not start the fight!

What is going on here? You are being called to death! The Lord is saying to you, "My child, will you offer your mind up to me?" How do you think Solomon could have both Godly knowledge and wisdom?

It was because he came to the Lord as an empty vessel saying, "I do not have the answers!" Until you come to this point of surrender, the Lord cannot use you.

PRECONCEIVED IDEAS

Whether you like to admit it or not, you have come into this call with a lot of preconceived ideas. You have built up pictures of what you think people will do in a certain situation. You have firm convictions of what doctrines you think are right and wrong.

Through all your experiences in life, you have built little "codes" that put people and circumstances into a box that you can understand. Well, that is what God is trying to break you out of right now.

How can the Lord send you to "all the world," if all you know is your corner of it? If you are a white American, could the Lord send you to a black South African? If you are an Indian South African, could the Lord send you to a Native American?

With all the anointing you do have, are your preconceived ideas smashed enough that you could reach anyone? Paul certainly had to do that. The Lord had him hopping from nation to nation. What about Jesus?

He had a soirée with Nicodemus in the evening, and delivered prostitutes from demons in his day job. Are you so versatile? If you have a Baptist background, can you minister to Pentecostals? If you are a Pentecostal, can you love and minister to a Methodist?

So now you understand why the Lord keeps putting you in Churches and ministries that cut across everything you believe! You are a woman and God sends you to a church that does not believe in women ministers!

You flow in every gift of the Spirit, and you are sent to a church that preaches that prophecy is a work of the devil!

Is your mind perplexed yet? Will you allow the Holy Spirit to change the way you think so that you can reach His people? Could you truly bring people into a face-to-face relationship with Jesus, in a church that does not believe in the gifts of the spirit?

Could you bring faith, hope and love to God's people, as a woman, in a church that does not believe a woman can minister? Well that is what this training is all about.

Is it wrong to flow in the gifts? Is it wrong to be a woman? Not at all. However, can you put your preconceived ideas on the cross? Dare you step down and discover a road you have never seen before?

You are much like Abraham putting your Isaac on the altar. You will not find the "ram in the thicket" until you do.

> **KEY PRINCIPLE**
>
> Get ready for it – your mind will become perplexed and your intellectual understanding will be brought to the cross as a prophet.

EMOTIONS

> *2 Corinthians 4:8 We are hard- pressed on every side, yet not crushed…*

I am a big mouth. It is what my husband both loves and hates about me all at the same time. What can I say, both being prophets, there was never much of a middle ground with us. We are either passionately in love, or passionately saying exactly what we think!

For as long as I could remember, I did not shrink from this aspect of my character. My no-nonsense attitude opened doors and opened hearts. So much so that I excused my sudden bursts of uncontrollable anger and firm confrontations, and thought that was what God forged in me.

Then came the crunch. The Lord switched things up, and told me that I needed to pastor the prophets. It turns out that if someone is open, bleeding and full of pain - a chisel and hammer applied to their tender heart does not bring about much healing.

It seemed that my usual "putting my foot into it" went to a whole new level! I brought offense. I said things I should not have. Every expression of emotion was out of place.

I was quiet when I should have spoken up. I was loud when I should have shut up. I was going around in circles weaving a mess for everyone around me to clean up. I slowly, but steadily, came to realize that all my "personality power" had to come to the cross.

It was not about if I could "say it straight," but it had to be about if God wanted to "say it straight." I had to be His mouthpiece, and not try to squeeze His word into my personality!

JESUS – SO MANY EMOTIONS

Nothing changed me quite like the secret place with Jesus. I was in His presence one day and He said to me, "Colette I want you to feel with my heart." I saw Him walk towards me, and then walk into me.

I looked down in the spirit, and I could feel that His hands were in my hands. His feet were in my feet. His heart was my heart. He said, "Now listen. Listen to my heartbeat."

Day after day, the beating grew louder until all I heard was the thunder of His will instead of the struggle of my flesh.

I felt Him weep. I sensed His anger. I felt the intensity of His jealousy for His Bride. In comparison to the intensity of the heart of Jesus, my personality paled.

My "no-nonsense" attitude stood out like a sore thumb. It was nothing else but pride and arrogance. My abrupt "say it as it is" was nothing more than an abrasive insecurity trying to strong-arm others into listening.

My tactless tongue was nothing more than a clear reflection of the loveless heart that beat in my flesh.

My dark heart was starkly contrasted to the purity of His. It is only when you come into His presence and feel His heart for His people that you understand the depth of the death you must face to everything you think you have to say and do.

You suddenly understand the striving you have within to feel, and to do. So often we cover over the gold inside of us with emotions that dull the shine of it.

The Lord Jesus has led me along the road to Golgotha many times. I know the nails of accusation and rejection. I know the intense heat of the fire that came from my will being crushed and my mind being confused.

Yet I tell you, child of God, nothing drove the nails deeper, nor pressed the crown of thorns on my head down more than no word of correction at all. The Lord Jesus never said to me, "You have no love." Not once did He say, "You are rude and arrogant." Instead He gave me His heart.

There is no weight and reality quite like it. It was in His tender love that I was broken the most. I understood exactly what He was talking about when He said:

> *Matthew 21:44 He who falls on this stone will be broken to pieces, but he on whom it falls will be crushed.' (NIV)*

This always sounded like such a violent passage – as if the Lord Jesus would pulverize anyone He wanted. It is only when you look into His eyes and experience His tender love that you know what it means to be crushed.

It goes deeper than any correction. To see the blackness of your heart and then to look up and see the acceptance in His eyes makes you want to strip bare of anything that would offend Him. It is because we love Him that we will obey His commandments.

You cannot love the Lord in this way until your emotions are brought to the cross.

KEY PRINCIPLE

> What you feel should be what Jesus needs you to feel. Love, anger, jealousy, frustration, joy, peace... God wants it all.

God wants your heart. As a prophet, you will be asked to put that heart upon the cross.

WILL

> 2 Corinthians 4:9 Persecuted, but not forsaken; struck down, but not destroyed;

I bet you aren't surprised after reading so far that I have a bit of a will. Now Craig, his will is strong too, but it usually manifests itself as stubbornness. Mine is not so subtle.

My will is loud, and it would often push when it should have just been quiet. Why do you think that I can tell you what not to do along this walk? You can be sure that I willfully went in all the wrong directions, before the Lord saved me and put my feet in the right ones.

The toughest part of this process though, was not just the death to my will. In fact, because I had such a strong will, when the Lord called it to death, I could see it coming from a mile away.

I had begun to sense His heart. It was not difficult for me to say, "Anything for you Jesus." What He did though, was a little more than that. When the Lord begins taking you through this death process, He will start addressing your natural strengths and weaknesses. This is where things can get really messy.

DEATH TO STRENGTHS AND WEAKNESSES

You see the nails coming at your strengths from a mile. Sure, it is not easy! When you are loud and the Lord tells you to be silent, it is tough.

When you like to "push through" and the Lord tells you to wait and be patient, that can really try your flesh. Nothing tries your flesh more than when the Lord starts putting His finger in your weaknesses!

What about if you like to be quiet? The Lord will demand that you are loud! Are you the kind of person that does not express your emotions easily? Guess what your cross looks like…?

This is, by far, the hardest part of this process. I was always quick, after a few rounds with the cross, to lay my flesh and strengths on the altar. However, when the Lord told me that I had to learn to follow through instead of leaving a job half done… my flesh screamed!

When He told me to be amiable and "nice" instead of so strong, I felt like I was walking with two left feet. Then came the day when He said to me that He has called me to be a spiritual mother and that I had to learn to be all "nurturing." I just about had a heart attack!

I tried to bargain with Him, "Lord anything but that! In fact, send me to another country. I will give up all my finances. I will let go of every anointing or strength I have!"

I wrestled. You know the Word says that with every temptation that we are given a way to escape. Am I the only prophet out there where the Lord made a disclaimer that said, "New notice – Way to Escape is nullified for 'Colette' from here on out"?

The truth is, we do not really want that escape anyway. When the Lord says to us, "You can submit to my will, or do it your own way – you have a choice," we know that it is not altogether true, because there is not really a choice.

How could we deny the One that paid such a price for us? How can you say "no" to Jesus when you stare into His eyes and see nothing but understanding there? And so I surrendered my will.

I surrendered the prices I wanted to pay, and allowed the Lord to decide what He wanted from me. I surrendered my weaknesses and allowed Him to come and make them strengths.

So what is your weakness today? Do you tend to shy from confrontation? Are you unable to be gentle? Perhaps you fly off the handle all the time and cannot be "grounded" for long.

Then again, you could be a procrastinator that has never finished a job in your life. Does the Lord keep putting His finger on your failures in your marriage? Do you keep being told that you have to be something you cannot be (or so you think!)?

I tell you this with all the love I have – until you bring those weaknesses to the cross, you will never make it to prophetic office.

The Lord needs your will to be His own. He needs to know that He can send you where He needs you to go. He needs to know that you will incline your ear to His will, and not your own.

So where is your pressure today? It is time to surrender, child of God. It is time to not only admit your weakness, but to face them as well. Whatever your fear – face this Goliath and overcome.

2. DEATH PROCESS AND THE BODY

> *2 Corinthians 4:11 For we who live are always delivered to death for Jesus' sake, that the life of Jesus also may be manifested in our mortal flesh.*
> *12 So then death is working in us, but life in you.*
>
> *Philippians 4:12 I know how to be abased, and I know how to abound. Everywhere and in all things I have learned both to be full and to be hungry, both to abound and to suffer need.*

There is nothing quite like eating potatoes, and nothing but potatoes, for a week, to give you compassion for the poor. Of course our family did have our "rice month," where all we had in the house was rice. You will be amazed what you can do with rice for breakfast, lunch and dinner!

The Lord was gracious though and did not leave us there. There came a time when He lifted us out of poverty, and proved His grace to us. I grew up, got married and had a few kids of my own.

He then called us to leave our country and we moved to Mexico with our children, which is where our very first ministry was started.

Things did not go as planned though, and our financial support was cut off from one month to the next. Now it is one thing to look into your past and to go through hard times, but it is another all together to see your children face those times as well.

I wanted it to all "just go away." I wanted the Lord to fix our situation, so that we could just move on. Our faith was being tested and until I got that memo, I continued to strive with the Lord. I had spent so much time asking Him, "Why?" that I did not have any left to work on my faith.

I was a slow learner those days and it took me a while to "get it." So when the revelation finally sunk in, instead of complaining, we praised and used the Word to strengthen our faith. I look back now and am so grateful for this time. Not only did it take my faith to a new level, but it gave my children lessons for their own call that they now lean on.

It also made me realize that what I could or could not buy was not what should drive me. There is nothing quite like not being able to go to the store to cause any lust of the flesh to come to the light!

What if you could not buy take-out on Friday night? What if you could never go to the movies? What if there was no gas for your car and you had to walk? How about you went to your cupboard, and all that was left was a single measure of flour and oil?

It is in these moments that our flesh is brought to the cross. It would not surprise me to hear that the Lord has called you on a fast more than once as you received a conviction of your call. He was trying to crucify the flesh and all its passions.

Is it because He does not want us to taste the flavor of fresh bread? Not at all, it is because He wants to bring a bit of order to our lives. It is our spirits that should be dominating here and not our flesh.

THE FLESH MANIFESTS...

You really want to see the flesh manifest? Go to a dinner buffet! We hosted a dinner once for my father during a seminar. We invited all the attendees to it. It had been a long session and everyone was starved.

Christian or no Christian, you should have seen the rush for that food table! I think I even saw the odd shove or two! We had to jump the line to get my father some food, before it was all gone!

It was both funny and sad all at the same time. Our flesh drives us more than we realize. The thing is, if you allow the Holy Spirit to bring your soul to the cross first, the flesh follows naturally. Why? It is because the soul is the control tower.

I already taught you in the *Prophetic Functions* book how the soul is the one that determines whether the flesh or the spirit will dominate.

That does not mean the Lord will not lead you into circumstances that will test you. You are about to find out if you have a root of temporal values! There is nothing like seeing if someone has a problem with "money" or "things" by taking it away from them.

> **KEY PRINCIPLE**
>
> It is one thing to give something up by a choice of your own will, but what about when it is taken by force?

What about if you lose your car or house? What happens when someone refuses to get you the thing you need or desire? What comes out of you then?

The flesh cannot be allowed to dominate, and as the pressures come on you, you will know exactly what needs to go.

WHERE IS YOUR SECURITY?

Because lack was such a part of my life, when the Lord did start providing, the first thing I wanted to do was cling to it. I never wanted to suffer lack like that ever again. Without realizing it though, those things had become my security.

They became the wall that stood between me and poverty. One day the Lord said to me, "Colette is everything you have really mine?" I said, "Of course Lord!"

Well, that is what I thought until some money that someone intended for me, went to someone else! I was so upset. I said, "Lord the enemy really attacked me here! That money was meant to be mine!"

He said, "I thought you said everything that was yours was mine?"

"Umm… it is Lord."

"Then did it ever occur to you that I wanted that money to go to that person instead of you?"

I was floored. I had not realized how much money was meeting a need that only Jesus could. It was a solid, but good death - one I will ever be grateful for. You cannot afford your flesh to dictate what you will do in ministry.

As we have risen up in the Church, there were other temptations. There are many who "feel led" to give into the work… with strings. If I needed money more than Jesus, I cannot imagine where that would have led us.

Faith Needed

This testing has a two-fold purpose. Firstly, it teaches you to put the flesh on the cross, but it also brings you to a new level of faith.

When you are in a situation where you have nothing but Jesus to pay your rent – your faith grows! When you have nothing in the cupboards but the Holy Spirit, you can be sure that you learn how to pray!

So do not despise this season in your life. Die quickly! Rise up in faith, and let the Lord Jesus be your guide and not a full stomach and bank account.

You will soon come to learn how much faith you need to fulfill this call on your life. As God opens the doors, it is going to require faith for you to teach and minister. It is going to require faith to speak to closed doors and expect them to open.

It is going to require faith to heal broken hearts and to flow in the gifts of the spirit.

> **KEY PRINCIPLE**
>
> If you cannot even have faith for your daily bread, or an outstanding bill, how will you have enough faith to heal a broken heart?

So if you feel like your life has been one trial after the other of having to surrender and give things up, then it is time that you got the memo!

The Lord is not punishing you. He is not trying to make you suffer. He is calling you to surrender. He wants to know that everything that you have, is in His hands.

HOUSE OR HEART?

When we talk about the price of the call, so many think that it means giving up a house or a car. Usually when someone thinks about going into the work of the ministry, the first thought that comes to mind is, "I will have to go without money."

As one who has been there, I can say with boldness, this is the least of it! Giving up a house or even your country is one thing. When the Lord starts asking you to give up your bitterness, desires and needs – well that is when things get tough!

What about when He starts to ask you to dig into your past hurts and to forgive and love those that hurt you?

How about when He tells you to return to the dominating leader that took advantage of you? Now that is a price.

Through your preparation and training phases, you will always be reminded of this scripture

> *2 Corinthians 4:10 Always carrying about in the body the dying of the Lord Jesus, that the life of Jesus also may be manifested in our body.*

NOT DESTROYED…

When will you ever stop living a crucified life? The day your body dies and you are put into the ground! Why? For as long as you remain on the cross, Jesus will continue to get off, in your place.

It is in these moments that you will experience the power of God. The anointing will increase. The miracles increase. The peace increases. Spiritual death is a way of life for the prophet.

I love how Paul says in 1 Corinthians 4:9 *"…. But not destroyed."*

Perhaps as you have read through all of this, you see only what God removes. What you do not see is how much He wants to give to you.

I wrote a chapter in my book *The Journey of Tamar*, where the heroine of the story is stripped down naked. This book is very much an allegory of the prophet and I wrote it using all the experiences I had in the spirit.

As she stands naked, she is not left that way. First, she is forced to see the scars she carries. Then she is cleansed. Then she is clothed in something beautiful.

This is the process the Holy Spirit is taking you through right now. Perhaps all you feel is the stripping and being forced to look at your dirt and scars. What you need to set your eyes on is the end goal.

The Lord is forging a beautiful creation in you. You are being made weak, so that the weakness can be replaced with His strength. You are called to stand naked, so that His glory can clothe you.

You are made blind, so that you can see with the eyes of Christ. Your stony heart is being removed so that it can beat with the heart of Jesus. With each death you go through, you are not torn down, but you are added to.

You will soon say like John the Baptist, "May I decrease and may He increase." When this rhema begins to ignite in your spirit, you do not need to face the cross with fear any longer.

You can say as Paul did, "I count it all joy!" You can go to the cross with joy and positive expectation, not because of the nails in your way, but because of the glory beyond the cross.

As you engage in prophetic training, not only will you learn to embrace these nails, but you will learn to die quickly. I will be leading you through to resurrection soon, but for now, lets see how you can work through this process of death quickly and avoid having to face the same set of nails again and again!

CHAPTER 03

DIE ALREADY: YOUR SECRET PASSAGE THROUGH THE CROSS

Chapter 03 – Die Already: Your Secret Passage Through the Cross

> *John 19:30 So when Jesus had received the sour wine, He said, "It is finished!" And bowing His head, He gave up His spirit.*

Life is never convenient. Neither is death. Tell any pregnant woman that childbirth is convenient and she will laugh in your face. From the time her feet swelled to twice their size and a full night's sleep became impossible – she wanted that baby out!

If she is anything like me, she would have pleaded with her doctor, "Isn't the baby ready yet? Can I start this process?" Her doctor would have told her the same thing that he told me, "The baby will come when it is ready to come."

That is why babies are born at ridiculous hours of the night – just to remind us that life is not convenient. It happens when it wants to happen. Anyone attending a funeral will have the same thought.

Who ever said of a loved one that died, "Yep! They died at just the right time. Today was a perfect day for them to pass."

The Lord did not call you to a convenient road. He should know, because He walked it ahead of you. With each step He took for you, with the cross on His back,

He realized that this walk was one of submitting to the will of the Father.

Just as you struggle with your flesh, Jesus struggled too in the Garden of Gethsemane saying, "Father if this cup could only pass from me..."

Jesus... a perfect man travailed with the road he had to walk. So yes, the flesh will strive within you for dominance. It will want to live and thrive. It will want things to be convenient. It will say, "Yes I know that I must face the nails and whipping... but can't we do it in the morning?"

THE ROAD TO THE CROSS

As if being subjected to the agony of the cross was not enough, Jesus was made to carry that cross where everyone could see him. That is one of the first lessons that you will learn during this process – there is no such thing as a private crucifixion.

Everyone will be engaged in the process. Your pastor will be there to drive in a nail or two. Your spouse will be there to make sure your crown of thorns is fitting all right and your neighbors will be the one to shake their heads and say, "...and he used to be such a nice man."

If you back out now, you will never see the glory of resurrection. All you will take from this process is the humiliation and pressures you have faced. I have spoken a lot regarding the pressure, but how about you learn how to move through it quickly?

> **KEY PRINCIPLE**
>
> You do not need to keep travailing in the Garden of Gethsemane. In fact, you can race towards it and say, "Lord change me! Lord make me into a vessel of honor for your Name."

You can be sure that your prayer will be answered with the weight of the cross. You will leave that place and pressures will begin to mount. The whip and long road will surely begin.

1. Looking Toward Glory

> *Hebrews 12:2 Looking unto Jesus, the author and finisher of our faith, who for the joy that was set before Him endured the cross, despising the shame, and has sat down at the right hand of the throne of God.*

So beautiful. As Jesus felt the weight of the cross on His shoulders, the Word says that He did it with joy! He looked past the shame, seeing Himself being seated at the right hand of the Father. With each nail, He saw your face and instead of pain, He embraced joy.

Is it possible to enjoy this process? If you make a choice to look at the goal instead of your present shame and struggle, then yes, you can enjoy this process!

You can enjoy it as much as a fitness fanatic drives their muscles beyond their potential, knowing they will become stronger because of it.

So often we look at it all wrong! We see the shame and the struggle, but not the glory that is ahead. If you begin this process with a picture of glory in your spirit, you will skip your way to the cross, anticipating the good things that God has waiting for you there.

When you realize that your flesh is smothering the gold inside of you, you will be ready to get rid of it.

You are a caterpillar that has been bound up, for way too long, in your cocoon. It is time for the butterfly to emerge. It is going to take shedding that safety net though. It is going to mean being exposed to the elements and pushing that flesh aside.

2. Die Already

It did not take Jesus long to die. He saw what was beyond the cross. He knew His purpose. He knew that life came after death and when the moment arrived, he bowed His head and submitted His spirit into the hand of the Father.

When the Roman soldiers came to remove them from the cross, Jesus was already dead. To make doubly sure though, they pierced Him in the side, and the Word says that blood and water flowed. Jesus knew how to die.

The two thieves next to him were not so good at it. So the soldiers broke their legs. Why be so mean? Well the reason was to help them die quicker! With their legs broken, they could no longer push up on the cross to breathe.

Broken legs meant death by suffocation. Not long after that, they also died. Jesus did not have to suffer this fate – and neither do you!

How many times have you resisted the nails of the cross? You press up again and again until you are so exhausted that you just give up.

THE LEG BREAKING EXPERIENCE

How many more times do you have to face the same pressure before you surrender? Just like the Roman soldiers, that came and broke the legs of the thieves, so also will your legs be broken if you continue to resist the nails.

Now Paul, He was a smart man. He had quite the "leg-breaking"!

> *Acts 9:5 And he said, "Who are You, Lord?" Then the Lord said, "I am Jesus, whom you are persecuting. It is hard for you to kick against the goads.*

A good back-hander threw him to the ground, and Paul had the good sense to stay there until God had his say! How many times has the Lord had to break your legs before you would surrender to his will?

What you need to understand, is that this is a last resort. He will first lead you along the road of Golgotha. After that, the stripes and the crown of thorns will bear down on you.

Again and again, you will face the same pressure. Different people will "prick" you with the same accusation. Circumstances will continue to "perplex" you with the same confusion.

The same pressure will come on your will again and again from every side until... you can no longer breathe.

In this moment, what will you decide? Will you choose to yield to the Lord Jesus, or will you push up on the cross until the Lord has no choice, but to break your legs?

It takes you a while to "get" that the Lord is calling your flesh to death at first. In fact, when you first start your prophetic training, you have no clue what is happening to you. It just feels like the hordes of hell decided to inhabit everyone around you to make sure that every day, was a bad day!

Your spouse manifests, your boss goes off his rocker and your kids start acting in ways you cannot begin to express. Wake up! Recognize the nails.

Recognize the Nails

If the same pressure keeps coming on you again and again, then know that the Holy Spirit is knocking at your door. Now you can die quickly, or you can keep resisting. You can say, "Father into your hands I commit my spirit." Or you can say, "… but Lord it is not fair. I did not do anything wrong!"

Was it fair to Jesus? Did He do anything that deserved the nails and humiliation?

Who the Lord Uses

Jesus submitted Himself to the Gentiles, and to a death that labeled Him as "accursed." Why do you struggle then when the Lord uses those who love you to drive the nails in?

That is why when the Lord starts bringing some "pricks" against you, He will use those you are open to. He will begin with your mentor or spiritual parent. If that spiritual parent is your pastor, then do not be surprised to find a few nails driven in from the pulpit!

So you resist. Of course you are justified, because they did not do it right – as if there is a "right" way to drive in a nail! There is no such thing as a "righteous crucifixion"! What you did not realize, is how much work that the Holy Spirit put into arranging that circumstance!

Didn't you ever wonder how amazing the timing of Jesus death was? Right during the Passover – a live depiction of the very type and shadow He came to reflect with His lifeblood. It was no coincidence that He died on the Sabbath. His death was convenient for everyone, except Him.

The same is true of your journey through the cross. Each circumstance and timing of it has been set in place by the Holy Spirit. If you resist His hand and do not follow through, it means a new arrangement of circumstances.

The Lord has to set up your situation, relationships, and move the right people into place. Now you know why it has taken you so long to reach prophetic office! If only you could "Die Already" like Jesus!

If only you could surrender the first time the nails came your way. Then you too, could move on to the power of resurrection.

So if you do not submit to your mentor or spiritual father, the Lord will use your spouse. From there, He will use close friends, family members, and fellow believers in the Church. You resist. Then the Holy Spirit presses in.

Pressure will come at you from the workplace and finally, if you continue to resist Him, that pressure will come from the world.

Put your hand into the side of Jesus and see for yourself how the world treats one who is set apart. This is what we call a "leg-breaking." It is where you have resisted the hand of the Lord so much, that He has to stop you dead in your tracks.

This is where He has to put you in such a dramatic set of circumstances, that you have no choice, but to surrender to His will.

Is this for everyone? No, but then again, not everyone is called to be a prophet, are they? Herein lies the truth of the price you are called to pay as a prophet. Make no mistake, there is no one in this world who is able to follow through without a true calling.

This very process is what separates the sheep from the goats – the true from the false prophet.

> **KEY PRINCIPLE**
>
> When you can stop complaining about how much the nails hurt, and move onto seeing the glory that waits, letting go is easy. This is not a punishment – it is an invitation to promotion!

Today Jesus is no longer on the cross. He is seated at the right hand of the Father. You too are called to rule and reign with a prophetic authority. So then, will you surrender to this prophetic death?

What Death to the Flesh Feels Like

Silence. There were voices shouting accusation. Thirst gripped Jesus' throat and He felt weary. Looking down at John and His mother, I imagine the inner struggle He must have faced, knowing that others were paying the price alongside Him.

So many things must have been going through His mind. In addition to the pain that wracked His body, were the pictures of the future and the disciples He raised. Pressures, accusations, pain... He was surrounded by chaos.

Then at its height, the unthinkable happened. It felt as if even His Father had turned His back on Him. He felt truly alone. There was no reason to keep bleeding. The job had been done. Rejected, alone, bleeding and in pain, He surrendered.

In that instant, the ground began to shake, shocking everyone there. A distance away, in the temple, the veil was suddenly torn, but although Jesus might have felt something in the spirit, He was not there to see any of it. Jesus was dead.

When you finally surrender to the cross, you wonder why it took you so long. Something breaks and a deep peace washes over you. You might feel alone. You might feel like you failed more than anyone. Yet it does not matter.

You find yourself floating over the pressures of the circumstances. You realize that you cannot fix your flesh. You cannot keep pushing against the hand of God. There is only one thing you want – His love. You want this call. You want His hand in your life and you do not care about anything else.

In that moment, no sacrifice is too much. You say, "You want my bitterness Lord? Take it!"

"You want my money? Take it!"

"You want my marriage? Take it!"

"You want my respect? Take it!"

Nothing else matters but Jesus. In that moment, you surrender the flesh and walk in the spirit. A veil is torn between soul and spirit, and the new man that has been created in you is manifest.

Along with it comes the fruit of the spirit that was hidden underneath the stench of your rebellion and fear. You are untouchable.

THE SPEAR IN THE SIDE

The enemy does not believe you though. He says to himself, "Nah, he is just faking it!"

So to make doubly sure, he will throw a spear into your side. He will hit you with a pressure that you just overcame. You see there is an essential truth about a dead body – it does not usually react when it is pricked!

In fact, if you prick a dead body and it jumps up, other than giving you the fright of your life, it would also be proof that it is alive! What the enemy does not realize is how much victory is in that "spear in the side"!

When the enemy thinks he can attack you with the same pressure you just surrendered to the Lord, He is testing you, to see if you will flinch. He pokes at you and says, "Did you flinch? Did you react? Is there some flesh I can still use there?"

When that same pressure does not bother you, it proves to the enemy and to you, that your flesh is dead! This is a moment of true victory! It is in this moment that you will realize that you have truly put off the old man, and that the temptations of the past are no longer found in you.

There is no greater proof of your spiritual life! So if the enemy keeps "pricking" you, you need not respond. When the Lord has brought something to death in you, then trust that He did a complete work.

Just Surrender

The change comes in the resurrection, but for now, your part is to surrender. In the moment that you do, the veil is torn, the pressures will end and your striving within will come to peace.

With each veil that you surrender, you will draw that much closer into the presence of Jesus. This is your joy. This is the reason why you keep going through it. In the Old Testament, the saints were taught to obey the law. In the New Testament, Jesus said that if we love Him, that we would obey His commandments.

We do not go to the cross because we are forced to. We do not go there because we will suffer if we do not. We are drawn to the cross because of love. Let love lead you there and take you through towards the power of resurrection.

CHAPTER 04

TEMPLATES AND TRIGGERS IN THE TRAINING PROCESS

Chapter 04 – Templates and Triggers in the Training Process

> *Hebrews 12:1 Therefore we also, since we are surrounded by so great a cloud of witnesses, let us lay aside every weight, and the sin which so easily ensnares us, and let us run with endurance the race that is set before us,*

This spiritual journey of ours is a race that is set before us, that we are called to run. The problem is, we start out on this race with our templates for life strapped to us like a rucksack. Have you ever tried to sprint with a rucksack?

As we respond to problems incorrectly in life, weight starts to get added to us. You are trying to run the race, you are trying to serve the Lord and do what is right, but the rucksack is too heavy.

Instead of it being so easy, it is difficult. You want to "get out there" and start a ministry, but with every opposition you face, you just feel like giving up. You want to rise up and be used mightily of God, but you always open your mouth and say the wrong thing.

> **Key Principle**
>
> As a prophet, you want to walk in the spirit and do the will of God, but find that you find it so much easier to sin than to obey His word!

You shout out like Apostle Paul, "wretched man that I am!" Because even though you know you should surrender to the Lord, you go your own way instead.

You know what the Word says and you know how it should be, but somehow in the end, it does not work. Why does it work for others, but not for you?

It is because you are carrying weights around. At the end of the day, it is sin that is besetting you. It is like having ropes around your feet, tripping you up along this race.

THE RACE YOU RUN

How can you run this race with endurance, when you are carrying such a load on your back? Perhaps, you have learned to deal with the issues of the past or to deal with your problems.

Hopefully you have learned to surrender to the cross and allow the Lord to have His way.

Perhaps, you have learned to exercise your spiritual muscles, and you have pushed your faith beyond the weights that are on your back. You have pushed hard and you have gotten to a point where you feel that you are actually moving on, in this race.

You pushed passed disadvantages. You overcame your insecurities and weaknesses to a certain point, but it just takes one thing to trip you up. Suddenly, you are at ground zero again.

You say, "Lord, I cannot run this race."

There is nothing wrong with the race. Your template, the essence of who you are, the building blocks of your life, are messed up.

You need to get rid of some of those stones in your rucksack, so that you can run this race more effectively. If you have been in ministry, or you are learning to walk a new level of maturity, and suddenly things start coming against you - count it all joy.

The Lord is giving you an opportunity to take the rocks out of your rucksack. He is trying to take away the ropes that are making you trip, and to help you run this race.

The human heart is very fickle sometimes. One day, you want to conquer the world, and the next day, you want to run away.

How can we bring you to a point where you can run your race effectively, full of confidence, joy, faith, hope, and love?

Running the Race With Power

How do you get to the place where you start expecting to succeed? How can you begin to expect blessing and people to respond correctly to your ministry?

How do you get to the place where you have peace inside, instead of feeling like everything is a hard grind?

Let's put some of these stones aside. They come in various forms, and I am going to specifically talk about the templates and programming in our lives that weigh us down.

TEMPLATES, TEMPLATES EVERYWHERE!

> *1 Peter 1:13 Therefore gird up the loins of your mind, be sober, and rest your hope fully upon the grace that is to be brought to you at the revelation of Jesus Christ;*

So what does your mind have to do with running a race anyway? Yet here, Peter tells us to "gird up the loins of our mind!" Have you ever pondered what that means practically? I just spoke about the race that we run as believers. Well here, Peter is telling us how we can do it effectively.

The hope at the end of this journey is your focus, and to reach it, you need to get your mind in gear. You see prophetic office ahead of you. You are running hard, but it feels that no matter how much you run, that you keep steering off course.

It is like shopping with a cart that has a bad wheel. You do not mean to slam the side of the isle, but no matter how hard you try to keep the cart straight, that nasty wheel keeps forcing the cart in the wrong direction!

Well that is why the Lord has to deal with templates in your life. They are the weights on your back. They are a bad wheel on your shopping cart. They make it that much more difficult to get to your goal.

Sure enough, you will get to your goal, but it does not need to take forever. You can do something to remove the hindrances. You can do something to make sure that your walk is a straight one. However, dealing with templates will not displace the need for the cross.

They also will not automatically ensure that you make the right decisions. Dealing with them however, will make choosing the right path that much easier!

So what is a template anyway?

> **KEY PRINCIPLE**
>
> A template is a collection of reactions and choices centered around an event that took place for the first time in your life.

This term is not my origination, but actually one that my father used when the Lord first started giving him this revelation. Being a programmer by trade, the Lord used something that he was familiar with.

To make his job that much easier, he would use templates for certain kinds of programs. So instead of always needing to rewrite tons of code every time he got a new project, he would simply use a template and just tweak it for the needs of each particular client.

It is a beautiful picture of what Peter was trying to tell us here in,

> *1 Peter 3:8 Finally, all of you be of one mind, having compassion for one another; love as brothers, be tenderhearted, be courteous; 9 not returning evil for evil or reviling for reviling, but on the contrary blessing, knowing that you were called to this, that you may inherit a blessing.*

Peter was saying, that even though we all come from different backgrounds, we need to have the same mind. We need to "tweak" the patterns we have for life, so that we can walk in agreement.

Start looking at your prophetic call, and it makes perfect sense. Until you think like Christ, how can you run this race? You want to run a prophetic race? Then you better "gird up the loins of your mind" and begin to think prophetically!

Now there is a lot standing in your way. There are many templates of the past that are hindering this kind of thinking. So the Holy Spirit will begin challenging you. We spoke at length about the death process as it relates to your mind, emotions and will.

There is so much that you have experienced through your preparation process. As the pressures came on you, there were times when you made correct choices.

At other times though, you made the wrong ones. Let me explain.

My Hiding Place

Colette Rejection Toach. If I had to label myself as I went through the process, that is what I would have chosen. And so I found a hiding place. We moved around a lot and the first thing I always did when we went to a new house, was to find a corner in the garden that I could call my own.

I would hide there for hours imagining another world. The good part? It helped me draw closer to the Lord and prepared me for the face-to-face relationship that I would later have with Jesus.

The negative part? I avoided the problems of life. I did not want to face my parent's divorce. I did not want to face the teasing kids. I did not want to face the poverty or fear. I built a template in life.

You see each of us responded differently to rejection. Nothing prepared you for the shock you felt of your first rejection. You were a small, naïve child that knew no better. You had no hidden agenda. You did not mean anything by what you said or did.

In fact you literally stumbled into that situation. You did not expect the backhander you got emotionally. In that moment, your first sting of rejection pulsed through your body and you made an instantaneous decision.

"I will run and hide."

"I will stand and fight back."

"I will cry and feel ashamed."

"I will try to justify myself and explain."

"I will feel like a victim and not let anyone get close again."

Unfortunately, you did not have the relationship with Jesus back then that you do now. You were still a child! You did not know that He was right there, wanting to pick you up in His arms.

So instead of responding in the spirit, you responded with your flesh. In that moment, a template for life was formed. A little program code was written on your mind and heart that you continued to lean on for years to come.

With every rejection you faced from thereon, that template was reinforced – along with your sinful response. In fact, a time came when people did not even need to reject you anymore for that template to play out.

All you needed was a similar situation, a hint of rejection, and the walls came up. Whether the person intended to reject you or not, did not count. "It smelled like rejection and that is enough for me!" Up come the walls.

Jesus Melts the Walls

Then Jesus comes with His tender love and manages to find a crack in your stony heart. His light rushes in and illuminates rooms in your life you had forgotten about. For the first time in many years, you begin to feel acceptance and hope.

Yet Jesus does not stop there. Sharing your heart with Him is not enough. He calls on you to open the doors of your heart, and to share it with the church. You step out – you hit the wall you built. You beat your fists against it, but the wall does not budge.

That is the way I felt when I looked around at my family and realized how hard it was for me to love with abandon. My fear overwhelmed me. I had a sinful template in place. One I had built many years ago.

Each time a voice was raised or I sensed just a hint of disagreement, my template played itself out – without a second thought. My subconscious re-winded to the little girl that did not understand why she was not good enough. The child that was so full of big ideas only to be brought to the reality of her inability.

Then Jesus came with His tender touch and who could resist? The healing begins on the inside, and for the first time in years you feel the draw to let the hurt go.

Yet no matter how much you pray, you cannot seem to love like He loves. You cannot have His mind. No matter how much you pray, you feel stuck.

TEAR DOWN THE CORNERSTONE

Child of God, you need to deal with your template! It is time to go back to that time of your life and to face the hurts of the past. It is time to go back to the cornerstone and to bring it down. When you tear it down, the rest of the wall will follow.

The templates you have built, are a cornerstone to a wall, which block you from the presence of God and restrict the anointing in your life.

We know the pain is there. We feel the discomfort when Jesus looks at us and smiles saying, "You know it's time for you to be vulnerable, right?"

Who can resist? The only way to overcome is to go right back to the first time it happened. This is where the ministry of inner healing is essential. Inner healing is not enough in itself though. What is hindering you more than anything is the choice you made back then.

Mine was to shut my heart away and keep it to myself – what was yours? Mine was to put on my "Sunday face" and to perform so that people would accept and not reject me, so no - you are not the only one.

PERFORMANCE ORIENTATION

We call that performance orientation and I have yet to meet a prophet that has not wrestled with it in one way or another. When the attacks come so often, and you have bruised your knees so much, you will do anything to just make it stop.

In fact, you will even tuck away some of your convictions so that you can give people what they want, just so that they will stop lashing you with the kind of stripes that Jesus faced upon the cross.

You will say anything. You will do anything. Just make it stop! Then God calls you to be a prophet and He says to you as He did to Jeremiah, "I have called you to be my spokesman, but they will not receive your word. Not only am I telling you that you are going to be rejected, but I am telling you that it is your call."

There is no way to perform your way out of that one. There is only one thing to do. You have to go back and deal with those templates. The Lord will keep putting you in situations that expose how much you perform for others to get their approval or recognition.

He will not relent until the load you have been carrying is lightened and you are free.

Sinful Templates

> *Romans 12:2 Do not conform any longer to the pattern of this world, but be transformed by the renewing of your mind. Then you will be able to test and approve what God's will is-- his good, pleasing and perfect will. (NIV)*

You have been shaped by the world that is round about you. Your parents, teachers and friends have all had a part to play. However, your decisions are what take center stage.

> **KEY PRINCIPLE**
>
> Each time you responded to the pressures of life in a sinful manner, you allowed your mind to be shaped by the spirit of the world and not by Christ.

Because most of these pressure situations took place when you were either a child or unsaved, it is no surprise that these incorrect choices were made. So where to from here? Like I said already, it is time to look at your sinful responses.

A good place would be to start looking at your failures today. It is only when you identify what you are going through now, that you can begin to trace it backwards. In the next chapter, I will teach you how the Holy Spirit uses situations to bring up the templates of the past. For now though, I want you to realize that if you are hitting a "wall," it was not built overnight.

You built this wall a long time ago, and it has been reinforced in your life again and again. Each sinful response to the same situation bound you like links in a chain. It is time to break the chains.

Allow the Holy Spirit to take you back to the first time you made that sinful choice. Repent and allow Him to turn it around. Allow Him to let you see things His way.

You will soon come to discover that the child that you left behind is still there. The innocent daydreamer holds the key to your call. It was the child that Jesus picked up in His arms.

It is the child that holds the key to the vulnerability you need. It is the child that needs healing, and it is the child that Jesus called.

CHAPTER 05

How Templates are Exposed

Chapter 05 – How Templates are Exposed

My Dad makes the best lentil soup you have ever had in your life. I have such good childhood memories of this soup. I am sure that you have some memories of your own of something special that your parents made for you.

There is this one memory that really stands out to me. I was about 14 at the time. It was cold and wintery and so Dad put soup on the stove. He always used to make it in a pressure pot. He put all the ingredients in and then pressurized the soup for a certain amount of time.

Anyway, as the soup was on we were having some family time in the living room. We were talking and having so much fun that we lost track of time.

Out of nowhere, we heard what sounded like an explosion, followed by the sound of rushing water. My Dad exclaimed, "The soup!" Family time was over as we tripped over one another to get to the kitchen. You should have seen the sight.

The pressure had built up so much in the pot, that it had forced the nozzle out – shooting it at the ceiling. A gushing eruption of lentil soup was sprayed all over the ceiling and kitchen walls.

I am sure you can imagine the mess and the smell. The soup had burnt and so this horrible, burnt bean soup smell permeated the air. In fact, a couple of years later when we moved out of that house... if you walked into the kitchen and looked on the ceiling, you could still see splatters of lentil where we couldn't get it cleaned off. That smell permeated the house for months afterwards.

Pressure Causing You to "Erupt"

So, what has this story got to do with templates and inner healing? Well, this picture is a perfect illustration of what happens to you during prophetic training. Pressure comes on you. You are like that pot of lentil soup. You know what happens when you add some heat to a pressure pot? It starts to pressurize.

As you have been in training, that is exactly what has been happening to you. The Lord has caused things to heat up a little.

It is starting to get hot and the pressure is starting to build. Every now and again something happens in your life. Something happens that makes you feel a little out of control. The pressure triggers something in you that causes an explosion just like that lentil soup pot!

What comes out is pretty much the same thing as what we experienced – a very foul, horrible, smell that sprays over everything and everyone and leaves a lasting mark.

IDENTIFYING TRIGGERS

What am I talking about? I am talking about templates and triggers. What I want to do in this chapter is to help you identify triggers in your life.

What you will experience in your prophetic training are trigger situations. In training, it's going to really get strong.

HOW THE LORD EXPOSES SINFUL TEMPLATES

The Lord will put specific pressure on you to cause that pot to explode. Why? Until it does, you don't know that there is a problem to be solved. So if circumstances have been coming at you, out of nowhere, that cause you to explode in five directions at once, it's a good sign.

Now we can't just leave the lentil soup all over the floors, walls and ceiling, can we?

No – we have to clean it up and identify why that explosion took place. When you can identify why you are losing control, you will find that there is a deeper problem that God is trying to address in you.

We have already looked at the process of sanctification, and how the Lord will bring you to death again and again. So how will you know if an invitation to the cross has been dropped at your door?

EMOTIONAL SIDESWIPE!

It's simple. The first thing is, you are experiencing emotions that you cannot control or explain.

You are at the store, bump into an old friend, they say something and afterwards you suddenly feel depressed. You think to yourself, "What is the matter with me? Why am I so depressed right now?"

Perhaps you get uncontrollably angry and you think, "Why am I so angry? They didn't say anything to make me angry…"

It feels like a truck has sideswiped you. You are gripped with emotions that you cannot control. Guess what? You are experiencing what we call a trigger. It's just a trigger that is pulling out the emotions of an underlying problem of a template that has been with you for many, many years.

If you stop for a moment, you realize that the Lord has already been preparing you for this. In fact, it is likely that for the last while memories from the past have been cropping out of nowhere. At night you have been dreaming about places and people of the past.

Sound familiar to you? Coupled with unexplained emotions that you can't control, it's a big, fat sign that says, "Hello! Your pressure pot is about to explode! Let's take a look at this and see what's happening here!"

There is a problem here, and a template that is being triggered. Now the worst thing you can do is to say, "No – I don't have a problem."

This is a stubborn and foolish response. You know why? You are going to end up with lentil soup all over your face. You have got to have the courage to face reality and realize that there is a problem lying under the surface. There is no shame in admitting that you don't have control of the situation.

There is a lot of shame though in being ignorant and saying, "Well I don't have a problem. It's everybody else who has a problem."

"I had a problem once, but I have dealt with it!"

Admit That Something Might be Wrong

That attitude is not going to help you. If you go through this training thinking, "Well yeah, I have handled that. I have dealt with that and have been through that," then you are not going to make it to prophetic office.

> **Key Principle**
>
> Admit that perhaps there are still things that God is trying to deal with in you.

If there weren't, you wouldn't be reading this book. So instead of saying, "Oh, that is my mother's problem."

"No, that doesn't relate to me."

"I dealt with that years ago."

"I am not going to allow myself to go back there."

Stop right there! If it was "dealt with" years ago, it would not be gushing out all over the place right now, would it?

Have a bit of wisdom here and let's have a look at what's going on inside of you. Let's have a look at what's going on in your life. Have you been having dreams?

Have people from the past been popping into your mind? Have you had some conflict situations lately where your emotions are suddenly raging out of control?

Wake up and smell the lentil soup! The Lord is exposing a trigger in your life.

So then, onto the nitty-gritty – how to deal with it!

TRANSFORMING TEMPLATES: STEP BY STEP

So then, how do we transform your sinful templates? First, by identifying them.

Step 1: Identify the Trigger

In fact, by identifying the trigger, you will immediately feel the pot simmer down. Just by seeing what the problem is, you are half-way there. When your emotions are out of control and you don't know what's going on, it's difficult to see what the Lord is trying to do.

That's why it's so wonderful if you have a mentor to help you along through your prophetic training. When you experience these explosions, they can say, "Yep, I see your problem. I see you have a trigger right here!" Then they can pray with you and get revelation.

When you handle this on your own, it's a little more difficult because you just have these teachings to go on. So you need to start looking at the memories that keep coming up, the dreams that you keep having.

Step 2: Trace The Reaction Back, One Memory at a Time

The next thing to do is to look at what you are feeling right now. From there, you can begin to trace it back to the first event (the cornerstone of this template). Can you remember another time in your life when you felt the same way?

Trace it backwards, one memory after the next. Start with how you feel right now, all the way back through your history, as far back as you can remember.

Physical Manifestations

There are some people who have such strong triggers that they do not just feel them in their emotions, but in their bodies as well. When we go on to teaching about *Prophetic Warrior* in the next book, I will teach you about how demons influence our templates.

You will also learn in that book, that when you sin, that you give satan license, which can lead to physical attack. So sometimes, when you trigger, you might even get physically sick, or feel something in your body.

If this is happening, use the principle I already shared. When was the last time you experienced this physical manifestation? Trace it back one memory at a time.

Ask the Holy Spirit to help reveal those memories to you. You will be surprised at what comes up.

Step 3: Repentance is Key

Once you are able to see the source of your cornerstone, it is time to repent. You know the Word says that we should submit ourselves to the Lord. Only then can we resist the devil and he will flee from us. No healing or victory will come until you submit yourself to the blood of Christ.

It is hard sometimes to separate hurt from sin. The hurt stung, but I want you to try and separate these two for a moment. Put the sting of pain aside and isolate your response to that hurt.

If you can do that, you will see that how you responded was not a godly response! I am not asking you to explain why you are justified, or even how natural it is to respond in this sinful way. I am not judging you – I am just saying that until you bring it under the Blood, you are powerless to bind the enemy, or to receive the healing that only the Blood can bring.

The problem here is not the pressure. The problem is how you responded to it. What keeps the sting in your heart is not what was done to you, but the fact that you are holding onto the hurt through your sin.

> **KEY PRINCIPLE**
> Have you ever wondered why generational curses are so binding? It is not the demon that is the problem, but rather the resentment, jealousy, anger and fear that keep it anchored in your life!

The sin anchors the curse. The sin anchors the hurt. The sin is an open door for satan to keep the hurt coming until the day you die.

Now I do not know about you, but I am quite done with everything the devil has thrown at me throughout life. I am done with the rejection. Done with the warfare, and certainly done with his lies. It does not matter to me how much of "self" I have to crucify to take away every upper hand he has in my life – I am doing it!

I am pretty sure that you share my passion. So then, remember the price I spoke about regarding your call? Consider this one at the top of your list.

It is to admit your sin, regardless of hurt, accusation or injustice – just because Jesus said so!

WHY THE LORD DOES IT

Why all this suffering? Why is the Lord asking you to face your own bitterness, when it is quite obvious that it was not your fault that you were abused? It is not your fault that you were hurt and left bleeding. So why then are you, instead of that bully, being made accountable?

Jesus did not call that bully to be a prophet. He called you to be a prophet. He also knows that your bitterness or fear is anchoring that experience in your life. It is holding your sinful template in place, and anyone that walks into the room that just sounds like that bully will trigger your little program, causing you to respond in a way you know you should not.

The Lord is not the only one that knows that! The enemy does too. Do you want to trigger all over someone that comes to you for inner healing? What if someone comes to you for ministry that triggers you to a teacher that picked on you in high school?

Without even realizing it, you would end up reacting to that person in the flesh, playing out your sinful template. You will look back after the fact and say to yourself, "What was I thinking! I cannot believe I just came down on that poor guy for no reason. What is the matter with me?!"

You are triggering. If you could deal with those templates before the enemy picks up on them and uses them against you, you will save yourself (and the Church) a lot of heartache.

The Correct Perspective

A lot of people think that dealing with templates and inner healing is about going in and finding out who did things to you, throughout your life. No – we are not a Freudian society here. We are citizens of the kingdom of God.

It's not about who "did it to you." It's about how you responded to that person. It is where the problem lies, in a template. That's the main thing that most prophets in training seem to misunderstand. The Lord is not trying to crush you! He is trying to set you free. One by one, He is allowing you to lift the stones out of your rucksack so that you can walk with a new bounce in your step.

Smashing the Psychobabble

So you find out, "Okay, I have a need for recognition, because my Dad wasn't there for me."

How Templates are Exposed

"I have a need for acceptance because my Mom wasn't there for me!"

So does that make your Mom or Dad the reason for every problem in life? No! Your problem is how you responded to your Mom and Dad.

The problem lies in the bad attitude you responded with. That is what God is exposing. God is not exposing what your parent did to you.

> *Hebrews 5:14 But strong meat belongeth to them that are of full age, [even] those who by reason of use have their senses exercised to discern both good and evil. (KJV)*

It's time to grow up! The Lord has plucked you out of a normal Christian life and called you to be His prophet. Just like it says here in Hebrews 5:14, it is time to grow up! What does maturity look like?

KEY PRINCIPLE

> Someone who is mature knows how to draw a line between what is both evil and good.

And so, I want to divide the line here, and bring separation between the darkness and the light.

It's easy to look through your life and say, well I have all these templates because of what everybody did to me. It's so easy to fall into that trap.

We have a whole church psychoanalyzing one another about who did what to whom.

"I am this way because my parents favored my older brother…"

"I am this way because my sister was the favorite one and she was pretty. I am not pretty and therefore I have this low self-esteem."

Time to dump the excuses! You are this way because of the choices you made. You responded in sin.

Crucifying Blame

Jesus didn't have the easiest life either, but He responded without sin. He did not blame the Romans for crucifying Him. He does not even put the blame on you – instead He chose to put the blame on Himself.

Along with your sin, He also put all excuses on the cross and submitted to it willingly. He bore the injustice. He remained silent in the face of accusation.

The Lord is not exposing your sin to hurt you. He is doing it because you keep running bad code throughout your life. You keep responding sinfully in situations where He needs you to have His mind and heart.

How Templates are Exposed

> *Romans 12:2 And be not conformed to this world: but be ye transformed by the renewing of your mind, that ye may prove what [is] that good, and acceptable, and perfect, will of God. (KJV)*

You need to be renewed. You need to be transformed by the renewing of your mind. That is the process He is taking you through. That is why an essential step is taking responsibility for your sin.

The "Template Three-Step" at a Glance

1. Identify the Trigger
2. Trace Trigger to Original Template
3. Repent

Only when you have followed these three steps, are you ready to resist. You submitted, now you are ready to resist (covered in Book 5 *Prophetic Warrior*).

This process is the crux of your prophetic training. This is where the shaping and changing takes place, so take it seriously.

Not only that, as you become comfortable with this process, you will take others through it as well. Only when you've got the victory, will you be able to take them through it also.

CHAPTER 06

MINISTERING INNER HEALING

Chapter 06 – Ministering Inner Healing

As you watch your child go through the stages of growth, there comes a time in their lives when they start experiencing their first bumps and grazes. The first time they try to ride a bike, they fall down and cut open their leg. They run too fast down a hill, ending with a tumble that grazes their knees.

Before I was a mother, I could handle anyone else's child when they took a tumble. If someone had a gushing wound, it was no problem to step in and help.

For a short season in my life I thought I would even enter the medical field. What killed that idea was when I got married and we had our first daughter. I remember the first time that she hurt herself. I was pitiful. I cried more than she cried. My husband had to say, "Sweetheart, get out the way, so I can clean this before she bleeds all over the carpet!"

It didn't get better when we had more kids. I remember the time that my third daughter, Ruby decided that she was old enough to help me in the kitchen. She picked up a knife to cut a bagel and ended up slicing her hand open.

She came to me and said, "Mommy, I have cut myself and it's bleeding."

She didn't sound so stressed about it and before I saw it I said, "Ah okay, well it's not so bad!"

Then I turned around and saw blood dripping all over the place. Oh Lord!

"Oh no, there is blood! There is blood! Lovey, there is blood! There is blood!"

Craig had to come save the day because I was running in 7 different directions.

Craig said, "Lovey, you are not helping. Would you please go away!"

He was trying to clean out her wound and my fussing was stressing them both out. I don't know who Craig needed to treat more, me or my daughter!

We both decided that it was best for me just to leave the room so that he could deal with the situation and calm everything down. So... it turns out that I would not have made a very good doctor.

But what I did learn is that when somebody is cut open like that, they do not need you to lose your nerve. It hurts, and their first reaction is to pull their hand away when the antiseptic stings.

INNER HEALING IS A FIVE STEP PROCESS

This is a very good picture of the ministry of inner healing. Now, hopefully you are not going to react to inner healing the way I do to bruises, cuts and grazes.

Hopefully you are going to be level-headed and won't have to be sent out of the room like I always am!

In this chapter I want to give you five clear steps that you can follow when someone needs inner healing.

Now - you have been cut up, bruised and bashed mostly by me for the last 5 chapters in this training. So I thought, you know what, let me give you a break.

You will take everything that you have learned over this last while, and you will learn how to help others. You will realize that it's not quite the same thing.

You see, you opened this book, ready, willing and open to learn. So it was easy for me to get in there with my chisel and start smashing. You were ready for it. You were hungry for it. You are crazy. It's what you are here for.

But you know, other people aren't as crazy as you are, and so the process that you take them through will be different.

By the time you have worked through these steps - the next time somebody comes to you cut and bleeding, you won't get hysterical and you won't start chiseling at them right away. You will handle the situation with wisdom. You will be a nice person - somebody they want to come to.

STEP 1 – WAIT FOR THEM TO ASK FOR HELP

And so, the first step you will take when somebody comes to you bleeding with hurts from the past, is to wait.

Yes - you are going to see them bleeding all over your carpet, and you will let them wait. (I assume you know that I am speaking figuratively here).

Don't do this when they are really bleeding. Don't let them bleed on your carpet.

I am talking about when they come to you with spiritual problems. Someone comes to you with hurts and it's obvious that they've got problems in their lives.

Someone knocks on your door and proceeds to pour their guts out. From the get go, you can see that they've got issues, hurts, bitterness towards parents and... you know the drill. When this happens, do not jump in there and give them everything you have.

It's what you did in the past though - didn't you? They came to you for help and you had so much great advice to give. You probably blabbed as much as they did. You went on and on about all these great teachings you are learning and everything you are doing... mistake!

The first step is always to wait. Now what are you waiting for? You should know the answer by now... you are waiting for them to ask for help.

The reason is that you might see them bleeding all over your carpet, but they don't see it yet. Until they see it and are ready for you to help them deal with their problem, you will get a backlash. You will not get a breakthrough at all.

They must be like a child that has fallen off his bike, running to you saying, "I am hurt! Please help!" The minute you get that "Please help!" then you can move on to step two.

Don't move on to step two until you've got the "Please help me!" from step one.

Wait until they say, "Do you have an answer?"

"Please can you help me? "

"What do you suggest?"

"I need your advice... "

They have got to ask for help. Otherwise, all they want from you is someone to sit idly by while they dump all their problems over you.

Finding Out if They are Ready

If somebody comes to you and spills out all their guts, it's really okay to say, "I understand. That is difficult. Is there something you would like me to help with?"

You can offer your help and ask, "Would you like help? Would you like teaching? What do you want me to do about it?"

Is that such a blunt question? Maybe it is, but until they ask for help, you will be wasting a lot of time and effort.

If you look back over past ministry experiences, you are nodding your head, aren't you? Many failures occurred because you forgot step one and jumped right into step two and couldn't understand why you couldn't get them to step three.

Step 1: Wait!

Don't proceed until they ask for help. Please, memorize this. Write it down. Step 1 = wait. Put it in capital letters, underline it, bold it! Wait.

You see, the word "wait" is just not in a prophet's vocabulary. Every other word in the dictionary is there, but wait was left out. And so I am putting it back in the prophetic dictionary for you.

Wait, before you jump and leap, before you fall to your death - wait! Once they ask for ministry, we can go on to step two.

STEP 2 – IDENTIFYING THE SOURCE

Step two is to identify the source of their hurt.

Once they have asked you for help, then you will get into a two hour discussion of every hurt they have ever had and all the bitterness they had throughout their life and everybody that did something wrong to them... WRONG AGAIN!

This is not a counseling couch. We are not doing Rogerian counseling where you lay them on the couch and say, "I see... tell me more!"

We don't want them to tell us more. Lord, help us... we really don't want them to tell us more. You know, after the first set of students I trained (I had about 50 of them in my first class), I didn't even know what my own life story was anymore.

> **KEY PRINCIPLE**
>
> There is no need to talk about every pain in their past. You want to go right to the source.

We all have problems, and you will just bog yourself down with details – rather go to the problem that the Lord wants you to deal with right now.

If you talk about everything that has ever hurt them, you will get so confused in the end that you won't know what is going on. Sure, it's great to know what is going on in their lives right now.

It is a great idea to find out a bit about their parents. That's always a really good start. That way you get a gist of where they are coming from and what kind of person they are, but when you identify the source, you will be surprised to find that it is not what either of you thought it was. That is why it is a called a ministry. You need the gifts of the spirit and anointing to minister in this way.

Go Straight to Prayer

Here is another pitfall. You "get in there" and you ask the questions and you see, "Aha, that must be the problem," and you start zeroing in on the problem but are getting nowhere. Then you think, "You know what, let's just pray."

Don't feel bad - I still make this mistake so I won't fault you if you have made it once or twice.

When you pray, the Lord shows you something completely different. So take some advice from me: jump straight to the praying part, after they asked for help.

Pray about it and see what the Lord reveals. Now when you pray, the Lord will give you revelation - especially if their hearts are open. You can pray and ask the Lord. Don't go on the obvious. Please underline this - don't go on the obvious!

If you are going on the obvious, I guarantee that's not the source of the problem. Otherwise, they would have solved it themselves already. Get revelation. Underline that down too! (You are doing a lot of underlining in this chapter!)

Get revelation! Why are you a prophet? Prophets get revelation. So wait and get revelation, please. Identify the source.

Now - what may happen is that the Lord may show you a scene from their past. I often flow in that kind of revelation. I'll see them at a certain age and they might be crying. I might see them with someone. I will explain the scene that I see in the spirit. This is where the root of the problem is that the Lord is trying to deal with right now.

WHAT GOD IS ADDRESSING NOW

I won't say that this is the final root, or that this is the end source of the problem, because problems can be complicated. However, this is what God is trying to deal with right now. The problem is, folks often think, "Oh, I have to deal with everything!"

I'll come to somebody and I will say, "The Lord wants to address your relationship with your mother."

"I have a good relationship with my mother, but my father, he was bad to me."

"Well, God doesn't want to deal with that right now. He wants to deal with this, because it's the source of the problem we are dealing with right now."

You see, that's why you have to get revelation. If you just went on what you thought, you will miss the source entirely. You need revelation from the Holy Spirit on what the source is. When the Lord gives you that revelation, whether it's an impression, a prophetic word, or a vision.

EXPLAIN THE VISION

When you get a vision or a revelation for somebody else, don't assume that you know all the answers.

Sometimes we get strange pictures that make no sense to us, but will make sense to the person that you got it for. You can say, "I see a vision of a child, I am not sure, but right about seven years old or so, and they are sitting in a corner crying."

You can also explain a bit of the emotion you sense and whatever else comes to you and then you say to them, "Does this make any sense to you? Can you relate to it in any way?"

Memorize this line: Does this make any sense to you?

Not, "I'll tell you what it is... !" No, take it easy.

Draw them out. You see, that is the best part in all of this. You are not the one doing all the healing here. The Holy Spirit is going to do the healing. All that you are doing is identifying the problem. You are leading the person through the process.

Can't you see that? As you went through these teachings so far, I addressed things, but I just led you. I didn't heal you. I didn't change you. The Holy Spirit changed you. I just led you to His presence.

DO NOT FEEL PUSHED

This is what you must learn to do with others as well. Lead them through their problems but they must get the conviction. You can't get a conviction for them. You can't want ministry for them. They have got to want it for themselves. When they do that, they reach out in faith, and then God will give you the revelation.

If you don't get the revelation then either they are not open, or the time is not right – they are not ready for what God needs to do.

In a situation like this, just speak blessing. I already covered that in one of the previous books, so I will not labor the point. Don't force it. Just share revelation as God gives it to you.

If He doesn't give you anything say, "God is not giving me anything right now but we can just pray and just speak blessing and I can pray as the Lord leads."

The chances are that they are not ready to look at the problem yet. So don't feel pushed and assume something. Identify the source - that is step two.

ASK QUESTIONS.

To help get clarity, do not be afraid to ask questions.

"Does this make sense to you?"

"This is what I sense and what I see, can you relate to it?"

Don't run right over them and say, "Well, that's the source of the problem let's get to it."

No - you may be way off base or may have misinterpreted what you saw. There have been times when I saw visions that I thought were figurative, but in fact, weren't figurative at all.

It was an event that really happened to them. The same holds true vice versa. I saw something that I thought really happened to them, but it was figurative.

So if I had gone in there and given my own interpretation, I would have missed it entirely. So, share what you are seeing. Share what you sense, and then the ball is in their court. When they throw that ball back to you, you are ready for step three.

Don't Be Afraid to "Go There"

When someone has experienced something painful, they will not know how to proceed. They will be open for ministry, but unsure of what to do with all the emotion that suddenly comes out of them.

Take some time to let the feelings come out. Far too often we glaze over this part and want to run straight to the healing.

In many cases, you will find that the person has hidden their feelings over the course of many years. Then as the Lord starts exposing it, it is like a volcano explodes.

Tears, anger, bitterness, and frustration… you name it! Do not rush past this, but allow them to express. If you feel that there is something more that they are not sharing, but want to, then ask questions.

This is especially important in the case of sexual and physical abuse. Very often people do not know what to say to someone who has been through this sort of thing. Do not be afraid to ask honest questions.

"How did that make you feel?"

"Why were you angry?"

"How did everyone respond to you?"

You will be led by the Spirit as you ask. The point is that they can see that the hurt that they have tried to hide is very much alive and needs healing. Taking someone to that "sore spot" in their lives often brings most of the healing.

It is like a festering wound that has been there for years. It is only when they are ready to face their hurt and reaction, that you can move them on to the next step.

Can you see how each step ends off with them taking the final action?

In step one, they have got to come and ask you. In step two they have to identify what you are exposing. Before they are ready to say, "Yes, I see that. Yes, I can identify with that problem." You can't take them to the next step because then, you are just forcing your will.

Trust me, after years of slogging through this - you don't want to push it. You will spend hours ministering only to get discouraged. Just please learn from my mistakes because I have made plenty of them for you.

There are some mistakes you want to make on your own as you go through this training, but then there are some that you are allowed to skip - this is one of them! You don't want to spend three hours ministering to somebody that leaves, or you never see them again, or even worse, it blows up in your face.

Key Principle

> So, step one, wait until they respond and say, "I want ministry."
>
> Step two, wait until they respond and say, "Yes, that makes sense to me. Yes, I understand. That happened to me. This is what went on in that time. This is what I feel!"

Step 3 – Dealing With Sin

Once they have done that, you go to step three, and step three is not pretty for either of you. Step three is dealing with the anger, bitterness, oppression and their sinful reactions to what happened to them.

You see, that's the crazy thing. When somebody says to you, "Yes, you are right. When I was 5 my mother rejected me. My father beat me... "

When they share that, they expect you to say, "Shame, let's speak healing."

I am not going to explain why we are dealing with the bitterness first because we have already been through that. You have got to start dealing with their bitterness because the Scripture says in James 4,7: *"Submit yourselves to God first, then you resist the devil and he can flee."*

Only once you have followed that, can you bring healing to them. You really have to do this job with the anointing because bringing them to repentance is essential.

You say, "You really had a hurtful time, but you see, the reason why you are struggling right now, is because you reacted to that hurt wrongly. You reacted in bitterness. And actually, the Lord Himself can't heal you until you let that bitterness go. Until you let that anger, or guilt go, you cannot move on."

There will be cases where there was terrible abuse and they were innocent. If the hurt has remained though, you have to look at their sinful response to that injustice. It is here that you will find fear, guilt, jealousy, pride and every other work of the flesh.

Before healing can come, they have to let it go.

They have to say, "Lord, I give you my fear and I trust you again. Lord, I give up this guilt and the things I have been holding on to because of this situation. I give up my bitterness."

Only once you have done that, can you deal with the demonic. (We will cover that in more detail in the *Prophetic Warrior* book in this series).

Once again, this step ends off with them giving a response. You have got to bring them to a point of repentance where they say, "Yes okay, my Mom was mean but I still had no right to respond that way."

"Yeah, that was a scary and a bad situation, but I still should not have responded in fear or guilt. Jesus is here for me now."

AVOID BLIND SPOTS

You can't have something that we call a blind spot. I will mention this here quickly because this is a major blockage when it comes to ministering to people.

Someone starts sharing things that happened to them, and they trigger off similar circumstances that happened to you.

You have this tendency to want to pull the punch a little bit because you feel bad. Your own feelings say, "Oh, that's tough. I know how that feels!"

Tell me something. When I was dealing with you throughout these last few chapters on dealing with your sin, did I pull my punches? When God dealt with you, did He pull His punches? No, He didn't. He drove that nail in nice and deep and solid, didn't He?

Aren't you grateful for it? Don't deny this person that same conviction that you had because until they have it, they are not getting a breakthrough. Without conviction, you wouldn't be where you are right now.

That's a startling revelation. I used to make the same mistake.

I would see people go through stuff and I wouldn't chisel them, and I wouldn't correct them and my spiritual father would say, "Why didn't you correct them?"

"Yeah, I just know how it feels when you mess up like that!"

"And what did I say to you when you messed up like that?"

"You chiseled me. You didn't take any nonsense."

"Exactly, and that's why you are who you are. Don't deny others that same opportunity!"

We seem to see it as being mean when you expose someone's sin. It's not! It's showing the ultimate love because you are showing them how to break through. So don't be afraid to say what needs to be said.

Use Tact

By all means, use some tact. Don't say, "You are a filthy, lousy sinner!" Rather say, "Look, I see that you responded sinfully here and until you deal with this, God can't bring healing to this area of your life. He wants to bring change, but you need to deal with this!"

> **Key Principle**
>
> Use tact, but don't be afraid to confront.

When they deal with it and they follow through, pray and submit then you are ready for step four.

Step four and five, are steps where they don't respond. This is where you minister. The first part, well that's just you leading them through the process. They do all the work. So this is where you start stepping forward now, allowing God to use you.

Step 4 – Speaking Healing

Step four is to speak healing. It's a supernatural healing, let me tell you. This isn't just you laying hands and nothing happens. No, when you stand up in faith, and you lay your hands on somebody and you start speaking healing into that memory, that hurt of the past, you will feel something happen.

It's as supernatural as physical healing. It's the same gift, only it's for healing of the soul.

It's miraculous - never forget that. It is essential to bring Jesus into that memory as you speak healing. It's very easy.

Bring Jesus Into the Memory

You might find yourself saying, "I just see Jesus right now in that memory with you. He is picking you up. I just want you to see Jesus right there as I am praying. I want you to see the other person through His eyes.

As you let go of the anger and as you just see this whole situation through His eyes and see that He is holding you."

As you say that, you just lay hands on them and speak healing, "Holy Spirit I invite you. I invite you to come now and I speak your healing into their lives, into their hearts."

As you see the visions and the pictures, just speak them out. Pray until it stops. Then when it stops, the healing is finished.

There is one final step.

STEP 5 - COUNSEL

They need counsel. You see, I could pray and take the hurt out, but some of the poison got left behind. You need to deal now with the habits and what they have been doing to nurture that pain. I am afraid there is only one thing that will change that.

The Word of God!

Do you see the balance between the Word and the Spirit? You thought being a prophet was all about being fluffy and just spouting off all the time? No - let's bring you to maturity, shall we?

You need to now give them some counsel. They need to be followed up.

It's good that you went and dealt with the spiritual stuff, but they also need the doctrine and the foundation. The Word of God is our foundation, and without that, we have nothing to stand on. If they are going to keep their victory, they need the Word of God. They need to start transforming those templates and those bad responses with the Word of God.

They can only change their habits with the Word. So, step five, you have got to leave them with a project.

Before they leave, say, "Okay, the Lord has dealt with this. Now - I tell you what, I want you to pick up this book, go through this chapter and get back to me and we can talk about it."

Give them some kind of action to follow up with so that whatever you have done remains. Jesus even did this with His disciples after He had healed and preached. They would come to Him afterwards and discuss what happened. They would go through more principles and details.

Don't just say to them, "Well, the Lord has done His work," and send them home. No - they need follow up. So, point five, finish with the counsel.

Conclusion

Let's go over these five steps again very quickly.

1. WAIT - Wait until they ask for ministry.

2. IDENTIFY the source - Do not proceed until they are open and can identify!

> Side note: Assume nothing! Share the revelation with them and let them decide.

3. DEAL with anger, bitterness and oppression - you know that whole package right there is the time to address. Do not proceed until they have dealt with their sin and their problem.

This is especially important for generational curses, because somebody who has bitterness towards family members, links them to that curse. When somebody comes to you with a curse of poverty or theft, this is what links them more than anything.

4. SPEAK HEALING - Bring them into the presence of the Lord and let Jesus walk through their memories. That will transform them.

5. COUNSEL – Leave them with something practical to do that is based on the Word.

I hope you wrote all of those steps down because you will come back to this again and again and again.

I look forward to seeing you bring some healing to the body of Christ, because this teaching that you apply, will become a foundation to your ministry.

There will come a time when you are sitting there listening to somebody bleed all over your carpet and you will hear in your mind, "WAIT" and then you are going to know in that moment that you really did receive everything that I said in this chapter.

Chapter 07

Resurrection is a Choice

Chapter 07 – Resurrection is a Choice

Victory Over Death

Resurrection is a Choice

> *2 Corinthians 4:10 Always carrying about in the body the dying of the Lord Jesus, that the life of Jesus also may be manifested in our body.*
> *11 For we who live are always delivered to death for Jesus' sake, that the life of Jesus also may be manifested in our mortal flesh.*
> *12 So then death is working in us, but life in you.*

Confusion and Death

When I came to the Lord to write this chapter, I was not sure where to start. However, when I sat down to write, He reminded me of a vision that I had a while back and did not understand. As I thought about what to share, it all just dropped into place for me.

I had been through a particularly deep death. We had gone through some really tough times. It was one of those situations where there is not just one death, but it is one death after another death after another death. There is one sin that the Lord deals with, another template, then another one. You feel so overwhelmed you do not think that you are ever going to rise up. It is like you just barely have your head above water and "BAM!" you are under again.

Mountain in the Way

If you are a student of our prophetic school then you know what I am talking about.

I just finally came to the place of crying out to the Lord and saying, "Lord, where is this at? What is going on in my life?"

Then as I came to prayer He showed me, in the Spirit, a huge mountain in my path. Me, being the prayer warrior I thought, "Okay Lord, what must I hit it with? Must I cast it into the sea? Must I demolish it? Must I stand over it? Must I stand on satan's neck? What must I do?"

He said, "No."

I was a bit confused.

He said, "Approach the mountain."

So I thought, "Okay," and I approached the mountain.

Then He said, "Start breaking it apart."

Victory Over It

I thought, "He must be nuts!"

All I had was a tiny little chisel, and every time I tried to break the mountain all I was pulling off was one small stone at a time.

I thought, "Lord, I'm never going to go anywhere with this."

He said, "Persevere. Keep doing it."

As I was sitting hitting away at the little pebbles and little rocks, suddenly out of nowhere this huge mountain split. It split clear in half and a glory flooded me. A huge big golden light flooded me and threw me back, and it just surrounded me in His presence and His anointing. When I stood up and looked again the mountain had been split in two and I could walk straight through it, and my path was clear to the other end.

At the time I did not understand, but He said these words to me: "This is not one that will be cast into the sea, but this is one that you will approach head on. I will split it, and I will cause this problem that is in your life to bring forth and sprout forth blessing. I will use this mountain that has been oppressing you not to be removed, but to gush forth blessing on your behalf."

From Bad to Good

That is so the nature of our Father, to use those things which are bad, and which satan has used to put in our paths, to bring forth blessing. So I want to look here how to pass from death to resurrection, and from despair into walking in victory and authority. We have looked enough at death. I just want to make a few short comments on death though, to clear your perspective on it.

DEATH IS POWERLESS OVER YOU

Firstly, death does not have power over you. Jesus Christ died so that we would have victory over death.

It says this in 1 Corinthians 15:55 to 57:

> *O Death, where is your sting? O Hades, where is your victory?*
> *56 The sting of death is sin, and the strength of sin is the law.*
> *57 But thanks be to God, who gives us the victory through our Lord Jesus Christ.*

KEY PRINCIPLE

Death does not have power over you! What is the power of death? The power of death is sin. Sin is what brings death.

The Lord does not bring death. It is sin in your life, it is past templates, it is wrong reactions in your life, that have brought about the death. That is what gives it the power, not the Lord. The Lord did not put you in the grave. He did not put you into temptation. Satan did that. Your sin did that. Your sin brought about the death, because the power of death is sin.

You need to see this clearly in your mind, because the Lord did not do it to you. You opened the door to the enemy. Are you grasping the concept yet? Death has no power over you in the name of Jesus Christ!

You can say to me, "Yes, I understand that. I understand that the Lord doesn't do this to me, and I came to Him in the depths of my despair and I cried out, and I did all I could. I tried and I tried to overcome this sin in my life. I tried to overcome the templates. I know my mother-in-law bothers me, and man I have gritted my teeth and tried to like her. I did everything. I sent her flowers. I sent her gifts on her birthday. I said nice things, but man here I sit in despair. Here I sit, still in depression. No matter what I do, I am not overcoming this death. No matter what I say, I am not overcoming it. It still has victory over me. Satan still has victory over me."

STRENGTH OF SIN IS THE LAW

Do you want to know what the strength of sin is? The strength of sin is the law. The strength of sin is works. Your sin brings you to death, and your works in the flesh keep you there. I do not see the Lord in this at all. I do not see where, "Well, it is the Lord dealing with me. I have to grit my teeth and go through this."

The Lord does not bring you to death. You brought yourself to death through sin. We are fleshly, we are human. We are naturally going to walk in the flesh. We are naturally going to face these mountains in our lives.

But the key is not to run away from the mountain. The key is not to stand in fear and awe of it.

The key is to stand up and face the mountain! It is to face your sin head on, to face your bitterness, your hatred, your covetousness, your lust - whatever has a hold on your life. The key is to not pass the buck, to not try in works, but to face it head on in the name of Jesus Christ. That is where your power will be.

Who brought death? Who brought death to Jesus? Did the Lord crucify Christ? Was it the Father who put Jesus upon the cross? Is it the Father that puts us upon the cross for death? Paul says in Corinthians, that if the kingdom of darkness had known the grace and the glory we would have in Jesus Christ, they would never have crucified Him.

So who crucified Jesus? Satan crucified Jesus. The enemy crucified Jesus. The kingdom of darkness did it. It is the kingdom of darkness that places you on the cross, crucifies you, and brings you to death through sin in your life.

A Chance to Rise Up

The Lord does not bring you to death. He leads you to the mountain. He led Christ to the cross, but it is up to you to face the mountain. It is up to you to split it in half and walk on through. Too many times we say, "This is the Lord's dealing in my life. It is the will of the Lord that I suffer. It is the Lord's will that I stay in depression and despair. The Lord is trying to teach me a lesson of humility here."

No, the Lord is not trying to teach you a lesson in humility here! The Lord is trying to give you the opportunity to rise up in power. Had Jesus not faced the cross, He would not have the position of power He has now. He leads you to the mountain, which is placed there by satan through your sin. But it is up to you to face it. It is up to you to stare it right in the eye and deal with this thing once and for all.

A Death is a Death

A death is a death. Did you ever see a dead man get up and walk? When something is dead, it is dead.

> **KEY PRINCIPLE**
>
> If you are facing a sin in your life for the fifth time, then you did not die to it the first time.

When the Lord has dealt with something; when you have faced a specific sin in your life and you have died to it, it is dead, and in the grave. You only die once. Once it is dead, it is dead!

You need to stand on the Word with that, because satan will keep bringing the past sins up, and you will become frustrated and more depressed. You say, "But Lord, I thought I dealt with this."

And satan keeps saying, "Actually, no you didn't deal with this. You need to face it again."

So you need to stand on the Word. Once something has been dealt with in your life, it has been dealt with, past tense, over! Do not believe the lies of the enemy. Do not believe them, but stand up in your authority and say, "No. I dealt with this issue. I dealt with it. I do not have to go through this again. I died to this. I died to this area of my heart." That is what you need to realize.

I went through a tough time once where the Lord revealed to me that I had a stony heart. It was such a difficult thing to face, but He said, "You are cold. You will not let my love flow through you."

I went through such a time of death and changing to remove that bitterness and the hardness that was in there. He released me and I walked in victory, and it was glorious.

But you know what? A while down the road I started having "symptoms" of being under oppression, and I was having the same feelings I did before. I became so confused. I thought, "Oh no. I have to deal with this stony heart issue again. Oh no, I have to go through it all again," and I became so discouraged and depressed, and didn't know where to go. I was not getting direction from the Lord.

Eventually I went to Him and journaled, "Father, I don't understand."

He said, "The devil has taken you off the right path. That issue is dealt with. It is under the blood. I dealt with it, and when I do a job I do it well!"

You know it set me free, just to know that dead is dead; that dead really does mean dead. It was under the blood. It was gone. It was history.

I said, "Satan, be gone in Jesus' name!"

I took authority over him and I was set free. I got back on the right path and I started running again.

If satan is coming to you with a sin that you have dealt with so many times before, it is time you stand up and say, "It is under the blood. I've been set free. I am not going through this again. Dead is dead - once, over, finished!"

Don't Grovel, But Rise Up

We need to have that kind of authority and not sit and take it. Do not just sit and grovel and take it. You are a prophet of God. If you are at this stage, you should know your authority in Christ. Don't sit groveling. Stand up and use the authority that Christ has given you.

I know that many of you reading this chapter are probably still in the grave right now. You are depressed. Everything has gone wrong. You hit the first chapter and all hell broke loose in your life. Family problems, financial problems - you name it, the squeeze is on. Now you are in the grave, and you are sitting there depressed and you don't know what to do.

WHEN DO YOU RESURRECT?

You are saying to me, "When is the time to resurrect? When does the resurrection come? I am forever dead. I die forever, I am in the grave forever and I can't rise up. What must I do?"

It says in Romans 8:10 and 11:

> *And if Christ is in you, the body is dead because of sin, but the Spirit is life because of righteousness.*
> *11 But if the Spirit of Him who raised Jesus from the dead dwells in you, He who raised Christ from the dead will also give life to your mortal bodies through His Spirit who dwells in you.*

It is time to resurrect when your flesh is dead. When you do not care what your mother-in-law has to say about you. When you do not care about that woman driver who annoys you every morning on the highway. When you do not care what your boss says to you anymore. When you do not care who picks on you. When you don't care that somebody in church rejects your word. When you do not care anymore - that is the time to resurrect.

When it is still bothering you when they say that word or they speak behind your back and it still gets you in your gut - you are not dead yet. It is not time to resurrect. But when you can come to the place where that person who annoyed you beyond comprehension does not annoy you anymore, then you are dead.

You are there when you don't care. Hey, some of us have to go through a nervous breakdown before we reach that point, because we need to have our legs broken a few times.

FLESH DIES, SPIRIT MOVES IN

When you are at that point of absolute death, that is when the Spirit of God kicks in, because your flesh is cut off and the Spirit can start moving from within, because you have that power in you. When you can throw the flesh away a bit, the Spirit can start coming out through your flesh.

You know what is the best part when that happens? It is not you, and it is not your strength in which you are going to rise up into glory. It is the same Spirit that raised Christ from the dead.

> **KEY PRINCIPLE**
>
> It is the Spirit of the Lord Jesus Christ that will come and manifest through you. It will not be your works, nor will it be your big mouth that does it. It will be the Spirit of the living God that does it.

He will lift you up. He will resurrect you. When you look at your life, you will know, *"Not by might nor by power, but by My Spirit,' Says the Lord of hosts."*

He is the one who will raise you up, and you will know it. You will know with every death and resurrection you go through, that it is Him that raises you up. It is Him that has power and authority to lift you up out of the mire; that it is Him, and not you. It is all Him, and none of you. It is all His power and no flesh. When you can come to that place of death and He lifts you up, it is so humbling. You feel like a worm, because nothing you did helped. None of your works helped. None of your crying helped. The Spirit of God did it! He raised you up. You need to know that, and you must remember that. Remember that it is none of you and all the Spirit of Jesus Christ.

How Do You Resurrect?

Here is a big question: How? You know the "when" is when you feel absolutely horrid and the whole world is against you, and you are really at the absolute pit of despair. But how do you resurrect?

You say to me, "But if you are depressed, you can't help yourself. You see, it is a sickness. I'm depressed and I can't help myself. I need somebody to help me. I cannot cope with this. I think I'm just going to go and sleep and take medication."

I have heard this argument a lot.

Jesus Used His Authority

Well, what did Jesus do? What did He do after He died and descended into the pit of hell? You think you have it bad? He had to go into the pit of hell. You think your life is hell? Can you just imagine the oppression? For any of you that have the gift of discerning of spirits, I could imagine the oppression and the depression must have been a nightmare.

His own Father turned against Him. You want depression? The only life source He had His whole life was cut and taken away from Him when He died. Here He was in the pit of hell surrounded by demons and the kingdom of darkness who were laughing and lording over Him. Do you think you have it bad?

What did Jesus do? Did He sit down and have a pity party? Did He sit down and say, "My Father forsook me and my disciples forsook me. Peter denied me three times. Here I am sitting with all these demons on my back. I can't break through. I have the whole trio of the kingdom of darkness against me. Satan himself is laughing at me. I have all these demons harassing me. What am I going to do?"

Is that what Jesus did? No, do you know what Jesus did? He walked up to satan, looked him in the eye and took the keys of the Kingdom away from him.

He said, "Huh! I'm using my authority. Give them here!"

Jesus took action. He stood up and He took His authority away from satan - the authority that satan had over man since Adam. Jesus walked in and He snatched His authority back.

Arise and Use Your Weapons!

You stand up now! Stand up and take your ground back from satan. Stand up in the authority of the Lord Jesus Christ and the Spirit of the living God and you give it to him.

Say, "Satan take your hands off me in Jesus' name. How dare you? I take authority over you. Take your hands off my children. You take your hands off my finances. You take your hands off my family. Who do you think you are?"

Stand up in the authority of Jesus Christ and you walk over him. Jesus led you to that mountain so that you could destroy it, not that you would be destroyed by it. You are to destroy it. You are to reign in victory. The sin was the open door. Now walk in there, close it and do the work.

Stand up and use your weapons. As prophets of God we have a whole lot of extra ones. We do not just have one or two. We have been given a whole range. We can hit him in intercession, in warfare, in praise and worship. Use whichever comes to your hand first. For me, it was a little chisel. Pick up your little chisel. Pick it up and go up to the mountain and start tapping away at those stones, and tap away a few.

"Satan, this is for my finances." There goes one.

"Satan, this is for messing with my family." There goes another one.

"Satan, this is another one for picking on me at work."

Start picking at a few of those stones and something will begin to build up in there. You will get a fire in your belly and you will say, "Hey, this is pretty good stuff. This is good!"

SATAN LAUGHS AT YOU

Satan has been laughing at you, did you know that? Did you know, while you are sitting there feeling sorry for yourself and saying, "Shame, shame, the whole world's picking on me," Satan has been looking at you and laughing? He has made a fool out of you. He is laughing at you right now.

He is saying, "Ha, ha, look at that. I have her right where I want her - ineffective, depressed and feeling sorry for herself. I have her cornered, because now she cannot use her authority against me. Now she isn't using her weapons against me. Now she is not using the things that hurt me before to attack me."

TAKE ACTION

I am not comfortable with the devil laughing at me. Are you? It just doesn't sit right with me. And if you are anything like me, prophet of God, it does not sit right with you, either. So stand up and kick his butt. Do it! Rise up. You can do it. You may just have a tiny little chisel with a tiny little end, but start tapping at those stones anyway. Start tapping at them, because as you start doing it, something is going to happen inside. You are starting to take action, and the churning will begin on the inside.

As you do that, you will get mad. It is good to become mad at the devil. But keep at it and start rising up, and finally you will resurrect and you will not be in that slump anymore. You will not be in depression anymore, and you will not be in despair anymore.

Suddenly you will have zest and you will have a fire. You will start saying, "Come on, guys. Let's praise and worship. Let's get back to business. Let's get going again and get this show on the road."

That is how you will rise up out of the pit of hell. You will take the keys back from satan that he has stolen from you through sin. That is how you are going to take it back. So come on. Get up! Start using that authority, even if it is just words to start with. Say it. "In Jesus' name..." Rise up!

Your feelings and emotions will start to change. As you get into the Word and start quoting the Scriptures at him, your feelings will start catching up and that fire will begin again. You will begin moving into intercession again, and that power will rise up again.

DON'T JUST RESURRECT - DO MORE

Jesus did not just resurrect. He died, He went to the pit of hell, He snatched the keys of the Kingdom, and then He ascended to take on His authority at the right hand of the Father. I cannot stress this enough to you. It is not enough just to resurrect! It is not enough just to come out of your slump and start feeling better again. No. That is not good enough.

You have not crunched the devil enough yet. All you have done is taken your ground back. That is not good enough. I don't want you just to take your ground back from satan. The Lord wants you to go and take some more.

It is not enough that you simply take back what he stole. You have to raid the gates of hell and go and retrieve the rest! You have to go and get more. You have to go and conquer more land in the name of Jesus Christ.

It is not enough that you just resurrect. It is not enough that you just come out of depression. It is not enough that the devil just kind of backs off a little bit. It is not enough that you just rise up to start living your normal life again with a nice pretty home, kids and a husband - where everything is great again.

MOVE INTO YOUR AUTHORITY

It is not enough! You have to rise beyond that into the authority which is, "...being seated at the right hand of the Father." That, is where you should be sitting. It is a promotion. You need to rise up into promotion. It is not enough that you resurrect. You must move beyond. You have to move beyond that into yielding the authority. You have to move beyond that into standing in the authority.

How do you do that? How do you come from just being resurrected; from just coming out of death and starting to feel better and using a bit of that authority, to walking in that authority? Romans 6:8 says this:

"Now if we be dead with Christ, we believe that we shall also live with him:"

We believe that we will also live with Him, walk with Him, have Him walk in us and live through us. Believe - that means faith. It is not enough that you just use the authority already vested in you to resurrect and come against the enemy. You need to use some faith to allow the Lord to live through you and rise up into that position of promotion. It takes faith.

I have to tell you prophet, this is a choice. You can sit in the pit of hell for as long as you like, waiting for a sign from heaven. But until you get up and go and take back the keys - and until you rise up and apply the faith that the Lord has grown in you, you will remain in the pit of hell. It is a choice.

Resurrection is a Choice

You learned that death was a choice by saying, "Lord, into your hands I commit my spirit."

> **Key Principle**
>
> Jesus chose to die. So you have chosen to die and let the flesh go. But resurrection is also a choice. You have to choose to take back your authority and you have to choose to allow the Lord to live His life through you.

It is a choice. It is not going to fall down from the sky and hit you on the head. Death did not happen by chance, and neither will resurrection happen by chance.

Maybe you are sitting there saying, "Okay, I've done it all right. I died. I did everything the Lord said. Now I'm going to wait for the resurrection."

Just imagine if Jesus had done that.

"Well I'm sitting here in the pit of hell. I'll wait for God the Father to reach down from heaven and pluck me out."

You Need to Ascend

It didn't happen that way. Jesus had to make the choice. He had to choose to take back the keys. Then He had to make the choice to ascend up to the Father to be glorified.

Now you may have just come out of your slump. You may have just come out of the pit of hell. But now you must go up to be glorified. That sounds exciting to me. How do you do it? You do it by faith.

"The same Spirit that raised Christ from the dead dwells in you." The same power, the same authority. Say it, mean it, and believe it. It is the same Spirit. Let it rise up within you. Then, when you are taking your little chisel and hitting against that mountain, and you back that action up with a bit of faith, you know what is going to happen, don't you?

That mountain is going to split in half. That mountain that is so huge in front of you will split clean in half, and the glory of the Lord will pour upon you in such power and authority. And you will not be the little Joe anymore, but you will be raised up to heavenly places.

Jesus Has More for You

That is where you should be standing. It is not good enough to just resurrect. It is not good enough to simply be okay. It is not good enough to just get by. It is just not good enough to have one revelation, one vision or one prophecy. It isn't good enough to dream one dream. It is not good enough to just get by as a prophet with one word of wisdom every now and again. No!

The Lord has more for you than that. He has more for you than sitting in the back of the church getting one little word once a week. He has more for you! If you are happy to simply come through a little test and stay there, and not grow up and be glorified, and take on the promotion that He has given you, you will not progress to anywhere. If Jesus had not ascended up into heaven and been glorified, He would not be seated at the right hand of the Father right now. He would still be sitting on earth.

Where are you sitting today prophet? Are you sitting at the back of a church in a pew? Or are you sitting next to the Father in heavenly places? Where are you sitting? It is a choice. The Lord will never force His will on you. He gives you opportunity, but He will never force it on you unless you grasp it, take it by faith and run with it. The Lord wants so much more for you.

He wants more for you than just to be in the ministry of a prophet. He wants you to rise up into the office of a prophet.

Use Your Imagination

Tell me something. How wild is your imagination? Come on, how wild can it go when it comes to ministry? Close your eyes and imagine. How far do you want to go? Can you see yourself in front of a crowd? Can you see it?

Can you see yourself healing the sick? Can you see yourself healing the lame? How far can your imagination go? Come on, give it a shot. Let it go wild. Let all the desires that are burning in you just burst into your imagination. Do it.

Now take that imagination and flip it over about ten or twenty times. Only now are you becoming close to what the Lord has for you. That is pretty awesome. Hey, being a prophet, you are naturally a dreamer. It should not be too difficult for you. Dream a bit. Close your eyes and let the Lord put the pictures in your heart.

Do not be afraid to dream or to think big. Do not be afraid to think beyond the natural, beyond your own expectations or beyond the expectations of others. Do not limit yourself to natural thinking. Think wild, think crazy, think big, and think huge! Imagine waves of anointing power; people falling over just by your shadows. Think big. Build the pictures in your heart and let it produce faith.

Move on to Victory!

IT IS IN THE MIND

The Lord will only take you as far as you want to walk. If in your mind, the path stops dead right in front of you, that is where you will stop. But if in your mind your path is way beyond the stars, then Jesus has a whole lot more to work with. He has a whole lot more possibilities to work with then. But if your thinking and your mind, and the pictures in your mind are saying, "Well, I hope this week I can minister to someone," you are not going very far are you? Your ministry is going to be limited to next week.

DON'T LIMIT YOUR VISION

Where do you see yourself next year? Where do you see yourself in the next five years? Still saying, "Well, Lord, I hope I am able to minister to someone this week?"

No! You are greater than that. You have more authority than that. Your calling is bigger than that. Your calling is as big as your desire. How big is that desire? How big is that imagination? How big are the pictures in your heart and your mind? The Lord put them there. Do not let people lie to you.

This really blows me away. I hear people walking around and saying, "You know, I am so sick of people walking around calling themselves prophets, because really they are not real prophets. Why would people want to be prophets and be exalted? They are just calling themselves a prophet so they can be exalted and have everybody look up to them."

Then I think to myself, "Who, in their right mind of thinking, would want to go through death after death after death?"

Think about it. Who would say, "Ooh, can I have some of that? I want to be rejected today."

Who in their right mind would say, "Oh yes Lord, I want to be a prophet of God. Come on people. Reject me. Come on death, where is your sting? Come on, give me your best shot."

Who in their right mind would do that? I tell you who would do that. Only a prophet of God would. They are the only ones stupid enough to do that!

THE LORD GIVES THE DESIRE

So do not look around you and say, "Well, he is calling himself a so-called prophet."

That is great. If that is his desire and that is his calling, let him have it. The poor guy doesn't know what he is in for. Leave him alone. If that is his passion and his desire, you can be sure the Lord put it there. Why would satan put a passion in the heart of a person to be a prophet so that that prophet could destroy his kingdom? Does that make sense to anyone? Why would satan put a thought in somebody's heart that they are a prophet so that they could rise up and destroy him?

Do you want to be a prophet? Do you want to wield the power and authority that comes with the prophetic mantle? Does that passion burn so deep in you that you do not know what to do with it?

When you look at the hurt you say, "Father, give me what I need. I want to heal them. Jesus, people are in pain. Give me what I need. Father, there are so many people with broken hearts. Give me what I need to mend them."

Do you think satan put that there? The Lord put that there. The Lord gave you the passion. He gave you the burning desire deep inside your gut that you cannot run away from. Now stop messing around and asking questions and having doubts, and start building pictures of hope that can produce faith.

Build the Pictures

Start building the pictures. Start seeing yourself ministering. Start seeing yourself doing it on a large scale, touching hundreds and thousands and millions of lives. See yourself doing it. Let the Lord put the pictures in your mind. As you are in the Word, see yourself doing what the apostles did. Visualize yourself doing it. Meditate on it.

Let the Lord say in your heart, "Child, I have such big plans for you. I can't wait for you to see what I have for you."

But you are limiting Him and you are saying, "Well Lord, do you mind if I have a crumb of the cake?"

He is saying, "I've got a banquet for you."

And you are saying, "Yes - but please Lord, can I just have a crumb?"

He is saying, "But I have a huge banqueting hall for you!"

"Okay, then can I have a corner of a cracker?"

HE IS A BIG GOD

No! Think big. The Lord is a rather big God in case you did not notice. Have you ever been to the ocean? We are so blessed to have it right at our doorsteps. We went there one night and I was feeling a bit discouraged.

I thought, "Lord, when are you going to intervene in our circumstances?"

As we stood on the beach I looked up at the sky and it was so big. It was huge! Then I looked at the ocean and

I could not see its end. It just went on and on. It was so big.

The Lord said, "I am bigger than that."

Wow! Have you ever stood and looked up at the sky? Do you know how big the sky is? That is His footstool. That is nothing to Him. It is a slab of marble for his footstool. He is a big God, and He has big plans for you. You are His adopted child. He has big plans for you. Do not limit Him. Rise up.

Use the authority He has given you. Build the pictures in your mind. Move beyond death. The flesh has been dealt with now. The sin has been dealt with once and for all. It is under the blood and gone. Move beyond that. Use your authority against satan, move beyond that again, and let Jesus live His life through you.

I went through such a death once - one of those ones that went over and over. I seem to go through a lot of these deaths. Maybe I am just a glutton for punishment. Maybe I have just learned to die quickly, I don't know, but I seem to just pop them off like popcorn there - one, two, three, four. Sometimes it becomes a bit heavy. But it came to a stage where it stopped. I did not simply resurrect, but I pushed on forward, allowing the Lord Jesus to work through me, and I was raised up into that authority. A new anointing suddenly came on me and I thought, "Wow, what was that?"

GO HEAL MY PEOPLE

I came to Him in despair and I said, "Lord, what do you want me to do?"

His power just flooded me and coursed through my veins with such power that my body could barely contain it. I fell to the ground, and He said to me, "Go heal my people. Go heal my people. I will give you what you need, but go and heal my people! They are hurting and you are sitting in the grave feeling sorry for yourself!"

Let the Lord Jesus move through you, and go and heal His people. That is what you have been called to do. Now rise up in that authority! When that power comes upon you, it empowers you. It gives you those butterflies in your stomach. It courses through your blood in your veins, and you have boldness. And when you face that mountain, forget just facing it. You sneeze and it splits!

LET HIM LIVE IN YOU

No more groveling now. Death has a season.

> **KEY PRINCIPLE**
>
> Death has a time to bring the flesh to complete uselessness, but now is the time to resurrect. Now is the time to rise up in power and let that power course through your veins.

It is not enough to look at it. It is not enough to hear about it. It is not enough to have one or two drops. No. It must be in your blood. It must be pumping through your body. Jesus must be so living in you that you can feel it in your flesh.

That is what I am talking about. That is what the Bible is talking about when it says, "living with Christ." Living as Christ, walking in victory and in power. There is not a single gift that Jesus did not use. He moved in the whole fivefold ministry. He was all of them, and all things to all men. He was an evangelist, He was a pastor, He was a teacher, He was a prophet, and He was an apostle. He was all five. He functioned in all of them, and He is in you.

Let His Power Flow

Do you want a gift? Do you want to function in something? He is in you. And when He is in you, and you are faced with somebody who needs healing, or you are faced with a problem, that problem will not be able to withstand the anointing power of God. You are living with Him and He is living in you, and you have that boldness and that power in your veins. But you have to let the anointing flow through you. You have to let the power go through you.

It is not enough to resurrect. It is not enough to look at it and say, "Gee, I would like to move like that one day."

It is not enough. You have to let it come through you. You have to let it move through you. You have to use the anointing and the authority and the Word of God, and hit every problem that you are faced with in the lives of your family, in the life of your spouse and in the lives of others.

BE GLORIFIED IN POWER

Let the power of God move through you. Step into His glory. It is time, ladies and gentlemen, to be glorified! It is time to be glorified in the power of the living God. It is time to heal the sick and the lame. It is time to speak forth prophecy that buckles nations; to bring forth decrees that change governments; to bring forth change in the lives of the System and change in the lives of people; to crumble the System that the kingdom of darkness lords over us.

It is time to stop saying small prayers, and time to start speaking forth decrees of power. How are you going to speak forth decrees of power unless you have that power in your veins, unless you have that power pumping through your body and coming forth out of your mouth every time you speak? How are you going to have that power but to let Jesus live through you in faith?

MAKE IT YOURS

Build the pictures. See yourself do it. See it, feel it, taste it, hear the crowds. Do it. Do it as an experiment, I don't care, but do it. Let the pictures start to come, and as the pictures start to come the Lord will begin confirming them. And when He starts confirming them the faith starts to burn and you say, "Yeah, oh yeah, this is mine in Jesus' name! Satan, this is mine. I'm going to heal the sick. Glory! I'm going to move in the power of the living God. I'm going to move in the anointing."

Start seeing it, and the next time you hit that chisel the mountain will split open, and that power is just going to come upon you in such strength that you will be knocked off your feet. You will be knocked right down. Apply it with faith, build the pictures, and let it start bubbling.

Where Are You?

So today, where are you? Are you facing a mountain? Are you sitting in hell, still in despair? Where are you along this path from death, to resurrection, to walking in life? Where are you along this road? Are you trying to avoid the mountain and pretend it isn't there? You see that is easy. Just pretend it is not there. No! Turn round and face it. Face it! You have authority over this thing. You have power over this thing in the name of Jesus.

Now use it! Stand up. Face this mountain. Look it square in the eyes and say, "I'm going to conquer you!"

Then approach it with your little chisel in hand and say, "Satan, I take authority over you in Jesus' name. I submit myself to you Father. Forgive me for my sin.

Satan, you have no power over me anymore. This oppression, go in Jesus' name! Demons that are hanging on my back, remove yourselves in Jesus' name."

SEE YOURSELF AS A BLESSING

Start using that authority, and as you do it let the pictures start to flow. See yourself rising up. See yourself, not just resurrecting and coming out of the oppression. No. See yourself moving beyond that into victory in the lives of others. See yourself bringing healing and life.

See yourself as being a conduit for the living waters of life that will flow into others and bring them to life. When you walk down the road, it will be green and lush, and you will bring fertility. You will make the soil fertile where you walk. You will make hearts glad where you go. You will bring joy into the spirits of people. You will bring life to their souls, and make them smile again. You will bring them something they never had before.

It is not enough just to resurrect. You have to pour forth. You have to live the life. You have to speak words of life like Jesus spoke words of life that, *"No man ever spoke like this Man."* Why? Because His words dripped with life, and honey, and food, and every good thing. Are your words dripping with every good thing? Are they bringing the healing balm of God into the wounds?

They can. You can do it. You have Jesus living in you. You have the same Spirit that raised a dead body and brought it to life, with no decomposition. You have that within you. Now use it! Let it come forth. Stand up and be the prophet of God who wields the power and authority, and wields forth the anointing that the Lord Jesus has made you to be!

CHAPTER 8

CATEGORIES OF THE PROPHET

Chapter 08 – The Categories of the Prophet

> *2 Kings 2:7 And fifty men of the sons of the prophets went and stood facing them at a distance, while the two of them stood by the Jordan.*
> *8 Now Elijah took his mantle, rolled it up, and struck the water; and it was divided this way and that, so that the two of them crossed over on dry ground.*
> *9 And so it was, when they had crossed over, that Elijah said to Elisha, "Ask! What may I do for you, before I am taken away from you.*

Not Everyone is Called to Prophetic Office

What would this world be without nurses? I was keenly aware of this when I gave birth to my second daughter. The doctor was late and the midwife had to deliver my daughter. She did an amazing job, and by the time the doctor stumbled in, my baby was already feeding and happy as could be.

The truth was that the nurses did all the work, and at the last minute, the doctor would arrive, do the final preparations, and cash the nice big check that was due to them. Sure, the doctor spent years studying. He also took the final responsibility, so if anything had gone wrong – he was the one to face the music.

The truth is though, that both nurse and doctor were needed for the process. It is the same in the church. In the great race towards prophetic office, it might not have occurred to you that perhaps God does not intend for you to reach office.

Now there are a number of reasons for this. You see, that nurse was stationed at the hospital that I delivered in. She had her shifts there and knew the rest of the staff. She knew that hospital better than any doctor.

The doctor was higher qualified, but he seldom stayed in one hospital for long. He delivered babies in many different hospitals, depending on his patients. I am using this to illustrate the fact that a prophet is not a... prophet.

There are different categories and each has their place. In the passage I put above, you will see three clear prophetic categories.

The first is, the sons of the prophets. The second category is Elisha and the third, Elijah.

I remember when the Lord first gave me the revelation that not everyone I trained would reach office. I was so upset! I could not figure it out. In my mind, "If you started on this road you should finish it!"

It was then that He started to show me that each prophet had their own road to travel! The nurse that delivered my baby – did I consider her to be a failure because she was not a doctor? Not at all! She was a godsend at a very transitional time of my life.

In the same way, the Lord will call some to be sons of the prophets and to not reach office. They are like the nurses in the Church. They are the ones that remain behind. They will know the church like no one else. They will know the flow of the spirit in that church and when the other fivefold offices are not around, they are the ones delivering the spiritual babies and seeing them take off.

I come across many of these in the church today. They are the ones who mentor the young prophetic ministers and help them identify their calling. They are found heading up the intercession team and being the prayer backing that the pastor needs.

Often they are the armor bearers or the ones who have the encouraging word of prophecy for the Sunday meeting. Should they feel "less" simply because they are not in prophetic office?

Not at all. They play a vital part of the church and make up the majority of the prophets in the body of Christ. In this chapter I am going to lay out the categories for you and explain how each one of them functions.

Find your place, and become excited about the part you play. In the Old Testament, the sons of the prophets were the ones who Saul hung out with when prophesying. They also were the ones to confirm that Elisha took over from Elijah.

FINDING YOUR PLACE

God could be calling you to function in your local church and to minister prophetically using the gifts of the spirit. You might not be called to hold prophetic office and travel the Church universal. If this is you – you just found your place!

It is a trend for prophets to want to travel to churches all over their city and the world. If everyone did that, who would be there to take care of the church at home? Who is left to mature believers and help them find their place in the local church?

> **KEY PRINCIPLE**
>
> It is the sons of the prophets that remain at home, that know the leaders and the congregation better than anyone else.

They are the ones who have the back of the other fivefold ministry and "do the stuff" on a daily basis.

This is the main difference between prophetic office and prophetic ministry! You will learn in the next books in the series that there is a definite difference between prophetic ministry and the office of a prophet. In this chapter, I am going to keep it practical and lay out these three categories.

MOVING FROM ONE TO THE OTHER

As a prophet, you will experience one or all of these categories. If you are called to prophetic office, then be sure that you will work you way through prophetic ministry first. Until you learn to serve as one of the "sons of the prophets" you will not qualify to be an "Elijah."

Everyone wants to be on the top these days, but not any are prepared to pay the price by moving through the ranks. However, it is only when you move through the ranks that you identify who you truly are in Christ.

I have had so many of our students pass through our training and not move on from the "sons of the prophets" category. There were a number of reasons for this. The first being that they were called to that! The second being that the church desperately needed them to remain!

They need a local prophet that would stay behind and help to mature believers, one at a time. That church was like me when I went into labor with my daughter. I needed a midwife by my side to help me push that baby out.

The Church is full of such midwives, feeling inadequate because they are not doctors. Allow yourself to fill the place that the Lord has for you and you will find out just how rewarding it can be!

COMPETITION IS UNNECESSARY

You don't have to compete with the rest of the world for your calling. Find out what God has for you. Find out which category you are in. Because when you do, you are not only going to find peace, but you are going to find the anointing and the place you have been looking for.

You are going to become useful - that's what we all want to be. You don't want to be the odd outcast for the rest of your life, wondering why you don't fit, striving for something that was never meant to be yours. You will always feel like you are missing the mark.

You don't have to feel that way anymore. Find your place. Settle in it and you will flourish. You will be amazed how many people you will reach and minister to and how effective you will be.

CATEGORY 1: SONS OF THE PROPHETS

> *2 Kings 2:15 Now when the sons of the prophets who were from Jericho saw him, they said, "The spirit of Elijah rests on Elisha." And they came to meet him, and bowed to the ground before him.*

Now who exactly were the sons of the prophets? They are the first prophetic category and they function mostly in prophetic ministry.

They will flow in words of wisdom and knowledge. You will find them in the intercessors' group. They are the ones that bring the public prophetic words in the local church. They hold a position, but not office of prophet. So they will function mostly in the local church and will have a church home. In fact some churches call them the "house prophets."

1. They Remain in the Local Church

Is it true that everybody who functions in the prophetic leaves their church? No – not the sons of the prophets. They don't leave. They remain to be a part of what is going on in that local church.

If all the prophets were leaving the church all the time and going from place to place, who will stay behind and encourage the people? If you've moved into any of the other prophetic categories, you probably started off as a son of the prophets.

2. They Function in Prophetic Ministry

You were there to motivate and encourage and perhaps on the worship team. You gave words of prophecy and people were touched.

Sometimes I think we wish we could all stay there. There is not as much training involved and not as much preparation required. They get to function in the prophetic gifts. They will function mostly in words of encouragement and exhortation. They will be used to give decrees, but it's not as often as someone in prophetic office.

3. Works With Church Leadership

Because of their strong passion for the local church, this category will work closely with the leadership of the church. They will be there to carry that pastor in prayer. In fact you would see them being labeled the "armor bearer" in the local congregation.

Sometimes this prophet oversteps that boundary and the Lord will call you to death again and again. You have been called to the church to exhort and restore – not to tear down. That is why you will continue to go through the training that will establish this character trait in you.

4. Prophetic Training is Less Intense

I was of the type that "If I had to die… you have to die!" It took me a while to realize different grace had been given to each of us! My depth of death was not the same as the prophet next to me! I am sure we all hurt the same, but how often we had to hurt was definitely different. I found out much later that God was calling me to train His prophets.

No wonder I was not allowed any room for error. My ministry reached more people than most, and by shaping prophets, I had better be in order. I had better speak on behalf of God and not blab out my own ideas.

> **KEY PRINCIPLE**
>
> Now someone that is called to minister in the local church is not going to be called to that same level of death!

It took me a while to "get" that! Apostle James paid a much different price to what Paul did. I love what Jesus says,

> *John 21:21 Peter, seeing him, said to Jesus, "But Lord, what about this man?"*
> *22 Jesus said to him, "If I will that he remain till I come, what is that to you? You follow Me.*

Jesus told Peter very clearly, "You pay your own price and you leave John to pay his! What I have called him to pay has nothing to do with you!"

The same holds true for your own call. Determine the price that God has called you to pay and walk it out. For one called as a son of the prophets, that price will be different. Less is required, and so less training is needed. Walk out your own call in fear and trembling.

5. THEY ARE MEANT TO SETTLE

Consider how the sons of the prophets settled and set up their homes. This was not so for Elijah and Elisha. They always moved around. This category of prophet is not called to the Church universal. They are called to settle down in a local church and to minister where God puts them. It could be that God will move you to different local churches, but the idea is for you to be settled.

If you keep feeling that you just don't have what it takes to go out there, relax! You don't have to go out there. Perhaps God is not calling you to go out there. Perhaps God is calling you to settle in a local church and to be useful.

So if you feel that the Lord just has you in a local church right now where your feet are grounded, where you're there just to be a blessing, then you are a son of the prophets and have got a very clear function. Sure, you still need some training. You still need to get rid of your preconceived ideas.

Do not think that you will escape the cross. You will still feel the weight of that church on your shoulders!

You are there to minister to those people, to love them and be there for them. You are to be a listening ear, to flow in the gifts and give them a word of encouragement when they need it most.

If this is where God has you right now, take a deep breath, relax and realize that it's okay! You don't have to push. You don't have to go further - not right now. It's all right to just be settled.

The Lord Always has a Place for You

Like I said before, the Lord might move you forward on to the next category of prophet, but it is quite possible that He will have you remain in this category for a number of years. It is during this season that He will challenge you regarding your personal relationships.

You will learn submission and get your home in order. In a marriage where your spouse is being worked on by God? Then you can be sure that you will remain in this category until you are both ready to move forward with the Lord. Isn't that just the grace of the Lord?

There is always a place to fulfill the burning call inside of you. Regardless of your circumstances and relationships – He will always have an open door. Your part is to embrace it and to flourish within it.

Category 2: Elisha – The Leader of Prophets

The prophets that I mentor personally are of this category. They are called to prophetic office. In other words, they do not remain as a son of the prophets, but they are mentored by somebody who is already in prophetic office.

You are a mentored prophet. So in other words, you are called to rise up into prophetic office, but you are doing that via a mentor. Well, you are pretty blessed because you got the easier option. If I look at good old Elijah and what he had to go through… the good part is that Elisha had somebody to be there for him and to take him through it.

These guys rise up so much quicker than the others do, because they have somebody there to point out the way for them. So if you are in this position, thank the Lord, because I think that you have probably got it easiest out of all of them.

It is quite possible that this mentorship will take place while you are in the local church, but in my experience, I have seen the Lord move many into a time of isolation during this phase. It depends on where the Lord desires to use you once you have moved on to prophetic office.

For some, He might send you back to the local church for a season, to make a home base. Others will be sent out to the Universal Church. The important thing is not to push the Lord into your agenda, but to allow Him to take you to where He wants you to go!

1. ONE FOOT IN LOCAL CHURCH - ONE FOOT IN UNIVERSAL

I would daresay that this category of prophet has one foot in the local church and the other in the universal. There are many in prophetic office that will always remain in this category.

However out of these, the Lord will pick out some to become Elijahs. Those who will be called to pay a higher price and reach a broader influence in the Church.

As an Elisha, you will rise up in office. You will be called to the Church universal and yes, you will go through all the preparation, training and the deaths

The only difference is, you are blessed enough to have somebody there to show you the way.

So, if you feel that you are called to prophetic office, to the Church universal and that you are in a place right now where God said, "Sit down, shut up, submit and learn," you are an Elisha!

2. Called to Submit to Mentorship

That is what God is telling you – to submit and to be able to receive. The Scripture says that Elisha washed the hands of Elijah. He served and was there to receive.

Unfortunately, we get too many trainees rising up who think that they are Elijahs, ready to teach everybody else, but not ready to learn! In that case, you would leave this teaching having learned absolutely nothing, except for maybe a bit of head knowledge.

The idea of being an Elisha is to receive and learn. You know, Elisha didn't come to Elijah with a list saying, "Well, this is how I think you should be training me. I would like to mention that you need to tell me how to prophesy and you need to handle me in a way that I like, please!"

No – it doesn't work that way! Elisha submits, and he listens because the Elisha has the benefit of rising up quickly. It comes with a price though. It means submitting. Later on, we will look more at the discipleship relationship.

If God has set you as an Elisha, then enjoy being an Elisha. Take all you can from your mentor. Rise up and grow and you will make it to prophetic office. You will get there quicker and with fewer bumps than those who have gone the way before you.

3. TRAINS SONS OF THE PROPHETS

Once in office, it is not uncommon for this category of prophet to be used to motivate and train the sons of the prophets in their ministries. They will be the ones who will encourage the new "prophets-in-training" to step out with their revelation.

They will oversee and encourage the prophets in the local church. I am sure that even as I share this, some people come to mind. They are the ones that the prophets go to when they are not sure if they have heard from the Lord.

Sure, Elisha did not remain there and there is a time when he took everything from his "Elijah" and his category changed. However the Lord might keep someone in this category long after they reach office, for the express purpose of being a source of encouragement to the prophets in the local church.

When such a prophet is called to suddenly break mentorship ties and to "cut all ties that bind them" you can be sure that they are being called to the next category of prophet.

IN A PERFECT CHURCH...

If we look at the example of the Word, we see that the sons of prophets looked up to Elisha. Consider this passage:

> *2 Kings 9:1 And Elisha the prophet called one of the sons of the prophets, and said to him, "Get yourself ready, take this flask of oil in your hand, and go to Ramoth Gilead.*
> *2 Now when you arrive at that place, look there for Jehu the son of Jehoshaphat, the son of Nimshi, and go in and make him rise up from among his associates, and take him to an inner room.*
> *3 Then take the flask of oil, and pour it on his head, and say, Thus says the Lord: "I have anointed you king over Israel." Then open the door and flee, and do not delay.*

I daresay that the perfect pattern would be to have an Elisha present in a local church that was responsible for training and motivating the sons of the prophets. Someone in office, who is under apostolic leadership, helping teach those still in prophetic ministry.

Someone who could fulfill the function of this passage:

> *1 Corinthians 14:32 And the spirits of the prophets are subject to the prophets..*

It would revolutionize the Church to have a prophetic leader who could test the spirits and work closely with the pastor and apostle of that ministry to ensure that everyone is in place.

We would certainly see a lot less deception in the church and a lot more accountability.

As the Lord raises up prophets in today's Church, I do see this pattern taking place naturally. Prophets-in-training naturally gravitate to someone who has been the way ahead of them. They are more likely to trust a prophet in office who can identify with their journey than someone who does not understand.

KEY PRINCIPLE

> As church leadership begins working with and appointing Elishas in the Church, we will see balance and a mature Bride being forged through this fire.

CATEGORY 3: ELIJAH – APPOINTER OF KINGS. TRAINER OF PROPHETS

> *1 Kings 19:16 Also you shall anoint Jehu the son of Nimshi as king over Israel. And Elisha*

> the son of Shaphat of Abel Meholah you shall anoint as prophet in your place.
> *17* It shall be that whoever escapes the sword of Hazael, Jehu will kill; and whoever escapes the sword of Jehu, Elisha will kill.

Now the Elisha will rise up and stand in prophetic office. He will motivate the body of Christ.

The Elijah category is slightly different. The Elijah category is for one that is already in prophetic office that is called of God to receive a mandate to build the Church with the apostle. He is called to do just as Elijah was called to do in this passage. To appoint kings. To train prophets.

1. Appointer of Kings. Trainer of Prophets

Elijah takes the Elishas under his wing and mentors them. He trains them and then sends them out. In other words, that is his mandate. His mandate isn't to be there to do all the words and all the stuff. No, it's for him to teach others how to do that.

And so, the Elijah is an appointer of kings and trainer of prophets.

He is the one who will take all the Elisha prophets to prophetic office. He is the one that will be sent out time and again to appoint Kings.

The Lord has done this to me many times. He will send me to a church or ministry for a single purpose – to appoint someone there to apostolic or prophetic office. I will not remain nor will I have an influence on their structure. I will be sent just like Elisha and Samuel were – to appoint kings to their place. What they do with it after that is between them and the Lord!

2. HEARS FROM THE LORD DIRECTLY

Another thing about the Elijah is that He has long ago broken mentorship links. He receives revelation himself and hears from the Lord directly.

The Elijah isn't a mentored prophet. He is a mentoring prophet. This changes everything.

So if you have felt a shift it could well be that the Lord is moving you from being an Elisha to becoming an Elijah. Each category is progressive. Some prophets might progress to the next, while others will be called to remain in a specific category.

How can you teach others to hear from the Lord when you do not know how to do it yourself? How can you call others to the cross when you do not know the address?

3. WORKS WITH THE APOSTLE

This category of prophet is the one that works directly with an apostle to build a foundation for the church – contributing to the structure of the vision. How do you know if you are making this transition?

It is easy, the Lord will begin by moving you out of the local church again. While you were going through your training, you would not be the only one who had a love/hate relationship with the church system. The Lord might even have taken you out of the church during your training.

However as an Elisha, He will send you back, but at a whole new level. You will serve and find purpose. For those called to work with an apostle though, this dynamic will change once again.

You will feel the challenge to your flesh and a call to let go of what you once had. You will transition from working with the local leadership and pastor to working with an apostle.

You will go from being a source of encouragement, to helping plot the course of the entire vision.

4. Elijah Training is Extended

As a leader, I always say, "I am not going to ask anything of you that I am not prepared to do myself. On the other hand, I expect everything of you that I am prepared to do myself.

"So in other words, I expect you to submit because I have submitted. I expect you to deal with your bitterness because I have dealt with mine. I expect you to listen because I have learned to listen. I expect you to receive because I have learned to receive."

Can you say that? Can you say that you expect others to submit, sit down and listen to you because you have done the same before them? Only when you have paid the price can you expect others to pay it to.

That is why the training of the Elijah is the most intense and in some ways feels like it is never over. Even after you reach prophetic office, the Lord will continue to call you to a new level of excellence.

Elijah was not allowed to remain hidden in the wilderness. He was challenged to face his enemies. He was challenged to face death and rejection, again and again.

> **KEY PRINCIPLE**
>
> It is because you are prepared to change all the time that you qualify to train others. For as high as you want them to go, will be as high as God calls you to go.

It is because of this that the crucified life is home to the Elijah. You can only take people as far as you are prepared to go. If you stop growing – they stop growing and so the Lord has to send them to someone else.

5. OFFICE MARKS THE BEGINNING

When you are an Elisha, the doors open for you to train others. You get the opportunity to hang out in your local church and be a source of encouragement. Sure, you will always be called to a "life of death" but you will flourish.

As an Elijah though, you will find yourself being called to the wilderness again and again where you will face the earthquake, rushing wind, and fire. Again and again, the Lord Jesus will remind you that His face is found in the still small voice.

There are many who desire to travel and change the Church Universal. If you are submitted to an Apostle who has an international vision, then this will become your home. However, keep in mind that as many places as God wants to send you will determine the level of accountability that He will call you to.

That means the training never ends. Think about that for a moment. Do you feel the Lord calling you to be a trainer? Do you feel Him calling you to build something that remains with an apostle? Then understand that you will be called from glory to glory.

UNDERSTANDING THE TRANSITION

When the Lord begins moving you into this category it can be confusing. It will feel as if you are going through training all over again. Why is this so? It is because you are moving from being an Elisha to an Elijah!

Elisha had his own opposition to face in times to come, but it was Elijah who paved the way for his success. Without the price he paid for the anointing on his life,

Elisha would never have received the double portion – there would not have been an anointing to receive!

The same holds true for you. If you know that you are in prophetic office and suddenly the Lord seems to be taking you through another bout of training... then realize something amazing is happening.

You are transitioning to Elijah!

Moving Through the Categories

If you cannot identify with the Elisha category, then you cannot jump right ahead into the Elijah! You need to take that time to receive first. You know while Elisha was washing Elijah's hands, he wasn't running around appointing kings.

Afterwards, when he rose up, He was used mightily of the Lord. However while he was under Elijah, it was a time of learning for him. There is an English saying, "You can't have your cake and eat it!"

Which one are you going to be? You can't be an Elijah until you have learned to submit first. So if God has you at a point of receiving, stop trying to be a hotshot and tell everybody what to do. Sit down, shut up, and submit! Learn, receive, and wash the hands of your Elijah. Take what you can.

When that season is over, then sure, the Lord can lead you further and the Lord can raise you up to being an Elijah. You will see that it's very normal for you to go through each of the categories of prophet. Some will start at the sons of the prophet and stay there. Some will start there and progress unto Elisha and then stay there.

However, there are some that will pass from son of the prophets, to Elisha, and then finally to Elijah and stay there. It depends on what God has called you to be, what burns in you, the tests you pass, and the training you go through.

Let me tell you something right now. If you don't know how to submit and receive now, you can forget about being an Elijah. How can you expect others to receive from you and to be trained by you, if you are not prepared to submit, be trained and to learn?

So if God has called you to this high level category, then you know what? You have got some learning to do! It doesn't come easy and there is a price to pay. You can't expect of others what you are not prepared to do yourself.

Determine Your Place

Where are you at right now? It is exciting to know that there is always another level in the Lord! If you have been functioning in prophetic ministry and been in the intercessor's group at church, then you are a son of the prophets!

From here it's very likely that God may have called you to rise up and be an Elisha.

You might have felt comfortable in this place for some time, but now you feel as though the Lord has something new for you. You start hungering for more training. The thought of going to the cross is attractive to you. You are ready for the kind of training that will equip you as an Elisha – a leader of prophets!

When you have been in the Elisha for a while you may come to a point where you reach prophetic office and you outgrow your mentor. From here, the Lord will put you in a place of leadership in the local church. Be the motivator! Do not be afraid to pass some of your "glory" on to others.

Elisha had no problem handing the appointment of a king to the care of the sons of the prophets. He stood back and let that prophet be lifted up. Are you prepared to do the same? Are you prepared to step back so that the newcomers can rise up too?

As tough as prophetic training is, it should still be a walk of rest because it's not you who is in control here, it's God. Find out where He has put you and then flourish.

I look forward to the next chapter, in which we will look at a lot more detail of the different phases of training. Perhaps by the end of that part, you will see exactly how far you have come, where you are at and how much further you have to go, before you reach your end goal.

Chapter 09

Prophetic Training Phase 1: Cherith

Chapter 09 – Prophetic Training Phase 1: Cherith

So you are in this place where you have a passion in your heart, and you see what's being done to the Church of God and you get frustrated. Sure, you flow in this little gift of prophecy and it is so cool to hear God.

Obviously, the pastor doesn't know what he is talking about. He is analytical and is always trying to figure things out instead of just moving with the spirit.

Now, you feel called of God to stand up as God's prophet for the hour and you have it in mind to walk yourself up to that pastor and give him a "thus saith the Lord."

You are deceived into thinking that he will say to you, "Welcome! Please come on in. I have been waiting for you. Wow! Thank you! I just needed that correction! I was just sitting here this morning asking the Lord to send me somebody to walk through that door to slap me!"

Prophetic Training – Elijah's Story

Well, that is a bit how King Ahab felt when Elijah strolled into his throne room one day with such a word. Elijah got the same welcome you did… he had to run for his life. Ahab wanted to kill him.

And you sit there praying, "Lord, where did I miss you? Lord, was that not your word?"

Perhaps so, but we need to work a little bit on your delivery. God also needed to work a little bit on Elijah's delivery. Although he was a prophet speaking for God, I wonder if he could have not used just a smidge more wisdom.

Every single prophet that has "been there" is nodding in agreement with me right now. The first reality you need to come to, is that maybe you are the one who needs change here!

Here is Elijah, he has this "glory hallelujah" moment, and he is expecting the heavens to open, but has to run for his life instead.

God needed to change him and needed to take him through a series of seasons so that he can be equipped to fulfill a greater task.

SEASONS AHEAD…

Maybe, when Elijah first started out, he had this great idea, "Well, God has called me to be a prophet to the nations so therefore I am called to go and prophesy to all the kings and tell them what to do. That's what it is! I am called to go to say, 'thus saith the Lord,' to this and that person."

Being a prophet means becoming a vessel that God can use. It means doing more than walking around and just giving prophetic words.

Later on in this book I will share what the exact end goal looks like for you. Right now, however, I want to share the seasons that God will take you through from the moment that He fully confirms your prophetic calling and releases you into training.

I am sure Elijah had been close with God and knew the Word, but there came a defining moment in his life where he faced Ahab. From then, things started happening in his life - a string of events that set the stage for centuries to come.

It is only at the end of these seasons that we see something being established in his ministry. It's only after these phases that we see Elisha coming into the picture.

At the end of these seasons, God released him to anoint kings and do what God had really called him to do.

Now wouldn't you think that if he had it together from the beginning, God would just have immediately sent him to go and anoint the kings, and get a hold of Elisha?

Your Next Season

In the same way, when the Lord calls you, there are some seasons to pass through. We have already spoken at length about the preparation phase of the prophet. I shared that this phase ends when you get a conviction of your calling and you are released into prophetic training.

I am going to pick up from there, and lay out each of these phases very clearly. So if you have received a clear conviction of your calling, and the Lord has released you into training, then get prepared for these seasons ahead.

No matter how many countries I travel to, and how many prophets I meet, those who have reached prophetic office have faced each of these seasons. So identify where you are at and take everything from each season that you can.

Making the Transition

Now up until this point you likely functioned in prophetic ministry. Perhaps you found a nice home church and settled in (as settled as a prophet gets anyway). You were of use and even had a few comfortable moments.

Then something happened. You started getting a stronger conviction of your call. You needed more. You wanted more. The level of maturity you had was not good enough. You felt a drawing from the Lord for more training and to become more than what you were.

This was usually coupled by you making a few mistakes. You upset a few people and did something that messed up the picture completely. Your circumstances start to shift.

Perhaps you are an Elisha prophet and an Elijah calls you to training. Your first thought about rising higher is exciting. You think to yourself, "This is going to be amazing! I am going to be challenged, but I am going to get more anointing! I am going to be the best prophet this church has ever seen."

It is right after that, that you will face-plant a wall and so… your training truly begins. Welcome to prophetic training! It will be a string of phases and seasons that will shape you into the prophet you are called to be.

Well how else did you think it would happen? If you could function at that level of authority already – you would have no need for "more." It is because you need that "more" that pressures come on you to bring it out.

> **KEY PRINCIPLE**
>
> Each prophet can identify this "switch" from preparation to training. It is a change from just functioning in the gifts, to having a burning desire for the authority of the prophet.

This is coupled by a sudden shift in circumstances and an increase in pressure.

Feeling the burn? Then press on and let us navigate each phase of training together!

1. PHASE 1 – BROOK CHERITH

What is the first thing that happened to Elijah after his glory moment with our senior pastor?

It says in 1 Kings 17:5-6,

> *So he went and did according to the word of the Lord, for he went and stayed by the Brook Cherith, which flows into the Jordan.*
> *6 The ravens brought him bread and meat in the morning, and bread and meat in the evening; and he drank from the brook.*

Where is the crowd now? Where are all the people that are asking for that great prophetic word?

You know, you have this crazy idea... you rise up in the Church and your prophetic ministry starts to flourish. You start seeing yourself doing things for the Lord, and you just can't wait until you are at that stage where God can use you more.

So, you utter those famous words, "Lord, use me! Lord do anything! I am prepared to pay any price!"

You feel the word of God and you step up to your pastor and then the next thing you know - you find yourself out on the street, hanging out at Brook Cherith.

Elijah didn't even have a companion at Brook Cherith. He had only ravens for company and water to feed him. The first thing that will happen when God releases you into prophetic training proper, is that He is going to remove you from the circumstances that you have been in.

1. Everything Will Begin to Die Down

He will take you to a quiet place and your ministry is going to die!

"Oh Lord, can't you just train me up in the position I am in? Just use it and I can go through the transition and still be the hotshot at church. I can still stand up and prophesy. I can still stand up and do the stuff. Please just do it on the side. Do it in the back room, Lord.

"You know, I can just die quickly before each meeting and then I can still come in and be God's man for the hour!"

Nope – it didn't happen that way for Elijah and it won't happen for you! The first season you will face will be a season of isolation. Take a note of these points that I am sharing here, because they will come to pass.

The first thing is that your ministry will die down. Suddenly doors will shut, people stop calling and you start wondering to yourself, "Lord, did I miss you? I was up on the hill a minute ago and now suddenly... there is nothing!"

You got this fantastic word, "I have called you to be a prophet to the nations. I have called you to set my people free," and it sounds so wonderful. You are ready to get in there and do the stuff.

2. Isolation

The next thing you know, there you are, all alone, a bunch of stinky birds. Nobody cares or calls. You are out in the middle of nowhere, and you start wondering to if you really heard God.

You wonder if you missed it, and you are not sure what you are doing there! Your first tendency will be to try and scramble back to what you know. You will try to grab onto what you are familiar with. You will try and push it. You will try to join another church or get hold of another ministry. You will try to get a hold of what you are comfortable with.

Do you think it was cozy for Elijah to hang out at Brook Cherith? Out there in the middle of nowhere?

Now personally, I am just not one of those "let's-go-and-pitch-a-tent" kind of people. My style is more toward the fancy, in-room dining, and poolside service. My husband - he can hike and do tents, but I'm just not like that.

My heart goes out to poor Elijah there. He probably didn't even have a tent. He was sitting there all by himself. He didn't even have anybody to complain to. He didn't even have a wife to nag him… poor man.

3. SILENCE

However, it is only when you are taken out of everything that the distractions are removed. You cannot hear the voice of God, and hear what He truly has for you when there are so many distractions in your life that are coming in the way.

The reason why He can't raise you up in your current circumstance is because if you have ever been in ministry, you know that the one thing that you don't have - is peace and quiet! There is never a quiet moment in the middle of ministry.

There is always somebody wanting a word or needing you for something.

So you squeeze God in when you can. God reverses the order though in this very first season of training and this is indeed the foundation of the training you will go through.

If you don't go through this season, you won't pass on to the others and you won't rise up to prophetic office.

You will never be sure of the voice of God in your life. You will always doubt and wonder. You will always hope you heard God, because you cannot be sure of yourself. You will continually be dependent on others to hear from God. That is why God removes the distractions.

GOD IS CALLING YOU TO CHERITH

The first thing He does is take away all the noise – all the ministry opportunities. Suddenly you just don't feel led to go to church. It's not like you have a problem with the people, but it's just that you are drawn into the presence of the Lord.

Maybe you still hang around people for fellowship, but somehow you just feel to tone things down a little and to step aside a bit. You are not sure why. God is calling you to Cherith.

The call to the brook comes from deep within. The dramatic start to your training might have begun with a conflict and "Ahab" chasing you out, but the call to Cherith is a sweet still voice within.

4. DEATH TO YOUR MINISTRY AMBITION

It is a place to be silent. This is a time where God will remove from you, the ambition of ministry. I often say to people that God needs to take away the need to minister.

You say, "Well, I don't have a need to minister!"

Okay... then let me take away all your ministry opportunities and then let us have that conversation again. It is very easy to be bold while you are in ministry. It's very easy to know who and what you are while you are pouring out.

What if you lost it all right now though? What if nobody looked up to you? What if nobody wanted to hear your prophetic words and nobody was interested in what you said? What if nobody cared and you were alone in the middle of nowhere in a room with four walls - would you still be a prophet?

> **KEY PRINCIPLE**
>
> Would you still be content with nothing but Jesus? Or does your ministry fill a need in you that only the Holy Spirit should be meeting?

Here is some truth - you won't know that until it's taken away. You are saying, "Lord, come to me in this time where I am busy and reveal yourself to me, within my situation."

He says, "If I could have revealed myself in this situation, I would have already! But the situation you are in is blocking my voice.

"I can't reveal myself in this, so I have to take you out of it so that you can hear me in a way that you have never heard me before. If you could hear me here, you would hear me here, but you can't... so move!"

5. Face-to-Face With Jesus

It is one of the most life-changing seasons you will ever experience because it is here in this quiet place, that you come face-to-face with Jesus. This is the foundation of your prophetic call.

Without this, you haven't even begun the first step in your prophetic walk. You haven't begun to understand what the prophetic purpose is, and you haven't begun to fulfill even an iota of it. A main focus of the prophet, is to reveal Jesus to His people.

Just because people are born again, doesn't mean that they know their Savior. Consider any of your relationships - the good ones have taken some investment. If you are married and have a family, you know that relationships don't just "happen." Not in the natural, and not in the spiritual either.

Although you may know the person and be familiar with them, it takes a season of really getting close, to truly know them. In a marriage relationship, this is even truer.

A Relationship Takes Time to Build

When I first got married, I thought I knew my husband. However it was only when we were married for 17 years that I could say with confidence, "Now I know my husband!" It seems that each year we are together, I get to know him a little bit more. Now, if this is true with someone that I can touch and see, how much more with the Lord Jesus?

With so much emphasis being put on the gifts of the Spirit, we have quickly bypassed the relationship aspect of our call. Without a relationship with Jesus, the gifts of the Spirit are meaningless.

It would be like me driving around in a Mercedes my husband bought me, wearing the big diamond ring my husband also bought me, but not having an intimate love relationship with him.

What's the Point of It All?

I can have all the goods, but if I don't have a relationship, what's the point of being married? We have trained the body of Christ to prophesy and flow in the gifts of the Spirit… they got the diamond ring and all the treasures. I ask you though, without a relationship with Jesus, what is the point of it all?

What if God took all those things from you? Say you lost the ability to prophesy right now. Say you lost the ability to hear the voice of God and all the financial and spiritual blessings that you sought Him for. Would you still know your Jesus?

Would you still follow His tender voice? Would you still know when He was calling you aside and whispering in your ear? Without all the things that satisfy your flesh, would you still know when He was telling you how He feels about you… would you still be able to feel His heart and His passion for the Church?

Could you receive the Lord for His name's sake and not for the blessings He offers?

Would you be able to smell that sweet fragrance when He calls you into the bridal chamber?

This is the core of what this season is about. You need to know Jesus intimately, not just as your savior, but as your groom.

6. Discovering Your Secret Place

You came to know Him as your savior when you got born again, and He was there to meet your need. He healed you, and He turned your life upside down. That is fantastic, but the kind of relationship He wants with you now, will fill you up so much more on the inside.

When I went through this season in my prophetic training, you could put me in a room with four walls and nothing else and I didn't care. I was so content and at peace with just being with Him. By feeling Him there, I didn't care if the world around me fell apart.

During this time the Lord showed me a picture of a cave hidden behind a waterfall. He pointed to the cave and beckoned me to come inside.

A Place to Hide

He said to me, "You will have to leave the outside and leave everything there and come into the secret place where no one can see you. Where you can't take hold of anything but me!"

It got to a point where I was just so content to just stay there. That's when He said to me, "The purpose is not just for you to stay here, but to come and become so saturated, that when you go out, you take Me with you!"

What are we called to do as leaders? It is to represent Christ to the Church. Have you noticed that after a couple has been married for a few years, they start to talk the same way? Sometimes they even start to look alike… one starts a sentence and the other finishes it. You see them as one.

Well, that's what the Lord wants with you. It's not enough to know His Word - you have got to live His Word. It's not good enough to just prophesy, you have to feel Him in every fiber of your being. You have to become that prophetic word. You have to become Christ.

AIMING FOR PERFECTION

The Word says, that when that which is perfect has come, that which is in part is done away with (1 Corinthians 13:10).

The gifts of the Spirit are amazing. Hearing God through dreams and visions, and prophetic words are some of the best perks of being a prophet. However let's not make ourselves dependent on these things.

Let our dependence be in Jesus Christ and Him crucified. Let Him be our foundation instead of our abilities and our works. Let His finished work on Calvary be our boast.

When that is our boast, we are conformed to the image of Christ. Now how can you stand up and preach to the people of God and say, "You need to be conformed to the image of Christ and not be conformed to the traditions of the world," when you don't even know the voice of your loving Savior?

7. Know Him to Become Him

The only way to become Him, is to know Him. It's to have a face-to-face relationship with Him. When you know Jesus in this way, you see the world with new eyes. You see His people with new eyes, because you are not seeing them through your own misconceptions anymore.

You are now seeing them as Jesus sees them. You don't even need to ask the Lord anymore, because you just see them as He sees them. You have become Christ. He begins to live His life through you. Is that not what sanctification is all about?

> **KEY PRINCIPLE**
>
> What is the purpose of the death? What is the purpose of the travail? Is it not to give birth and be transformed into the image of Christ?

Are you not meant to be a light in the world and a city on a hill, the salt and flavor of the world?

How do you think you will achieve all that? Do you think one day somebody is just going to come to you and say, "Have some salt here. Become a city set on a hill there."

No! I don't discover intimacy with anybody just overnight. The longer I get to know someone the closer I get to them, and the more we receive from each other. If this is true of our natural relationships, how much more with God?

Don't Rush This Season

We are so busy doing the business of serving God that we forgot that this begins and ends with relationship, and not with semantics.

That is why even before the deaths and the stripping begin, God will call you aside into this season of silence.

If you skip this season, you are not going to make it the rest of the way. Trust me, the next season will be knocking on your door soon enough. If you don't have the stability of your relationship with Jesus, you won't make it.

When we face hard times in our lives, it is the people we love that get us through. It is those that are close to us that give us the strength to carry on. Jesus is calling you into such a relationship.

If God is calling you to be a prophet, this is the first step towards your calling. So then when you face the travail and those hard times, you know you are not facing them alone. You are facing them with, through, and in Jesus.

This brings such a peace. Although it may sometimes hurt, it brings a peace. If you have been going through death after death, struggle after struggle, and thing after thing happens to you and you are feeling confused and frustrated, you need to go back to Brook Cherith.

You need to go back to season 1 and enter into the peace of the Lord. You know what the best way we can teach the body of Christ to discern spirits and to know what is of God and what is not is? It is simply to introduce them to Jesus and to help them to develop a relationship with Him.

Relationship Revolution up Ahead

Many of you have had difficult marriages, or difficult relationships. I daresay that nearly everyone reading this has faced a time in their lives when they wanted to give up. You have been in a place where it's just hard and you just want to walk away.

At times it is also possible that things just become dry. Then, there are those who even in the middle of all of that, come to a place of falling in love all over again.

This is where the Lord will take a marriage and He will cause that couple to fall in love all over again. They will then start from the beginning.

That is exactly what the Lord is calling you to right now. You have been walking a hard road. You have been pushing through, but you have forgotten your first love.

Do you remember how saturated you were when you first got born again? Do you remember the peace and the truth that just flooded you? The butterflies and excitement in your stomach? The hopes and ambitions? That passion doesn't have to stop!

Can you Feel the Call?

Jesus is calling you to that again - to fall in love with Him so that you get butterflies in your stomach when you think about Him. When you tear up just when you consider who He is to you!

Do you want to be a testimony? Do you want to fulfill your destiny in the Church? You could just stay in this phase and you would be accomplishing more than I see the Church experiencing right now through the prophetic ministry.

You would be the face of Jesus and the Church needs to see that - not yours. They don't need to pay $1000 for a prophetic word - they just need the face of Jesus!

They need to know He is there and what He looks like – they need to hear what He sounds like and that will come from you, out of your mouth.

So you better make sure that when you stand up that you are speaking Jesus, showing Jesus, and not your own agenda.

That is why training begins with this season. He doesn't just start with the stripping and the smacking. He starts by calling you into the secret place and filling you up on the inside, and bringing you to a place of romance and intimacy.

It is a honeymoon. At first though, you may not be so happy. You had your whole ministry going for you. You had a whole plan for the next five years, had it all together and then next thing you know, you are all on your own. You are frustrated and you yell at God.

The Lord says, "Would you just sit down, and come into my secret place?"

When you finally settle down and embrace this season, you will say, "Lord, what took me so long?"

You know why? You think you have to keep running. You think you have to keep doing. You think that if you are going to fulfill the call of God, you better start ministering and keep prophesying.

Then you wonder why you are running dry? What you are doing should stem from a place of rest in His intimate presence.

It's only when you get through this season of peace and of really coming to know Him that the next season of training will begin.

Clear Signs of Cherith:

1. Ministry doors close
2. You find yourself isolated from ministry, friends and family
3. Your desire for ministry fades
4. You enter into a face-to-face relationship with Jesus
5. You experience your own "secret place" with the Lord

Chapter 10

Prophetic Training Phase 2: Zarephath

Chapter 10 – Prophetic Training Phase 2: Zarephath

> *1 King 17:10 So he arose and went to Zarephath. And when he came to the gate of the city, indeed a widow was there gathering sticks. And he called to her and said, "Please bring me a little water in a cup, that I may drink."*

Out of everybody God could send Elijah to! He doesn't send him to a mansion. He doesn't send him to the big church in the city. He doesn't send him to the pastor that has 50, 000 members in their congregation.

No – God doesn't do that with poor Elijah. He gets sent to the little widow woman who isn't even in Israel. A strange woman, who doesn't even have enough to feed her own family.

And so just as you begin to revel in the beautiful relationship with the Lord Jesus, you are thrust, as a baby out of the womb into the cold, bright world. Your training begins in earnest as the Lord begins the shaping process.

This process begins and continues with pressure and, as Elijah found out, humiliation.

So just when you feel ready to step forward, the Lord will not send you to the big names out there. Instead He will send you to some strange mentor, or some strange circumstance.

The stripping has just begun.

WELCOME TO ZAREPHATH

If you thought that letting go of ministry and going into obscurity was the stripping part, then you were in deception, because that was the fun, exciting phase.

1. LIVING BY FAITH

This is where the stripping truly begins. So Elijah camps out at the widow woman's home – great. What kind of ministry is he to do there? It's in the middle of a famine.

Ever felt like a famine just hit your life? What was natural before, is a fight now. Do you realize how much faith you will need to fulfill the call on your life? It is no surprise then, that during your training, you will be challenged in your faith.

The Lord will force your hand to plant the mustard seed of your faith so that it can grow. The Lord will use different means for many different people. For us, my test of faith was a financial one. My husband lost his job due to the bad economy and could not find another one.

Nothing forces you to plant the seed of your faith than living with your in-laws and needing to clothe and buy diapers for two babies!

Elijah understood this well. They were literally living on a bit of bread and water every day. There were no great ministry opportunities. He must have been bored out of his mind.

Where are all the grand pictures of ministry now? Where are the delusions of grandeur now? This is where God will begin to start stripping you. He will begin to humble you.

2. Humiliation

He will start to strip from you everything you thought was your ministry, hoped was your ministry and wanted to be your ministry.

> **Key Principle**
>
> He will take every strength that you could boast in. He will expose in you every weakness you are too afraid to face.

He will put His finger on those hurts and struggles, as well as bad attitudes and character traits that you would rather nobody went to.

A Twofold Purpose

It is in this phase that all the sinful templates of the past are being exposed. What is the purpose here? It is twofold.

Firstly, so that you can let go of "you" and start to define what God has called you to be.

This is why the responsibility is so intense and that's why the stripping must begin to take place. Your mindsets and your ideas have got to go. They have to become based on the Word and on what God wants and not on your archetype, feelings, and ambitions for ministry.

Why Zarephath is Needed

The second reason why God starts addressing those things is because you need healing. The main reason why you have those wrong mindsets and problems is because of the things that you have experienced through your life.

What we experience from the time that we are born into this world, shapes our character. Sometimes this is a good thing. Sometimes the things we face, even the challenging things, are good. They shape, transform and conform us.

Sometimes though, the pressures that come on us through life leave scars and hurts. You react to them negatively and so they leave a bad attitude and you lose your hope.

You have an experience growing up or even a bad experience in the Church, and it builds a veil around your heart. That is why you have so many preconceived ideas. That is why when God gives you one thing, you speak another.

Sometimes you don't even realize it because everything He says is being filtered. You see, God is going to put the word in your spirit. Remember the teaching we did in *Prophetic Functions* about spirit, soul and body?

> **KEY PRINCIPLE**
>
> His word has to come from your spirit, through your soul and out your mouth.

Our character is shaped through the influences on our mind, emotions and will.

How we react to the things that happen to us in life changes the way we think. It forms what we feel about things as well as the way we do things. Now if those thoughts, feelings, and actions stem from sinful templates, you have a problem.

Say you reacted badly to something someone did to you in the past. Now here comes the pure word of God, which is like a beautiful spring, bubbling up from your spirit. It travels through your soul and when it arrives there it is met with hurt, bitterness, frustration, anger, confusion and demonic oppression.

The Lord's word is being filtered through all of that and so by the time it's released out of your mouth, we have a mess.

I'm not saying that everything you share is deception - I'm just saying it's mixed. I'm saying it comes out colored with your preconceived ideas. It comes out colored by your hurts and pain.

Instead of God's Word coming through with the heart of Christ, it becomes tainted with what is in your heart.

I'm not saying He is not speaking to you or that you cannot hear Him. He is speaking, but let's deal with the filter, because your filter is messed up. God is not a man that He should lie, or repent - but we are! (Numbers 23:19).

The things that have conformed our character and made us into who we are today... let's be honest, we have not been formed by the hand of God. We have been in this world. We have been through unusual experiences and gone through hard times.

And so the Lord opens the door. You know the Scripture that says, "Behold I stand at the door and knock"? That is what the Lord does in the first phase of your training – He knocks.

TRANSITION INTO ZAREPHATH

When He comes in, you start to fellowship. You fellowship with the Lord and have your cup of tea with

Him (if you are in South Africa), and your coffee (if you are in the States) and you have a good time getting to know one another.

After the tea party ends, He stands up and starts looking around your home.

He starts turning on some lights in your rooms and He says, "Wow, when was the last time we renovated in here?

When last did we sweep these cobwebs out from under the bed? Did you know that this furniture is falling apart? My goodness, what is that smell? No, this won't do!"

He picks up a broom and a mop and He starts sweeping through your life. He throws out all the old stuff.

"But Lord, I like this picture on the wall!"

"No – it goes. That picture doesn't belong here. It's old. It's moldy. Dump it!"

3. YOU WILL TRIGGER DAILY

It is because you have a close relationship with the Lord, that you can survive this kind of stripping. And so in this season, all templates are exposed.

You will trigger daily. You will encounter people daily that will say something that will set you off from naught to one hundred in 2 seconds flat.

Memories will come to your mind out of nowhere. Pressures will come upon you. Your boss will start to get on your case. Your spouse will wake up in a bad mood and dump all over you. And then you will go to church (or at least try) and you will get kicked out again.

You will try to get your best friend on the phone but instead of understanding, they will snub you. Your children enter a new phase of rebellion and you come down with a dose of flu… Welcome to Zarephath!

The Lord is stripping you. But you see, you need to get what He is exposing in you. This is why He puts you in this situation of humility. This is the reason why he took away all your ministry opportunities. You need to "get it".

We prophets-in-training can be a little dense. We don't get the message the first time around. You go to a party and something happens. Somebody gets on your case and voila… you end up in conflict. What is wrong with this person?

You go to the church the next day… and the same thing happens! What is wrong with everyone?

Its Monday and you head to work, and "get into it" with a co-worker. Everywhere you go, you are just rejected…

"The world is going mad, no one knows what it means to be kind any more."

"Every church I go to and every Christian I meet… sooner or later they just reject me."

"My co-workers are just jealous. That is why they are turning against me."

"My spouse is just in the flesh, there is no reason why they should be angry with me!"

Seriously? When are you going to get the message?

TIME TO "GET IT"

Is it true that the whole world has to change or could it just be that, maybe, just maybe, you are the one that has the conflict?

Have you considered that perhaps you are the problem?

God keeps making the same point again, and again. Yet you sit around thinking, "What is wrong with everyone else?" Sometimes when I see such a prophet with a "victim mentality," I just want to pick them up and shake them until their teeth rattle.

"God is trying to get through your thick skull! Die already – let it go!"

It is because you are reacting the way that you are, that God is putting His finger on it. While putting His finger in this sore spot, He is saying, "Why did you react like that over here?"

Why – let's take a look at that for a moment. "Why do you keep reacting to rejection this way?" The Lord wants you to look at what keeps coming out of you when pressure is on you.

What Makes You Crazy?

You know, we are all very diverse so it's not going to be the same for everybody. Depending on who you are, particular circumstances will bring different things out of you.

Each of us has a "something" that makes us just go crazy for no reason.

Have you ever stopped long enough to ask yourself why? Also, have you ever looked at how long you have been reacting to this particular circumstance and when it started? When was the first time you experienced this reaction in yourself?

Guess what – that's a template! God will take you in there and you will deal with your sin. You will ask for forgiveness and deal with anything demonic you may have given license to, and then you will receive healing.

> **Key Principle**
>
> When you repent, receive healing, and allow the Lord to change how you think, then that's one preconceived idea that just bit the dust!

That's one moldy window frame that just got replaced. It's one room that just got swept out. However for the Lord to work, it takes some humility on your part. That's why this season is all about humility. It's all about having the courage to look into that mirror and face… yourself!

It is so easy to spot all the mistakes in everybody else, isn't it? God has been trying to point yours out for years now though, so when are you going to "get it" instead of making excuses? When are you going to take responsibility instead of trying to justify yourself all the time?

It doesn't matter how wrong everyone else was and how much they hurt you. Suck it up, face it, die already, get some healing and move on!

Look at Your Own Heart First – Then Pour Out

What use are you to the body of Christ otherwise? They need what you have, but your filter stinks. Let's wash it out and get a new one. God wants to conform you to His image. He wants to change you to be a gushing river and not just a little trickle of a stream.

If you have too much junk in that filter, all you are getting out is a trickle of anointing. It's exhausting for God. It's exhausting for you. It's exhausting for God's people.

If you feel blocked in the power, it's not God who is the problem. His power and anointing are limitless. The Scripture says that He has rivers of anointing to give out.

You have a whole irrigation system going on in your spirit. The problem is not with God or the anointing, the problem lies with you. It's in your mind, emotions, and will where all your templates and experiences of life are.

4. Your Veils are Removed

So Zarephath is a tough time. You can thank God if you have been given a mentor because it's quicker that way. This is the longest phase of your training and if you go through it without a mentor, it can take years.

It's like I said, let's just be straight here, we are stupid. The Lord does something and we just react, but then say, "Ah okay. I've got it under control again. Whew... That was close. I nearly lost it there... But I've got it under control now and can move on."

Then something else comes up and you react again, but you just say to yourself, "Oh no, I can't be bitter. I let it go. I'm not going to judge (with gritted teeth)..."

But yet, you do judge. You have judged your whole life, but just because you are pushing it down and holding it together, doesn't mean that it's sorted.

Just because you have put on the Sunday face, doesn't mean that this soul of yours is in a good healthy state. It doesn't mean that this house of yours is nice and clean.

All you have done, is just close that door, slip the key under it, to make sure you can't go in again.

"No… I'm not bitter. I never get angry…!"

If you say that, then you have issues! I tell you what, I get very angry. A prophet is meant to get angry because that's the heart of passion the Lord has for His Bride. He is jealous for His Bride and angry with the enemy.

If you know the Lord, you know His anger and wrath. So don't tell me you never get angry because then you just pushed it down until it is "under control." If you keep doing that, how would you know what anger is yours and what anger is God's?

I have had so many students come to me, saying, "When is the death going to stop?"

I reply, "When you get it!"

"Oh, I have been going through years and years of death. God is just shaping me. God has just been pushing and killing me… "

"Nope – you just didn't get it yet. You don't have to go through that much death."

Resurrection is the Purpose of Death

You really don't have to endure all this death. You get this idea that being a prophet is just all about death. No – it's all about resurrection.

God can't use a dead piece of meat. Many get this idea that God just keeps humbling you. No, you are just not getting it.

What was the point of the crucifixion? Was it so that everybody could have a parade?

The point of Jesus dying was so that He could ascend! The point of Jesus dying was so that He could be seated at the right hand of the Father and unite man and God so that we could be where we are today.

The point was to receive the glory and anointing through resurrection. That is why Jesus died. The death was just a transition. It was just so that He could get on to the good stuff and so that is what death in your life is all about.

5. Going Through the Inner Healing Process

He will bring out abuse from the past and things that people did to you that you would rather not remember. He is going to bring out fears, anger, guilt and most importantly He is going to bring out your hurts.

"Oh, but I don't hurt anymore now!"

"Oh, but the child in you does! Let's go and dig and let's really put the past in the past."

"Well, but that happened to me in the past…"

"Sure, but the past is affecting your present. It's affecting your ministry now and it will also affect your future. So let's go back and put the past where it belongs."

This all can only take place when healing comes. This is why inner healing is such a vital part of prophetic training. A lot of those preconceived ideas, like I shared, are based on hurts. I'm talking about things that happened to you from the day you were born.

As a little child you experienced things that have shaped your character for today.

You may think that it's all over and done away with. If you are a believer who just wants to serve God in a simple body ministry, you might be able to get away with not having to "go there."

However, if you want to represent Christ to His Church, forget about hiding it. You are going there. You better be prepared to pay the price.

6. Strengths are Brought to the Cross

> *1 Kings 17:20 Then he cried out to the Lord and said, "O Lord my God, have You also brought tragedy on the widow with whom I lodge, by killing her son?"*

Prophetic Training Phase 2: Zarephath

Elijah wasn't the hotshot in the widow woman's home. To make matters worse, in the middle of his stay, her son just up and dies.

Just great! Don't you just love it when that happens?

"The Lord is going to deliver you... He is going to help you with your finances..." and they end up going bankrupt. Just great – I love it!

"The Lord says that you will have a child!" And they are declared infertile...

How humiliating is that? Elijah was so humiliated. He couldn't boast in anything anymore. He just prayed and begged the Lord to please do something.

He cried out and said, "Lord you have to do something, because I can't do it anymore."

> **KEY PRINCIPLE**
>
> During this season, your strengths will be brought to the cross.

Even Elijah's anointing was tested. The son was not healed right away, but he had to fight for it!

In the same way, your spiritual and natural strengths will be brought to the cross until they are under submission to the Lord.

7. WEAKNESSES BROUGHT TO THE CROSS

> *1 Kings 18:10 As the Lord your God lives, there is no nation or kingdom where my master has not sent someone to hunt for you; and when they said, He is not here, he took an oath from the kingdom or nation that they could not find you. 11 And now you say, "Go, tell your master, Elijah is here."*

Imagine having a price on your head for giving a prophetic word. How bold would you feel showing your face in public?

Elijah was not allowed this weakness. He had to overcome his fears and face Ahab. As you will learn in the final phase of your training, it is through facing your weakness that you will qualify.

You will learn that God is most reflected through your weakness. Fear of man? God will ask you to confront. Fear of rejection? He will ask you to bring a word of correction that you know will bring rejection.

Fear of failure? God will give you an impossible job to do that will surely end in failure.

The bottom line is that nothing can stand in the way of doing God's work. Your strength and weaknesses have to be put into His hand. He should have control of them all.

Each of these points are markers in your training. Can you identify them along your journey? If so, you are closer to your goal than you realize!

PAY THE REAL PRICE FOR THE CALL

Paying the price has got nothing to do with things like being prepared to sell your car, your house, or to go and study somewhere. That is not the price of the call. The price for the call is to let go of your bitterness, your hurt, and your pain. The price of being a prophet is about letting go of... you.

It's about letting go of all those things that you rather nobody knew about. It's all about allowing God into those rooms of your life – that's the price that He has called you to pay. When you come to that place, there is nothing left of your boast.

Now you see yourself through the eyes of truth. You stare into that mirror and you know that there is nothing to boast in. You look at your reflection and see the flesh and all your junk.

Change truly comes when you look long enough to gaze beyond your reflection to see that the only treasure that is left in you, is Jesus.

When you get to this place, then you understand the saying, "By His Grace."

You see, you know about His grace and you appreciate the gift of His grace, but you only live His grace when you see who you are and how that compares to who He is.

Then you know that you stand here not because of your great ability.

Good – when you are finally at this place when you say, "You know, someday, way, way into the future, I will think about becoming a prophet." When you find yourself saying that, you are starting to get ready for phase 3.

Signs that This Phase is Ending

It is easy to tell when someone is truly ready for the final phase of training that will lead them to prophetic office.

More times than I can count, I have had prophets come to me and say, "Oh I am called to be a prophet. I have such an anointing on my life. You should see how God uses me. I am going to just impart, impart and impart…"

I say, "Well, what you need to do is die, and die, and die because you haven't even begun to understand prophetic ministry yet!"

When you truly go through these seasons, you know that your boast is not in yourself. You know that your boast is in the Lord alone, and that you stand here because, for some weird reason that you can't figure out, despite your failures, God reached out and picked you.

You come to the place of saying, "What were you thinking Lord? There are so many others that have so much more… but yet out of everybody you reached through the crowd and picked me!"

You know at this point that you are called, not because of anything you deserved. This is why you have to go through all this. You have to see it for yourself. You have to become unsure of yourself.

That is such a politically wrong thing to say, isn't it?

Everybody teaches you, "Know who you are. Be who you are! Be confident! Get out there."

YOU ARE THE EXCEPTION TO THE RULE

That is valid for everyone – except the prophet. May I continue to be unsure of myself and who I am but completely sure of what God has put in me. May I boast in what God has done in me.

Your boast should look like this:

"Lord, if you don't show up when I stand up there, if you don't show up when I step out, I don't have anything to give. It will just be a load of noise!"

It is in this moment you will feel the most vulnerable. You will feel more dependent on the Lord than you ever have in your life.

CLEAR SIGNS OF ZAREPHATH:

1. You will experience one death of a vision after the next
2. You will be called to a season of humiliation
3. You will be called to live by faith
4. Pressures will come on you that will cause you to trigger often
5. Every veil will be stripped that hinders your mind, emotions, and will
6. You will experience inner healing
7. Your strengths will be called to death
8. Your weaknesses will be called to death

CHAPTER 11

PROPHETIC TRAINING PHASE 3: CARMEL

Chapter 11 – Prophetic Training Phase 3: Carmel

Isn't it like the Lord to lift us up when we are at our lowest? Ravens, famine, humiliation and only a widow for company, we find Elijah hidden from everyone.

When things were at their lowest the following happens,

> *1 Kings 18:19 Now therefore, send and gather all Israel to me on Mount Carmel, the four hundred and fifty prophets of Baal, and the four hundred prophets of Asherah, who eat at Jezebel's table.*

From grave silence to dramatic exposure, the Lord sends Elijah to Carmel to face a big confrontation. I wonder to myself if he was as bold the second time around.

I am sure he trusted that God would show up, but after his first experience with the king, I wonder if his knees were knocking a little bit as he faced this confrontation.

You have gone through so much. You have hit so many closed doors and failed so many times. You are at a place now in your training after the second phase, where you know why you didn't make it.

You now realize that you were full of arrogance, pride – blinded by hurts and preconceived ideas. God has now stripped you of your fleshly ambition and just when you say to yourself that you could remain in this place forever, is when the doors open and things change.

When you are content to remain where you are and it doesn't bug you if you don't go into ministry for another 10 years, God will move you. Out of nowhere, God will put you in a circumstance that is very, very familiar.

1. Resurrection of a Vision

You see, through the whole Zarephath season, you experienced a death of a vision. You let go of all your ambitions and what you thought God had called you to do. Now that you are finally at peace and rest in Him, the doors are opening again and they look very similar to what they did before.

You thought God was going to do a new thing. Yes, He is, but there is yet one more phase of training that you need. You have to go back and face your failures of the past, but this time something is very different.

That different "something" is you!

You are very different. The people will be the same as well as the circumstances. The opportunity will even look the same but you will no longer be the same person.

WALK OUT YOUR CALLING IN FEAR AND TREMBLING

When you enter into the resurrection of a vision, you do so in fear and trembling. Trust me, this is something that God does. He opens the door for you. You just need to walk through it in fear and trembling as Paul says in Philippians 2:12.

May you never stop walking out your call in fear and trembling. Anytime when you come and you say, "I have got it all together. I have the answer. Line up for a word. The great prophet is in town… " You will find yourself back at Zarephath!

If you ever find that kind of arrogance in you then you obviously didn't go through Zarephath properly. May we always walk in fear and trembling in ourselves and boast with confidence in what He has done.

Just like Elijah, you will go in fear and trembling facing the prophets of Baal. You will stand up to face the hordes of hell and all your inner fears.

This can be confusing sometimes, because God will pick a circumstance, where you face circumstances that mirror the past completely. There will be a temptation to think, "What if it's the same as last time and I get it all wrong?"

This time though, you are a different person and will look at it with a different set of eyes. The Lord knows that you have changed. If you have a mentor, they know you have changed. Unfortunately though, you do not see how much you have changed.

That is why the Lord sends you right on back to pick up where you left off. Not so that you can prove to everyone else that you have made it, but to prove to yourself that you have changed.

2. Ministry Opportunities Open Up

So during your Carmel phase ministry opportunities will suddenly open up. Your head will be spinning. In fact, at this stage of the game, you wonder if you want to do this anymore.

You will say, "I have just been hanging here with Jesus and it has been so sweet. It's been good and I feel so satisfied in who I am as a person. I am so satisfied in my calling right now.

You know, Jesus' ministry lasted for three years. I don't mind if He waits and I can do my three years at a later stage. I am cool with that."

Guess what – you don't need to minster anymore and that is exactly why God will call you to do just that.

The Need to Work for God is Gone

You will not need to use ministry to fill your own needs any longer and that is why He will pick you up and use you. Now when you step out, you will do so in rest and that is where the power is.

Now just before I lull you into a false sense of security, let me add here that not everybody is going to like it.

Not everybody liked what Elijah said. Ahab received it. Jezebel? Not so much....

Some people received it and some didn't, but the best part is that, it won't matter to you anymore. You will now know who you are and what God has made you into.

Also, remember, there is always Cherith. You could always go and hang out there if all else fails. Your secret place never closes its doors.

The point is that you just won't care anymore. Who cares if the doors open? Who cares if I go into ministry? Who cares if I just do nothing but sit in His presence?

The Lord said to me once, "If I have called you and taken you through all of this to do nothing, but to just be in my presence and to praise and glorify me, are you prepared to do that?

Are you prepared to go through all this death and failure, just to worship me where no one can see, are you prepared to do that?"

Who are we Doing This For?

When you come to this point of peace, let me tell you, the fire starts to burn again. The passion starts to bubble up from deep inside and you fall deeply in love with your Savior.

The best part is that it will show. People will get around you and they will see and feel it. They will want to come and warm their hands by that fire.

I love what one of the revivalists said. He said, "I just burn and the people come to watch me burn!"

Before training, you've got all the goods in your spirit, but you know, your soul is a bit like wet wood. When you use wet wood, the fire will not burn. All you will get is clouds of dense smoke in your eyes.

The Purpose of Training

That's why you have to go through these seasons. God isn't just being mean. He isn't trying to humble you just for the sake of it.

He is trying to get you to let go so that He can heal you. That is the purpose of training – to heal, transform, and equip you.

It's not all about knowing that you are nothing, as it is about knowing that God is everything.

3. You Face the Final Test

It is during this resurrection that you will face a final test that will qualify you for prophetic office.

So Elijah stepped out. Ahab receives his word. The rain comes, revival is manifest and Israel is awakened with the word of God. In the middle of this triumph, Jezebel manifests and we find Elijah running for his life once again.

Not everyone responded quite like he expected them to.

As you can imagine… he had a real pity party. Not that any of us can blame the guy. Have you been there recently?

Elijah shows us how to have a really good pity party.

"Oh Lord, they've killed them all. I am the only one left and they are wanting to kill me too. **sounds of weeping and undignified snorting**"

Don't laugh – we've all been there.

The Lord comes to talk to him. The earth rumbles, a hurricane comes… but His voice wasn't in any of those things. His voice was in the gentle breeze.

It was in what Elijah had experienced at Cherith. The sweetness of His presence and the gentleness of the Lord's presence is what reached him. Did the Lord condemn him?

Did He say, "Oh, you are just pathetic. Just get up!"

No – He said, "Elijah, there are many who haven't bowed!"

Then He gave him a mandate and told him to pick himself up.

"I want you to go now and I will show you, Elijah, what I have really called you to do!"

It is only when you come to this stage, this final test of who you are, that you will find out what God has called you to do and be as a prophet. This last test is your "spear in the side" to see if you really let go of the flesh or not.

Do you really need that recognition? Easy enough to find out. All the Lord needs to do is give you an opportunity that puffs you up. Do you follow after that and forsake everything else to be famous?

Do you let go of what you know is true, for a sudden financial promise? Do you cling to something, you know God told you was wrong, to meet your need?

That is what the final test looks like.

YOUR ACHILLES HEEL

Throughout your training, there is going to be a specific point that the Lord will address again and again. It is different for each prophet, depending on their experiences and responses to the past.

What is yours? For me it was all about submission! For others it is the fear to confront. Yet others are called to let go of their need for recognition again and again.

Your final test will put pressure on this exact place. It is in this resurrection phase where you will succeed. The greatest test of your entire training will not be when you are at your lowest.

It will not happen when the Lord is exposing your flesh. Rather it will happen when you succeed and people sing your praises. How do you handle success? Does the success and open doors change you? Do they erode your new convictions?

In this moment, you will make or break it for prophetic office.

4. Placed in Prophetic Office

When you pass this final test, the Lord will open the doors for you to be placed in prophetic office. Just like He gave Elijah a plan and a purpose through that still small voice, you will also find yourself receiving the one thing you aimed for.

Isn't it something that Elijah received this direction in a quiet place? When you finally reach prophetic office, you expect noise and drama. Yet office comes to you the same way the call to training did – in the quiet.

> **Key Principle**
>
> Prophetic office comes in a moment when you do not expect it and when you feel the least capable and worthy of it.

That is when you know that you carry the authority of the prophet, it is not because of your own merit. You stand in it by the grace of God alone.

Your Mandate

God has given you a mandate as a prophet. This is why you needed Cherith. You need to know the voice of the Lord clearly enough so that when He comes with that gentle breeze to give you direction for the future, you get it.

Otherwise, you won't get it! You will miss out on that opportunity. The Lord won't bash you over your head. He won't shout at you, because at this point you would have come to know His voice so keenly.

You know the tender voice of your Groom so much, that He just whispers to you, "My child, let it go. Come – let me show you what I had really planned all along. You know this road you have walked, you know this journey that you have been on… it's only been part of the process to lead you where I need you to go.

"You see, I have something completely different for you. I want you to go and anoint a few kings. I want you to go and get hold of Elisha and train him. I want you to…"

Now you are beginning to understand what this calling is all about! Now you understand that all the death, travail, and seasons you have been through.

It was from that point on that Elijah really started accomplishing a work in Israel. Before then he was just a big mouth. After that, he established a foundation that remained.

BECOMING LIKE A HOT COAL

For many who start out, that is all you are, just fireworks. You are a firecracker and that is great. However, a firecracker cannot maintain a flame.

It cannot keep the hearts of God's people alive. You need to become a burning coal that people can come to gather around, be set on fire, and to then take that fire back to where they came from.

Firecrackers are great to watch. We love the sparks. We love the colors and how anointed they look. He is so loud and entertaining. It's fun – we love it. As prophets, we love to worship and kick the devil's butt. We love to hop around everywhere.

However, it lasts for but a moment and then it's gone. If you take a burning, white, hot coal though, you find something that can maintain a fire.

You put that coal in the hearth and you can add fresh wood again and again. The hot coal will set all of the wood aflame. So much so that you can take that wood and start another fire with it.

Don't get me wrong, I love the sparks, but let's move on for God. Let us become coals in the lives of God's people.

This way we are not just there for a little word, or a little spew, but we remain in their lives and get to see lasting change in the body of Christ. Real change!

How can you see change when you just hop around, give off your little sparks and leave? Where is the real change? Well, that change begins with you as you receive the call.

I have some further pointers for you on your training as a whole, but for now let's look at what you can expect in the third phase of your training.

CLEAR SIGNS OF CARMEL:

1. Visions are resurrected
2. Ministry opportunities suddenly open up
3. You face one final test

In conclusion, I have some little points that I added for you to keep in mind as you are going through your training. This is just purely based on experience because this is what I have seen through my own training, and as we trained up others.

Prophetic Training Pointers

1. Very Sensitive to the Spiritual Realm

The moment you begin training, some things are going to change. The first thing that will happen is that you become very sensitive to the realm of the Spirit.

You will see things more in black and white than you ever have before. This is especially true when you start flowing in the gift of discerning of spirits. You won't be able to watch the movies you did before, and you won't be able to do certain things that never used to be a problem in the past.

The things of the world will become horrific to you. Before, it wouldn't have bothered you so much, but when you start going through this process, it will simply irritate you.

When I first got married and I started figuring out the things what my husband liked and disliked. I especially paid attention to things like the way I dressed, or the way I cooked. Once I knew him, I just couldn't in good conscience, wear something knowing that he really disliked it. It just felt wrong.

I am sure that he wouldn't have minded. He didn't tell me, "You can't do this anymore," but I knew that it wouldn't have pleased him. The more I got to know him, the more I changed as a person because I wanted to please him.

2. YOU LOSE THE TASTE FOR THE WORLD

So when you enter into this relationship with the Lord, the taste for certain things just leaves you. You don't have to try to stop doing it - the taste for it just leaves you.

You become so sensitive that people will look at you thinking, "What's the matter with you? You go around acting all 'holier than thou'. Do you think you are better than everyone else?"

You are not trying to be difficult - its just that certain things just don't feel right anymore. You know the Lord wouldn't condemn you, but things just feel off. It irritates your spirit.

3. YOU WILL SWING THE PENDULUM

You will go up and down, left and right, being an emotional mess. Stop trying to hold it together. In fact, the sooner you just face what's going on inside of you, the quicker you can get over it.

It's an up and down rollercoaster ride, because it will dig things out of you that God wants out. If you are the kind of person that is always calm, you will learn to get angry.

If you are the one that is always angry, you will learn to become calm. God is going to swing you in all these different directions. So don't expect it to be a nice, calm, little track.

You will think, "Am I just being hormonal, because I am just everywhere…!"

We ladies can blame it on hormones. I don't know what the men will blame it on… but let me tell you, when men go through prophetic training, it seems that they get "hormonal" too.

They are just as much up and down and all over the place. One day you are weeping, the next day you are over-confident and all your emotions are just spurting everywhere. You just don't even know what to do with yourself half the time.

One day you are so excited about the call of God and the next day you just want to die and not do this anymore.

It's completely normal. Relax. It's all part of the process. Just go through it. You are not going mad or anything. God is just pulling things out of you so that you can see it. Then when you see it, you can let it go and receive healing.

Recapping Preparation vs. Training

I taught you a lot about these two phases at the beginning of the book, but I want to recap them here for you a little more practically. In hindsight of what you just learned, you will understand this process more than you did before.

> **KEY PRINCIPLE**
>
> There are two phases you go through. There is the preparation where God gears you up for training.

It's a bit like going to school. Then there is the training phase, which is a bit like university.

That is when the pressure comes on you and you start training for the job He's called you to do.

The phase that I have covered in the last three chapters, is the training phase, the secondary phase. Your whole life has been preparation. For some of you, perhaps you have even known for a long time what your calling is.

However, there comes a very specific season when God says, "Let's take you to office now. Let's take you to that position and authority."

This has got nothing to do with gifts. You know what, I had some prophets in my school who couldn't even prophesy. However, they were prophets, let me tell you.

Prophecy came when it needed to. It is more about the authority that the prophet carries. It's about the purpose the prophet fulfills in the Church. They just need a few gifts to do it, but it's the purpose that counts.

The training will gear you for that purpose. It's a very intense phase. We don't make it a doctrine, but for those that we take through this, it takes about 9 months of mentorship to get you through.

Training is Easier With a Mentor

Without mentorship it can take years, because in that case scenario you don't have somebody there to point things out. If you have a mentor who is there for you, they can say very clearly when you miss it, and point out what God is correcting in you.

They can say things like, "God was testing you right there and you failed."

Because of all that input, if you are open to receive it, you will go through the phase of training very quickly. However, if you don't have a mentor it can be difficult.

You don't have to have a mentor, but I tell you what, I think Elisha had it a lot better than Elijah did because in the end, he received a double portion.

So we are advocates of mentorship in our ministry. Otherwise we wouldn't be here. The Church is running out of time. God has got a lot that He needs to do in the body of Christ.

I see it in the team I train. They rise up very quickly. That's why many of them are so young. They don't have to wait another forty years to get the message! They get it the first time, and so God can use them quicker. It's quite simple.

In the next chapter I am going to show you a bit what this entire process looks like when you have a mentor. The training is just as intense, but having a mentor means you will go through it quickly and (hopefully) face the tests only once!

Prophetic training is like boot camp. It's like military training. It strips you, just like for anybody who has been in the military. It takes away your uniqueness and free will. Your will becomes what God wants, not what you want.

However, by the end of it He gives you the sword and the shield. When you stand up after being appointed, and people look at you, they do not see your face. They see that big emblem on your shield. The emblem of Christ.

When they see that emblem, they recognize it. You know this yourself – you get some that just speak prophetic words and then you get those that speak with the voice of God.

That is exactly what this training will do for you.

Assessing Where You Are At

So, what phase are you in right now? Have you been released into training yet? Let me assure you, there will be a time in your life when God will release you.

You would have been released by another prophet or the elders laying hands on you. A prophetic release over you will also release you into training. Very often the person doing the releasing does not even realize what they just did!

Perhaps somebody prayed for you and suddenly after that everything went wrong.

I have taken you through the phases here, but realize that there is a very specific time when this will start in your life, just like it happened for Elijah. It was a very clear line that was drawn in His life.

Where are you at right now? Are you prepared to pay the price to follow through to the end? If you are, God will take you through it! At the end of the day, He is conforming you. The Holy Spirit is conforming you to His image.

Jesus – The Reflection in the Mirror

I want to conclude this chapter with the illustration that God gave me when I was going through my prophetic training.

> *2 Corinthians 3:18 But we all, with unveiled face, beholding as in a mirror the glory of the*

> *Lord, are being transformed into the same image from glory to glory, just as by the Spirit of the Lord.*

The Lord told me that it is like standing in front of a mirror. When you stand in front of a mirror, and somebody stands behind you, you can see their reflection as you look on.

The Lord said that when He took me through this training, that I just needed to stand and look at His reflection in the mirror!

Jesus is the reflection of the Father. So as I look into the mirror, the Father stands behind me and His reflection in the mirror is the face of Jesus.

The Lord said that if I could just continue looking at the face of Jesus, the Holy Spirit would come on me from without, and begin to conform me to that image.

This is exactly why it starts and ends with a face-to-face relationship. For as long as you keep your eyes on Jesus, you will continually be conformed to that image.

If for a moment however, you take your eyes off Jesus and look at yourself and your failures, the changing process stops.

You will then be conformed to the image of your flesh instead. So keep your eyes on Jesus. Keep seeing that reflection in front of you. Then you won't need to change yourself because the Holy Spirit will come upon you and conform you.

It's not for you to try and make yourself into a prophet. It's not for you to try and do what only God can do. Would you please come and rest in Him and let Him do to you and with you what He pleases? If that means being nothing or doing nothing, be content with that, because this season will not be forever.

The call goes out to you. Take up your baton and gaze at the reflection of Jesus so that the Holy Spirit might conform you to that image… from glory to glory.

Chapter 12

The Training of Elisha

Chapter 12 – The Training of Elisha

> *Matthew 10:24 A disciple is not above his teacher, nor a servant above his master.*

Cherith, Zarephath and Carmel. Each of the phases are a journey themselves. As you have faced the blood, sweat and tears of prophetic training, you might be one of those that the Lord has called to be an Elisha.

Now there are a host of benefits to being an Elisha – one being that mentored prophets go through training a lot faster! You do not need to face the same test a hundred times before you "get it." You do not need to try and drag yourself to the cross.

In fact, you can have someone drag you to the cross and while there, tell you why you failed the test. There is a considerable amount of responsibility placed on both mentor and disciple. In the next two chapters though, I want to take you by the hand and show you exactly what the training of one called to an Elisha looks like.

While you will most definitely go through the training outlined in the three previous chapters, there are added qualities that you will receive as an Elisha, compared to those that go through the process without a mentor.

To make sure that you do not "miss your time of visitation" I am going to take you by the hand, once again, and help you through this process. Called to be an Elisha? Then let's turn the page and see what things look like on the side of a prophetic disciple in training!

How Elisha's Training Differs

> *1 Kings 19:19 So he departed from there, and found Elisha the son of Shaphat, who was plowing with twelve yoke of oxen before him, and he was with the twelfth. Then Elijah passed by him and threw his mantle on him.*
> *20 And he left the oxen and ran after Elijah, and said, "Please let me kiss my father and my mother, and then I will follow you." And he said to him, "Go back again, for what have I done to you?"*
> *21 So Elisha turned back from him, and took a yoke of oxen and slaughtered them and boiled their flesh, using the oxen's equipment, and gave it to the people, and they ate. Then he arose and followed Elijah, and became his servant.*

Breaking down this passage we find an interesting little word. It says that Elijah called Elisha to mentorship and then Elisha ministered to him.

This word "minister" says volumes! Check out the Strong's translation for it:

> 8334
> sharath {shaw-rath'}
>
> minister (v) 62, minister (n) 17, serve 8, servant 5, service 3,

To minister, serve,

So when Elisha was called to mentorship, he was in fact given the high position of… hand washer! He got to do the dog work! Wow, talk about a high calling!

When you think about having a mentor, what kind of pictures come to your mind? For many they see what they will get out of it. They see the double portion of the anointing that they will one day, be able to take a hold of.

You see this great man or woman of God and hunger for their passion. You hunger for their fire and what they can do to help you fulfill your call. However the question remains – are you prepared to serve for it?

You are wanting a lot out of the relationship, but what are you willing to give in return? It is a strange thinking we have built up in the Church. One says, "What you have freely received, freely give."

The anointing that Elijah received, did it come for free? The position that Apostle Peter received – was it handed to him on a platter? Not at all! Elijah had to pay the price of the wilderness. Peter paid for the price of his calling with his very life in the end. Paul referred to the apostles as an offering that was poured out to God's people.

> **KEY PRINCIPLE**
>
> So before we even consider the subject of mentorship, let me challenge you with your first question, "What are you prepared to invest into a mentorship relationship?"

I will talk briefly on the role of the mentor, but for now, let us look at what you desire out of your prophetic call today. Has the Lord sent you someone that can help you rise up?

Have you felt the Lord leading you to receive from someone who has been along the way a little further than you? If so, then that is fantastic! You just found a shortcut to prophetic office.

Now along with that shortcut comes a price. For that "double portion" of the anointing, what price are you prepared to pay? You see, you cannot approach a mentorship relationship with a shopping list.

THERE IS NO SUCH THING AS A PERFECT MENTOR

You need just two things on your list and they should read like this:

1. Can this person help you fulfill your call as a prophet?

2. Is this person calling you to mentorship?

If you can answer yes to those two questions, then you just found yourself a mentor. You should know by now (looking at your own life) that prophets are a crazy bunch. They are quirky and have character flaws that need chipping away.

They can be arrogant at times and angry at all the wrong times. Do you expect perfection from your mentor, when you have not yet found it in your own life?

If you are looking for this kind of perfection, then you are going to be looking for a mentor for a very, very long time – they do not exist! If you enter into such a relationship with preconceived ideas of how they should talk to you, or what they should teach you, you will always be disappointed.

So you should enter into such a relationship just like Elisha did – by burning his oxen and becoming a servant.

What he said with this act was, "Ok, I am a clean slate! Let me follow you around and glean from you what I can."

Elijah did not sugar coat it either. Do you see Elijah explaining things nicely or being the kind of person that everyone wanted to be around? Elijah was a tough man! If I look at John the Baptist, I think we get a good idea of what Elijah must have been like.

Wild, rough, and passionate about the law. There was no time for "saying it nicely!"

WHAT YOU SHOULD LOOK FOR IN A MENTOR

Are you any different? Are you free of any of your "hard edges"? Your mentor has a single purpose – to get you to prophetic office. They are not there to make you feel good about yourself. They are not there to puff up your ego. They are also not there to make you feel comfortable.

In fact, a good mentor is one that keeps the pressure on and puts his finger in the nails that the Holy Spirit is applying to your flesh. Could you imagine John walking up to the cross as Jesus was dying and trying to remove the nails to "make the death a little easier?" It would just have taken Jesus longer to die.

The same holds true for the process of your calling. You do not want a mentor that will hide you from the nails. You want one that knows how to drive them in so that you can die quickly and move on!

Why wander around in training for another 40 years? Rather have someone be used of God to nail you to the cross than have someone with nice words that justifies your sin – just lengthening the death process.

So when you enter into a relationship like this, let's not be naïve. You are not looking for a pastor. You are not looking for a best friend. You are looking for a mentor.

You are looking for a mentor that will say to you, "Oh, so you do not want to come with me? Kissing mommy and daddy is more important? Then go away! I will find someone else!"

You want a mentor that says to you, "You stay here, I am going up to another city and I do not want you to come with me!"

You want a mentor who has the gumption to actually demand that you serve and "pour water" on his hands. Does this sound crazy? Well, what did you expect? You are not being invited to afternoon tea, you are being invited to prophetic mentorship!

Oh but our flesh screams, "It is not fair!" You will hear me say this again and again – prophetic training is not fair! It is not about what is fair, it is about allowing it to shape you.

It is not what happens to you, but how you take those pressures and allow them to shape you into a prophet.

> **KEY PRINCIPLE**
>
> The Lord is going to use those closest to you to drive the nails in during your training.

He is going to use your spouse. He is going to use your pastor. He is going to use the world. Now wouldn't it save a lot of time and relationships if he could just use your mentor?

What if you could suffer all the injustice and have your templates triggered by one source? It would mean that the nails come in a single direction instead of at you from all sides.

This is the core of why a mentor is so effective! Elijah was alone for his Cherith experience, but as an Elisha, you can have someone stand by you as you go through the process.

Sure, it will not take away from what you have to face, but it certainly helps speed things up to have someone there to point out when you are going in the wrong direction.

So with that being said, let us look at each lesson that you will learn during your mentorship relationship. What you might not realize is that the Lord is about to teach you a lot more than just about being a prophet.

In fact, because of this process, by the time you reach office, you will jump ahead. You will not need to face these lessons later on. So take time to learn them now. Integrate them into your prophetic training now.

Now I have trained many prophets since 1999 and I have seen some who learned these lessons during their training. When they reached office, the doors opened wide and they landed with their feet running.

Then there were those that did not learn these lessons. While skipping these lessons did not disqualify them for office, it certainly delayed the release of their ministry. Before the Lord could establish them in their specific ministry, they had to have a transition phase of learning these points below.

So like I said, you can do this the hard way or the easy way. You can integrate these lessons in your training now, and make it easier for when you get to prophetic office, or you can skip them and face them later.

DO NOT OVERLOOK THIS BENEFIT

Now before you make that decision, let me remind you of one further benefit of embracing these lessons now, through a mentor. Elisha was a greater prophet than what Elijah was. He took Elijah's prickly personality in his stride. He served. He followed. He obeyed.

Yet in the end, when his time came, he got a double portion of what Elijah had. There is a very clear reason why this works! When you submit yourself to someone and open your heart, you receive everything from them spiritually. Consider it like a spiritual blood transfusion!

It is what we call "spiritual DNA" in our ministry. It is something that you see all around you. Someone submits to a ministry, and before you know it, they flow in that same anointing and even take on some of that pastor's mannerisms!

Unfortunately this also holds true for the demonic realm and if you submit to someone who is in deception, you will pick that spirit up just as quickly. So it is important to be sure before submitting to a mentor. Be sure that this is the leading of the Lord. (We will look at this again in the *Prophetic Warrior* book)

Of course, only the Lord can give a double portion of the anointing! However to get what your mentor already has, that means submitting and receiving from them right now.

It means allowing the Holy Spirit to shape you through their mentorship.

LESSON 1: SUBMISSION

It sounds a lot easier than it is! I have had some disciples whose "Achilles Heel" was their inability to submit. So the entire crux of their training was all about submission to things they really did not want to hear from me.

It did not matter what I said or suggested – they would balk. Their main test at the end of their training was a "submission" test, and only when they passed it, did the Lord release them from me and into prophetic office.

So if you have come to a plateau in your prophetic training, could it be that it is time for you to learn the lesson of submission? It sounds easy until you try it! It is only when you place yourself in that position of trust, do you find your pride and bitterness breaking out to the surface!

It only takes someone to tell you, "You will not do it this way…" for you to want to do it that way!

It only takes someone to tell you, "You will not read this book…" for you to really want to read that book!

> **KEY PRINCIPLE**
>
> Are you submitted to Christ? Well can you be submitted to man? Only a mentorship relationship would teach you that.

Elijah faced this test right from the beginning when Elijah threw his mantle over him. He knew what that meant. He knew very well what Elijah was calling him to and the price he was being asked to pay.

What I love about this allegory is that Elisha struggled with the decision. He did not just run after Elijah and say "Yippee! Now I get to be a prophet!"

He considered the price he had to pay. The Word says,

> *Luke 14:28 For which of you, intending to build a tower, does not sit down first and count the cost, whether he has enough to finish it?*

I like a disciple that considers the price before just accepting mentorship. It means that they are aware of the price that they must pay and the conviction is their own. They are following hard after God and not just after a good idea.

If you cannot even pass the first test that your mentor throws at you, how will you pass the ones that the Holy Spirit will throw at you via the world? That is why you keep coming to the same point again and again.

In a mentor, you will find all the nails you missed out on in your training up until now. The largest of these being submission.

I learned this the hard way. The Lord taught me the lesson of submission by placing me in the home of my mother-in-law. A mother-in-law who had strict rules about how she kept her house and clear expectations of what she had of me.

I squealed! I demanded my rights. I stomped my foot in true temper tantrum form. Until I learned to submit to her, even when she was wrong, the Lord did not release me further in my call.

You can thank the Lord that you have an Elijah to trigger all your "submission" templates! The fantastic thing, is when you learn submission to man, submitting to the Lord is so easy.

We all say that we will do anything the Lord wants us to do – but has He ever called you on that? Has he asked you to submit to a mentor or someone you do not want to submit to? Are you submitting? Do you really obey the Lord when He asks?

What I love about learning this lesson is that when you submit in your heart, you find a new confidence in your relationship with the Lord. You find such a place of rest in that submission that you know without a doubt that you will do anything that the Lord asks of you.

It is no longer a guess or a hope – you know for yourself that you passed through this lesson and that you aced it! There is no better feeling in the world!

Lesson 2: Servanthood

> *Romans 1:1 Paul, a bondservant of Jesus Christ, called to be an apostle, separated to the gospel of God,*

Of all the titles that apostle Paul boasted about, he lists "servant" at the top. This is no surprise if you look at the meaning of the word "minister" in the New Testament Greek. Take a look at this:

> 1249
> diakonos {dee-ak'-on-os}
>
> AV - minister 20, servant 8, deacon 3; 31
>
> 1) one who executes the commands of another, esp. of a master, a servant, attendant, minister
>
> 1a) the servant of a king

> 1b) a deacon, one who, by virtue of the office assigned to him by the church, cares for the poor and has charge of and distributes the money collected for their use
>
> 1c) a waiter, one who serves food and drink

Suddenly why Elisha became Elijah's servant makes so much sense. Servanthood is at the core of what a minister truly is. I must admit I really like the part of this *Strong's* description that says "a waiter, one who serves the food and drink."

With so many in the church going around to see how much that they can "eat and drink" it takes a true minister of the Lord who stops taking and starts serving. The Lord is calling you, as a prophet to the high position of servant!

Now the fullness of this reality will only stick once you reach prophetic office, but there is no reason why you should delay this lesson until then. Take a page from Elisha's book and become one who "pours water on the hands" of your mentor. (2 Kings 3:11)

Perhaps the Lord led you into a mentorship relationship and it was nothing like you expected. Your mentor did not give you direction. Your mentor did not teach you anything! All he did was make you follow him around and do all the dirty work. Thank the Lord for that! You received at least "Lesson 2" from this relationship!

What you will soon come to realize is that this relationship is doing a lot more for you than educating your mind. This entire process is being used of the Holy Spirit to shape you. So it is not just how much your mentor teaches you, but how much you allow the pressures in this relationship to shape you.

At the end of the day, it is the Holy Spirit that is shaping you. He is the one who is forming you, by putting you in a situation that will bring up the parts of your flesh that need to be brought to the cross.

> **KEY PRINCIPLE**
>
> In fact, I would daresay that you would be shaped more from a mentor that is harsh and unfair, than one that is kind and understanding.

How so? Well if you can grow in a harsh environment (like John did in the wilderness) then you will flourish in a fertile one.

If you can serve under duress, and in the times where it is not fair, serving where you receive respect will be easy. So thank the Lord for the challenges you are facing in your training. Thank Him for sending you people whose goal in life seems to force you into submission and to do their dirty work. In that, you are learning what it means to be a minister and the Lord is shaping your character to have the capacity to receive more ability.

Lesson 3: Perseverance

I guess one cannot blame Elijah for having such a hard edge. Run for your life, live alone next to a brook for long seasons, and try to keep your sense of humor! One thing that he had to give though, was a passion for the Lord and the law.

He might have had a prickly personality, but he had grace where it counted. He trusted God with all his heart and believed the Lord even past his own understanding. This is the character trait you want from a mentor. When a mentor is completely sold out to the Lord, then you need not fear their human flaws.

You need not shy away from the mistakes in their flesh – because you see that they are willing to "go" when God tells them to "go." As the mentorship relationship dies down, Elisha is tested once again.

Do you remember when we spoke about prophetic training how the prophet always faces a final test? For Elijah it was having the courage to face Jezebel again. For Elisha it was to follow through again. When they first meet, Elisha is tested on whether he will follow through no matter what. He is tested on this one final time before Elijah leaves him.

Elijah tells him

> *2 Kings 2:2 Then Elijah said to Elisha, "Stay here, please, for the Lord has sent me on to Bethel." But Elisha said, "As the Lord lives, and as your soul lives, I will not leave you!" So they went down to Bethel."*

How do we know Elisha has changed? He does not question Elijah for a moment, but says, "I will not leave you!" As if to make a point, Elijah tries to get rid of him another two times! Elisha does not budge, because he knows very well that God brought him this way for a purpose.

When you are first called to mentorship, it might have sounded like a good idea, but a time needs to come when you receive a conviction that the Lord wants you there. It is only when you know this, beyond a shadow of a doubt, that you will have what it takes to stick it through.

By the end of his training, Elisha was able to hear from the Lord himself and knew that what Elijah had was for him to receive - even when Elijah himself tried to shake him off. When Elijah said, "I do not want you here." Elisha responded with, "I do not care!"

Do you have this kind of loyalty towards your mentor? Not basing it upon what you like about this person, but rather on the fact that you know that this is where the Lord told you to receive?

If you can begin to grasp these principles, you will leave each mentorship relationship you encounter, having received everything that the Lord wants you to. Unfortunately our human nature rebels against the Lord's common sense.

Our human nature says, "Why should I follow if it is not comfortable? Why should I submit if it is not fair? Where are my rights in this relationship?"

Did the Lord tell you to submit? Did the Lord put you under your mentor? Then it is time that you learn to follow through. When you learn to dig in your heels and follow through, you will find the same reward Elisha did at the end of this journey. You will receive a double portion of what your mentor had.

You will also take a character trait of greater value – the ability to persevere! When you have persevered with all your heart through a difficult relationship, it builds character into you. Because you did not give up through this mentorship relationship, you will not easily give up on others either!

As quick as you are, to throw in the towel with a mentor, is the speed that you will disengage with a disciple when it is your turn to lead the way. This ability to persevere no matter what will serve you well in the years to come.

Rather learn this now in a season where your ministry does not have a broad influence. Learn to fail here, in this relationship than when you are the one leading out front.

A Secure "Failing" Environment

I have spoken a lot on the lessons you will learn during your mentorship relationship, but be clear on one thing. You will fail more than you will succeed. That is the point of this relationship. The point is for you to see where the lack is, so that you can allow the strength of the Lord to cover those weaknesses inside of you.

Now this can be challenging if you are the kind of person who always feels that they have to get things right. How else will you know if you have a weakness unless it is exposed? How will you know if you have a flaw unless a chisel hits it dead on?

> **Key Principle**
>
> The best part of having a mentor, means having a place to fail.

There is nothing wrong with failing – as long as you are willing to take the lessons along with it. For a mentor to hear, "You are right! I messed up on that" is sweet, sweet music!

As a mentor, I am not training my prophetic disciples to become more – but to become less. To become less of themselves and more of Jesus. So when I see that they recognize their failures and shortcomings, then I rejoice. I rejoice. Because I know that just around the corner, Jesus will be shining though their face and actions.

The stripping that you will face during training will happen with or without a mentor. With a mentor, it will go faster. Now you can choose to be an Elisha or a Gehazi in this relationship. Elisha submitted to Elijah, he served, and he stuck it out, no matter what.

Gehazi did not. He saw the flaws in his mentor and saw that as an excuse to do his own thing. He failed in the end and you never hear of him taking the mantle from Elisha. Today, you have the opportunity to pass or to fail this test. You can submit to a mentor and go through the process quickly, or you can learn to face the trials on your own for another couple of years. It really is up to you.

At the end of the day, the Holy Spirit will have His way. He will teach you to submit. He will teach you to serve, and He will teach you to persevere. He can do that through a mentor, or He can continue to use the pressures of the world around you to do it. Either way, your training is picking up at quite the pace by now.

You can now embrace that training with your eyes wide open, knowing what to expect and the choices that you are required to make. Regardless of my instruction though, I know that you will still trip over your own feet and stumble over your words.

I know that the flesh will rise up and you will make a fool of yourself at least once as you plow on through.

Not to worry. If you take a look in the spirit to the left and right of you, you will see an entire army of prophets doing the exact same thing.

We are surely a quirky bunch aren't we? To that I say, "Bring on the nails. Crucify this flesh. Let Jesus be made manifest in our lives!"

CHAPTER 13

MENTORSHIP: THE DOUBLE PORTION

Chapter 13 – Mentorship: The Double Portion

> *2 Kings 2:9 And so it was, when they had crossed over, that Elijah said to Elisha, "Ask! What may I do for you, before I am taken away from you?" Elisha said, "Please let a double portion of your spirit be upon me."*
> *10 So he said, "You have asked a hard thing. Nevertheless, if you see me when I am taken from you, it shall be so for you; but if not, it shall not be so."*
> *11 Then it happened, as they continued on and talked, that suddenly a chariot of fire appeared with horses of fire, and separated the two of them; and Elijah went up by a whirlwind into heaven.*
> *12 And Elisha saw it, and he cried out, "My father, my father, the chariot of Israel and its horsemen!" So he saw him no more. And he took hold of his own clothes and tore them into two pieces.*

No one prepares you for the tearing apart your soul experiences when the Lord separates you from your mentor. You learned to follow. You submitted. You pressed through no matter what. In fact, out of everyone else, you are able to look past the exterior failures of your mentor and see the gold and tenderness hidden deep in their hearts.

So when the time comes for you to be separated, you are much like Elisha, that does not want to let go. This commitment and zeal is what the Lord has spent so much time working in you. As you have learned to love and commit to someone, so also will you love and commit to God's people.

I find it fascinating how much we read about Elisha's dealings with the sons of the prophets. You get the feeling that although Elijah knew them, that he did not meddle in their daily affairs.

Yet after Elisha picks up Elijah's mantle, something starts to change. We see Elisha getting involved in their daily lives. Although a passionate man who had no qualms about calling out bears to take down some rowdy teenagers – he takes time with a widow woman to help save her sons.

He had a soft spot in his heart for the sons of the prophets and saved them out of a difficult situation more than once. You have yet to experience the fullness of what you can receive in your mentorship relationship.

Here is the catch though – you will only discover those treasures once the relationship has come to an end. It is only once Elijah had left that we see Elisha's ministry taking off.

It was only when Jesus left that the disciples stepped up to the plate. Joshua took the land only after Moses died. Solomon built the temple once David was gone...

In the same way you will only uncover the fullness of your potential once the Lord removes your mentor. In a perfect world, you could rise up to the side of your mentor and become peers. I have certainly seen this happen. Unfortunately for most of us though, we cling too much to our mentor and the Lord has to send a fiery chariot to separate us!

It is because you finally walk in step with one another. You "get" how the other thinks. When you reach this point, you have received all you can from your mentor. In most cases, once you have reached prophetic office, that mentorship relationship is over!

At the beginning of your relationship, you could not wait for that day to come. You could not wait until you had that "double portion" and you could stand up and show the world what you were made of!

Near the end of that relationship, the more you learn, the further you see you still have to go. You wonder if you will ever arrive. In fact, you get to the point of not being stressed any longer if you will arrive. You are comfortable to follow. You are comfortable to let your mentor take the brunt of all the opposition.

It is nice having someone to hide behind! It is nice to have someone you are accountable to. So when the Lord starts tapping your mentor on the shoulder saying, "They are ready…" You are not ready to hear it!

I have seen this happen in many forms, however the most common is through conflict! Paul and Barnabus are sure good examples of that! Paul had grown to the point where Barnabus had nothing more he could add to him. Separation had to come so that Paul could rise up much higher than he thought he ever would.

When you have received all you could from your mentor with regards to your prophetic calling, the Lord will send a fiery chariot.

What I love about this scenario is that Elisha followed hard until God brought the separation. I have seen so many unfortunate situations where a disciple broke off the relationship declaring themselves "ready" just before receiving that double portion!

It is like tripping just before the finish line and having to run the whole race all over again! If the Lord told you to submit to this mentor and that they would take you to office – do like Elisha did!

In the passage above Elijah (in his typical no-nonsense tone) says, "What do you want Elisha?" Elisha does not bat an eyelid, "I want double of what you have."

"Ok, then stick to my heels. If you watch the Lord take me. The double portion is yours."

I can see Elisha right now, with his eyes glued to the heels of Elijah. He was probably too afraid to blink!

The point is, the Lord brought the separation – neither Elijah nor Elisha brought the sword down that separated them. The Lord caused the break to come from both sides at the same time.

> **KEY PRINCIPLE**
>
> Just like your mentorship relationship began with mutual consent, so also should the relationship end with mutual consent.

If you do not take time to hear the Lord regarding this, you will end up like Paul and Barnabus – in a big fight!

Hopefully that encourages you. Were you following hard on the heels of your mentor only to get into a huge fight that sent you both in different directions? Consider that your fiery chariot!

For others, the Lord might literally move the mentor out of country or out of their lives. If you are both willing to listen to the Lord together, you should both know when it is time to end the relationship. You will both see the signs.

THE SIGNS THAT YOU ARE READY

What do these signs look like? Let's take a quick look at them, before we end off with a brief overview of mentorship principles.

1. You Become Saturated

The first and most obvious sign is that you received all the principles, training and knowledge that your mentor has on the subject he is training you into. In this case, we are speaking of your prophetic training.

When you get to the place where your mentor has no more to teach you, you will begin to reach a plateau. There are naturally always more things to learn, but a time will come when you will need to practically use what you have been taught.

When you reach a point of being a saturated sponge that cannot take in any more water – it is time for the relationship to end. The time has come for you to apply what you have learned.

In many cases, the Lord might have you hook up with that mentor again later to receive other aspects of their ministry, or the Lord might send you another mentor all together.

I have seen the Lord move a prophetic disciple from one mentor to another for different reasons. The first mentor would take them through the preparation phase and gear them up for training. From there though, another mentor needs to take over to help them through the vigor of training.

Each mentor had a part to play and when the disciple received what was needed, the Lord brought the sword.

2. You Reach Prophetic Office

This one is self-explanatory. If you reach prophetic office, the mentorship ends. In my book *Mentorship 101*, I teach clearly regarding mentorship. I share there how a mentorship relationship has a clear goal.

Once that goal is reached – the mentorship is over. That is why it is essential to push through until the goal is reached! Imagine if Elisha had bailed out of the journey at Jericho? He would never have experienced his double portion beyond the Jordan!

Once you reach office, your relationship is over and a shift must take place. You must adjust from being mentor and disciple to becoming peers. This does not mean that you will not always respect your mentor, it simply means that it is time for you to apply what you have learned so far.

3. You Fail the Tests

This point is one none of us want to visit. However for Gehazi, this is where he made his home.

> *2 Kings 5:26 Then he said to him, "Did not my heart go with you when the man turned back from his chariot to meet you? Is it time to receive money and to receive clothing, olive groves and vineyards, sheep and oxen, male and female servants?*
> *27 Therefore the leprosy of Naaman shall cling to you and your descendants forever." And he*

> *went out from his presence leprous, as white as snow.*

You can feel blessed that your mentor does not judge you as harshly as Elisha did Gehazi! However it is safe to assume that this dealt a serious death blow to their mentorship relationship!

When you fail to submit and to receive what your mentor has, then a separation will take place – one of your own doing. There will come a time when you will be asked to go left and you will choose to go right instead. In that moment, the Lord does not need any help bringing a sword of division – you would have done it all by yourself.

Does this mean you will never reach prophetic office? I am most thankful that this is not the case! However you would most certainly have lost out on your opportunity to have received the double portion offered to you through that mentor.

You would have failed to experience the lessons that would shape the character you needed for prophetic office. And so like Gehazi, you will find a very long and lonely road ahead. Just like he was thrust out from that time to be alone, so also will you face that wilderness alone.

The training will continue. The Holy Spirit will continue to lead you, however it will be a harder road.

If this is you, then do not lose hope! The Lord knows your heart and He is able to turn all things around. Even if you missed that time of visitation, the Lord is well able to give you another. Like I said before, it is not your failure that is key, but rather what you take from your failure!

Sometimes in failing the tests, we pass them. That sounds a bit like an oxymoron doesn't it? It is only when we fail and see our sin with clarity, do we have the conviction to bring that sin to the cross.

So if you see more Gehazi in you than Elisha, then I commend you for it! In that conviction, you have received more than you realize.

All that is left for you now is to put aside the flesh and pick up Christ.

Mentorship Guidelines 101

I have taken you through what you can experience as both an Elijah and an Elisha in your training. To bring this subject together I am going to give you just a few points to help you understand the mechanics of mentorship. Consider this the abridged version to give you just enough to grasp the principles.

1. Mentor Chooses the Disciple

Elijah picked Elisha – not the other way around. You cannot walk up to someone and demand that they train you. This would reverse the correct order and put your mentorship on the wrong footing.

Likewise as a mentor, it is for you to take the first step. If you allow the disciple to initiate the relationship, then they will also dictate the route it should follow – completely negating the entire point of that relationship!

Jesus had an easy way of getting rid of people who did that! He stood up and told everyone that was following Him to eat His flesh and drink His blood. He lost everyone that day except the few that He had picked out and called directly.

> **KEY PRINCIPLE**
>
> When a mentor chooses the disciple and sets the expectation from the beginning, you are off to a good start!

2. MENTOR TESTS THE DISCIPLE

A mentorship relationship is meant to be interactive. The tests that a prophet would usually face in the world will be faced instead through the mentor. This means the application of pressure!

There will be times when the mentor will apply the tests on purpose (through the leading of the Holy

Spirit) and other times when the Lord will "trick" the mentor into giving a test.

This has happened to me more times than I could count! I ended up saying or doing something that tested my disciple without me realizing it! I would make a simple suggestion or request that ended up becoming a huge conflict. When this happens I know that the Holy Spirit just set up a test for them… which they failed gloriously!

The good news is that in failing the test, you understand it and often pass it.

3. There is Always a Purpose

A mentorship relationship is always purpose driven. There is a reason for this relationship and there is a time when it must come to an end. It must end when the goal is reached.

That is not to say that the relationship cannot be transformed from there on to a spiritual parent relationship or even to a peer relationship – that part depends on you and the Lord.

The point is, once your purpose is reached, the relationship is no longer needed. It is for you to take everything you received and to make your mentor look good by doing a better job than they did!

STEP INTO THE CLEARING...

So far you have traveled with me through many landscapes in each chapter. You have experienced the presence of the Lord Jesus as fresh water. You have felt your tongue cleave to the top of your mouth as you struggled through the wilderness.

You have seen your flesh displayed before you with clarity, and you have felt the sting of humiliation as you looked at your mistakes.

Soon your eyes will be so fixed on Jesus and on the goal ahead, that you will not realize how much you are changing. Your goal will no longer be about reaching prophetic office as much as it will be about reflecting the face of Jesus.

Your view of perfection would have changed. The title and even the authority of the prophet will no longer feel like a carrot being dangled in front of you at every turn.

You will start to look away from that and find the eyes of Jesus looking into your heart and soul. In that moment, you will find yourself being lost in Him. The pain of the nails will fade. The crown of thorns will melt away.

As you push past the final stretch of your journey, the road will suddenly open up. As if you had been cutting through thick vines and pressing through dense jungle, you will stumble into that opening.

When you reach it, you will see... Jesus. So simple. You will see the authority you have been hungering for in His eyes. You will see the office you desperately wanted, in His smile. You will realize that while you were pressing through each opposition, that you were being shaped by His hand.

Bit by bit, He removed the veils from your eyes to see. He untied your hands. He took the chains from around your feet. On the cross you found freedom and in the grave you found rest.

In that moment it will all make sense. So do not despise the nails. Do not thrash against the whip and the thorns. Allow them to change you so that you might stand up as a prophet of the most high God.

Weak in yourself. Strong in Him. Aware of your failures and convicted by His grace. This is what the Church needs to see and you, child of God, are being called to show it to them!

ABOUT THE AUTHOR

Born in Bulawayo, Zimbabwe and raised in South Africa, Colette had a zeal to serve the Lord from a young age. Coming from a long line of Christian leaders and having grown up as a pastor's kid she is no stranger to the realities of ministry. Despite having to endure many hardships such as her parent's divorce, rejection, and poverty, she continues to follow after the Lord passionately. Overcoming these obstacles early in her life has built a foundation of compassion and desire to help others gain victory in their lives.

Since then, the Lord has led Colette, with her husband Craig Toach, to establish *Apostolic Movement International,* a ministry to train and minister to Christian leaders all over the world, where they share all the wisdom that the Lord has given them through each and every time they chose to walk through the refining fire in their personal lives, as well as in ministry.

In addition, Colette is a fantastic cook, an amazing mom to not only her 4 natural children, but to her numerous spiritual children all over the world. Colette is also a renowned author, mentor, trainer and a woman that has great taste in shoes! The scripture to "be all things to all men" definitely applies here, and the Lord keeps adding to that list of things each and every day.

How does she do it all? Page through every book and teaching to experience the life of an apostle firsthand and get the insight into how the call of God can make every aspect of your life an incredible adventure.

Read more at www.colette-toach.com

Connect with Colette Toach on Facebook!
www.facebook.com/ColetteToach

RECOMMENDATIONS BY THE AUTHOR

If you enjoyed this book, we know you will also love the following books on the prophetic.

PROPHETIC WARFARE

Book 5 of the Prophetic Field Guide Series

By Colette Toach

A true warrior holds no excuses of why he cannot defeat his enemy and so is true with a genuine prophet of God. He is ready to take up the weapons of warfare that God has prepared for Him and to set the captive free and to heal the broken hearted.

Prophet of God, now is the time to face your own limitations and your own bondages and to see what has been holding you back from walking as the warrior that God has called you to be.

Once this is done, you may then step out, pick up your sword and break the chains of wickedness from God's people and the fire in you will blaze as never before.

PROPHETIC COUNTER INSURGENCY

Book 6 of the Prophetic Field Guide Series

By Colette Toach

In "Prophetic Warrior", we learned what tools we had at our disposal in spiritual warfare, what we are facing, and how to combat it. However, it is now time to become an expert at espionage.

Learn all about the "prophetic super spy", discover strategies that can be used in spiritual warfare, receive stealth training, find the secrets to dealing with fear of the mind, and where spiritual warfare begins and ends.

I'M NOT CRAZY - I'M A PROPHET

By Colette Toach

It takes a prophet to know a prophet! You do not have to follow in the footsteps of others before you take the wealth of this book and rise above the pit falls.

That is why Colette Toach can take the prophetic and dish it out in its truth and cover the subjects included in this book. So are you Crazy? Maybe a little, but this book will help you to be the true prophet that God has called you to be!

PROPHETIC ANOINTING

Book 3 of the Prophetic Field Guide Series

By Colette Toach

God has promised you a visit to the throne room! This is your summons from Almighty God. It is time for you to experience Him face-to-face and heart-to-heart.

Get ready for the meeting of a lifetime. The veils that have hindered the anointing in your life are going to be ripped away, and you are going to shine with His glory in every area of your life.

THE WAY OF DREAMS & VISIONS BOOK WITH SYMBOL DICTIONARY KIT

By Colette Toach

In this kit you are not only getting the teaching you need to understand your dreams and visions, but you are also getting the key to decode them.

Everybody wants to Interpret Dreams today. But where is the balance between what the world says and what the WORD says? You are about to find out that as a believer, there is a world in the spirit and in the word that breaks all the boundaries of what you knew - or thought you knew.

A.M.I. Prophetic School

www.prophetic-school.com

Whether you are just starting out or have been along the way for some time, we all have questions.

Who better to answer them than another prophet!

With over 18 years of experience, the A.M.I. Prophetic School is the leader in the prophetic realm.

From dedicated lecturers to live streaming and graduation, the A.M.I. Prophetic School is your home away from home.

What Our Prophetic Training Accomplishes

Our extensive training is a full two-year curriculum that will:

1. Identify and confirm your prophetic call
2. Effectively train you to flow in all the gifts of the Spirit
3. Fulfill your purpose as a prophet in the local church
4. Take your hand through the prophetic training process
5. Specialist training in spiritual warfare
6. Arm you for intercession and decree
7. Minister in praise and worship
8. Achieve prophetic maturity

CONTACT INFORMATION

To check out our wide selection of materials, got to:
www.ami-bookshop.com

Do you have any questions about any products?

Contact us at: +1 (760) 466 - 7679
(8am to 5pm California Time, Weekdays Only)

E-mail Address: admin@ami-bookshop.com

Postal Address:

> A.M.I
> 5663 Balboa Ave #416
> San Diego, CA 92111, USA

Facebook Page:
http://www.facebook.com/ApostolicMovementInternational

YouTube Page:
https://www.youtube.com/c/ApostolicMovementInternational

Twitter Page: https://twitter.com/apmoveint

AMI Bookshop – It's not Just Knowledge, It's **Living Knowledge**

www.ingramcontent.com/pod-product-compliance
Lightning Source LLC
Chambersburg PA
CBHW070636160426
43194CB00009B/1476

The Minister's Handbook
Second Edition

ISBN-10: 1626640009
ISBN-13: 978-1-62664-000-9

Copyright © 2016 by Apostolic Movement International, LLC
All rights reserved
5663 Balboa Ave #416,
San Diego,
California 92111,
United States of America

1st Printing November 2012
2nd Edition May 2016

Published by **Apostolic Movement International, LLC**
E-mail Address: admin@ami-bookshop.com
Web Address: www.ami-bookshop.com

All rights reserved under International Copyright Law.
Contents may not be reproduced in whole or in part in any form without the express written consent of the publisher.

Unless specified, all Scripture references taken from the New King James Version®. Copyright © 1982 by Thomas Nelson. Used by permission. All rights reserved.

The Minister's Handbook

Second Edition

COLETTE TOACH

www.ami-bookshop.com

Foreword

Anyone who has been in full-time ministry knows the burden Paul refers to when he spoke of the "care of the Churches."

The restless nights, wondering if you did the right thing and if those lambs under you are getting the best they can. Did you do the right things to make them grow or did you destroy them instead?

It is one thing to walk and fall in your own personal walk with the Lord. Your spiritual condition is between you and the Lord.

However, what happens when you have others looking to you for their needs and spiritual condition? Do you have what it takes to help them to overcome and grow? Where do you start and what is expected of you? What can you expect to face along this long lonely road ahead?

These are just some of the questions I asked and faced as I moved into full-time ministry.

I wish then, I had had this awesome book to help me plot a course through the minefield of public and personal ministry.

I wish I had the pointers to help me understand my failures and successes sooner and ease the walk on this thin tightrope between success and failure.

That is why as you read these pages and the chapters in this book, I know you will find answers to your questions.

You will find the pointers you are looking for to make you more effective in the calling you have on your life.

Most of all, you will have the peace of mind knowing that you can be a vessel for the Lord and help His Bride to rise up in glory. You will be the vessel you need to be, to help them rise in all the Lord has put in them and not hinder them in any way!

Colette has yet again condensed a lifetime of living into a powerful handbook. You can have the peace of mind knowing each word was lived and relived till perfection.

The end result? A handbook that will bless you and those in the body of Christ the Lord has entrusted to you.

With this book in your hand, you are no longer alone, but ready to take on the road ahead in confidence and assurance that the Lord and Colette have your back!

Much love and blessings,

Craig Toach

Co-Founder
Apostolic Movement International

Contents

Foreword 3
Part 01 – The Fivefold Ministry 12
Introduction – Handing Out the Gifts 12
    Getting Started in Ministry 18
Chapter 01 – The Seven Purposes of the Fivefold Ministry 24
    1. Equipping the Saints – Teaching, Training and Instruction 25
    2. The Work of the Ministry 29
    3. Building up By Producing Faith, Hope and Love .. 32
    4. Bringing Unity 38
    5. A Knowledge of Jesus 41
    6. To Warn and Protect 45
    7. Helping People Find Their Place – Fitting the Joints Together 47
    The Seven Purposes of Ministry 51
    Become Empowered 53
Part 02 – Personal Ministry 56
Chapter 02 – How to Hear God's Voice for Yourself ... 56
    Using the Urim and Thummim 59
    Knowing With the Spirit 62
    Flowing in Visions 64
    Journaling 66

Chapter 03 - Using Visions in Personal Ministry.......... 72
   Types and Shadows 73
   The Spirit of Wisdom and Revelation 74
   Flowing in Visions in Personal Ministry 86
Chapter 04 – The Five Golden Rules............................ 92
   Rule #1 Never Give Ministry Unless It is Asked For. 92
   Rule #2 Do Not Overfeed the Cow 95
   Rule # 3 Use Tact 100
   Rule #4 Faith, Hope and Love 107
   Rule #5: Perfection is Over-rated 113
   The Final Conclusion.. 116
Chapter 05 – Counseling: The Rules of Engagement. 120
   Advice is My Idea. Counsel is God's Idea............... 120
   Wisdom Makes Knowledge Work 122
   Counseling 101 123
Chapter 06 – Counseling by the Word 132
   First Step: Ask These Three Questions 132
   Step 1: The Problem 134
   Step 2: The Root Cause 135
   Step 3: Applying the Sword for Conviction........... 136
   Step 4: Healing and Deliverance............................ 137
   Step 5: Get Practical 138
   Case Scenarios... 140
Chapter 07 – Ministering by the Spirit 158

- Step 1: Receiving the Revelation 159
- Step 2: Applying the Revelation 165
- Chapter 08 – The Ministry of Inner Healing 174
  - The Joy of Personal Ministry 174
  - Inner Healing 175
  - What Hurts Do 177
  - Getting Started 182
  - Step #1 Get Into His Presence 183
  - Step #2 Deal with Demons 187
  - Step #3 Apply the Healing 192
- Chapter 09 – Dealing with Demons and Deception .. 198
  - Play it Safe 200
  - The Spirit of Divination 201
  - How Deception Comes 208
  - Avoiding Deception 215
  - Signs of Deception 219
- Chapter 10 – Dealing with Demonic Manifestations . 226
  - Two Camps 228
  - Demon Manifestations 230
  - Setting Someone Free 235
  - Some Signs of Demonic Bondage 239
- Part 03 – Public Ministry 246
- Chapter 11 – Taking Charge of the Public Meeting ... 246
  - The Main Problem 248

Opening a Meeting 251
When to do Announcements 254
Handing Over to the Worship Leader 256
Introducing the Speaker 256
Who is Really in Charge? 261

Chapter 12 – Preparing & Presenting a Sermon 264
You Are a Bomb Waiting to Happen 265
Preparing Your Notes Step 1... 2... 3 265
Sermon Summary: 280
Some Do's and Don'ts in Preaching and Speaking 281

Chapter 13 – How to Lead Worship 296
The Most Famous Praise Service Ever 296
How to Get Started 297

Chapter 14 – Prophesying Publically 320
The Rules of Engagement 320
A Personal Tip 328

Chapter 15 – Practical Ministry Guidelines 334
1. You Should Produce Faith, Hope and Love 334
2. Do Not Guess What Your Vision Might Mean ... 334
3. Do Not Read Your Own Ideas Into the Revelation 335
4. Visions do Not Always Need to be Shared in a Public Meeting. 337
Prophetic Preaching 339

Chapter 16 – A Note on Handling Rejection...............346
    What Not to Do 346
    What to Do 347
The Final Word 352
About the Author 355
Recommendations by the Author 357
    How to Get People to Follow You 357
    Mentorship 101 358
    Strategies of War..358
    Everything is Awesome When You are Part of the Team...359
    The Apostolic Handbook 359
    Pastor Teacher School..360
Contact Information 361

PART 01 – THE FIVEFOLD MINISTRY

INTRODUCTION

Handing Out the Gifts

Part 01 – The Fivefold Ministry

Introduction – Handing Out the Gifts

Everyone has their own Christmas traditions, but ours was always a little different.

The way my father tells it, we nagged him so much for our gifts on Christmas Eve that he decided to open one main gift the day before Christmas. Well as years went on… it became two gifts and then three gifts. In the end, we did all our Christmas celebrating on Christmas Eve.

However, the truth of why this family tradition came about was not just because we nagged my Dad so much each year. The truth was that he could not hold back the surprises. He loved to give gifts and the bottom line was that he was just itching to give us those gifts!

He could not wait until Christmas day. He wanted to give them early just so that he could see the joy on our faces. It is something that he passed down to us and now we see the same thing happening with our own children.

It is so contagious. I love giving gifts! If I have kids around me, I cannot help myself. I just love to see their little faces light up. My daughter Jessica was always the most wonderful child to give a gift to.

I remember one Christmas in particular. We were quite poor and we could not afford very much. However, my stepmom decided she was going to give the girls something handmade. She made each child a doll out of old socks.

The girls were really small and I remember Jessica opening up her gift. There she was - this little toddler with bright blue eyes and a head full of bouncy blonde curls. She opened it up and with a gasp came running to me and said, "Mommy! Mommy! Look at what I got! It's so wonderful! It's a..." Then she stopped for a moment, looked at it again and said, "What is it?"

I said to her, "Well, it's a sock doll!"

Off she went again, running around the room, "Look everyone! Look at what I got! It is a sock doll!"

You know, all that effort was worth it and when I think of the Lord Jesus, I realize that He has the heart of a father that delights to see us blessed as well. He wants nothing more than for us to be as that little girl that is so excited about the smallest things.

As we look at ministering to the Lord's people, I am trying to give you a picture of the purpose of that ministry.

Your heavenly Father has put you in charge of handing out some good things to His Church. Now when was the last time you saw the person who handed out the gifts, sit down, open up all the children's gifts and play with them himself first?

No. The Holy Spirit has given you a whole big bag of gifts, but do you know what the purpose of having those gifts is? They are for you to hand out to others. You have all these people in the church who are like little Jessica. They are all so hungry and so excited and waiting for the Lord to do something in their lives.

What's the Point?

If you just look at the body of Christ and see the needs, the Lord will give you enough to meet every single one. However, if you are in a place right now where you are not pouring out, what is the point of God filling you up?

What is the point of getting revelation if you are not pouring out to others? It is time to change your focus. Firstly, it will bring some balance and secondly, it is going to give you some rest. This kind of thinking is also going to increase your portion of anointing.

Increasing the Anointing

Do you know how you can increase the anointing in your life? You increase it by wanting to meet the needs of God's people.

Instead though, I see so many crying out to God for the gifts instead of more of Him. "Lord, give me the word of knowledge! Lord, give me the gift of prophecy. Lord, give me…"

But for what purpose? Why should the Lord give you any of these gifts if your intention is not to meet the needs of His people?

What is the purpose of ministry and of flowing out in the gifts, if it is not for the purpose of giving that all out to others?

What is Your Motivation?

The Church is the one who is meant to be unwrapping those gifts and reveling in them. You are the one that is meant to be handing all that good stuff out.

It is for you to bring joy and life. When you walk into a church or have finished ministering to people, what do you leave behind?

Do people leave that meeting acting like Jessica saying to everyone with all their excitement, "Yay! Look at what I got. Look at what the Lord did!"

Or on the other hand, do you walk through the door and everyone trips over their feet to get away from you? What is your motivation for ministry?

I promise if your heart is set on the needs of others and you ask the Lord how you can help them, you will not have time to sit around to wonder, "Do I need a word of wisdom? Should I give a word of prophecy here? Should I function as a teacher? What scripture would be best…?"

No, when you have the right motivation, then the Lord will give you what you need. If you will just love people, God will give you what you need to love them with.

When the Lord Gets Quiet

Now it is very common in ministry as the Lord takes you through training that there will be seasons when it feels like you cannot hear His voice or flow in any of the Gifts of the Spirit any longer. The reason for this is that usually during these times, the Lord sets you apart.

You find yourself in a situation where you just do not have an opportunity to minister at all. You need to realize that the Gifts of the Spirit are not for you, but that they are for the church! So if you are not ministering to others or not in a position to minister to others, then that is why the voice of the Lord suddenly seems so quiet.

In fact, I guarantee that the only time that you will hear the Lord will be in your personal prayer or in times of intercession. Why is that? Well because those are the only times that you are pouring out.

The gifts are for you to hand out to the body of Christ and if I can challenge you to keep that motivation, there will be an unending supply of anointing that will pour through you.

Think as a parent for a minute. It does something to your heart to see the pure joy of a little child, beaming from ear to ear because of their gift. You want to grant them that desire. The Scripture says that if we who are evil know how to give good gifts to our children, how much more will our Father in heaven give to those that ask?

A Season of Silence

What is going on, if you were flowing along nicely in ministry and then suddenly everything dries up? One day you are getting revelation and gushing the anointing over everyone and the next you are dry as a desert.

If the Lord has you in a quiet season, He could be pulling you aside to train you Himself so that you will be able to fulfill your purpose. If that is the case, there is no need for you to be flowing in all of the gifts, simply because there is no one to flow out to!

If you are a carpenter and there is nothing to build right now, what on earth do you need all your tools for? There is no use lugging them around if they are of no use. Put them down and go on holiday. If the Lord has you in a season of just being with Him, then put the tools down.

There will be times when you will need to come out of that quiet season and you can run off and do the work again. However, from experience, let me tell you that those times when the Lord draws you aside are the most precious you will ever have.

In years to come, you will look back on these seasons with melancholy and tenderness. It is these times that will define you as a leader. They will make you fall in love with the Lord more than ever. These quiet times are the ones that truly change you.

So do not worry about ministering or pouring out and just take this time to become the minister He has called you to be. Before long the season will be up and it will be time for action again - so enjoy it while you can.

Getting Started in Ministry

I was as green as grass when I went into ministry for the first time. It is one thing to sit in a meeting and watch the leaders "do their stuff" but it is another all together to get a chance to step forward and do it.

I realized that it would take a bit more than some good imitation to minister effectively. There is a huge gap in Christian literature when it comes to the practicalities of ministry. There is a ton of teaching on principles, doctrine and bible study. However, there is not a lot on how to take all that good stuff and make it work!

- What do you do if someone suddenly manifests a demon?

- How do you pray with someone who was abused as a child?

- What is the first thing you should pray when someone is facing a crisis in their marriage?

Suddenly all those principles become a pile of rubble in your head and you do not know which piece to put forward first. Well that is where I come in. As we work through this book together, I am going to take all of the building bricks that you have gathered over the years and I am going to teach you where they belong.

I am going to teach you to use the tools that you already have and to lay a solid foundation for your ministry.

If you have a calling and you can hear the Lord for yourself, then you are ready for the next step of your training.

I Invite You to Be My Apprentice

So consider this your ministry apprenticeship. It is a process whereby I lead you by the hand through the jungle of real ministry.

As I share the principles here, imagine that you are sitting comfortably next to me at one of our ministry centers and in front of us is someone with a ministry need.

Imagine that as I minister and share with this person, that I turn to you and explain what I am doing. I share why I said the things I did. I share what I sense in my spirit and what to say next. I am giving you the insight into what the person is going through and what to say to them next.

That is the picture of what I hope to accomplish in you through this book. Isn't this how Jesus ministered to His disciples?

He would stand up and preach and then afterwards explain the parables. He took Nicodemus aside and then afterwards shared with His disciples what happened. As a result, not only could we get an accurate New Testament, but the disciples were ready to take on the load of birthing an entirely new move after Jesus ascended.

I promise to hold nothing back. I will hand to you all my experience, principles and a few secrets I uncovered for myself along the way.

The Goal

The goal is to take all the good stuff that God has given to you and teach you how to use it effectively. The goal is to get your ministry off the ground and on to resurrection.

I do not need to tell you that you have a calling, because you already know that. What I can show you though is how to get that calling off the ground and to a place where it is reaching the church!

So let us begin. Stick close to my heels and pay attention, because this ride is about to begin!

CHAPTER 01

The Seven Purposes of the Fivefold Ministry

Chapter 01 – The Seven Purposes of the Fivefold Ministry

"I want to go into fulltime ministry, what must I do to make this a reality in my life?"

It was the umpteenth time I had been asked this question at a ministry conference I had been invited to. Each time I replied with the same question, "To do what? What do you want to accomplish?"

Often doing the work of the ministry is looked on as a position or a title, but the truth of the matter is, it is a function in the church. It is not only something that you are, but something that you do.

No one would apply for a job in the natural, if they did not know the job description beforehand, would they? So then it stands to reason that before you jump in on the ministry bandwagon, that you also consider what you should be doing as a minister.

When a doctor studies for years and years, they would be foolish to do it for the title alone. No, once they qualify, it is the work that they do that will decide if they deserve that title or not.

Well that is a picture of what it is like to be a minister for the Lord. When you want to do His work, I promise that the title you wear comes only way after you qualify in the work and the price you pay! So what does God expect from you?

By Colette Toach

You know that you are there to be a blessing to the church, but how? How should you be serving God? What should you be doing?

What does your "Heavenly Boss" expect of you? He has told us quite plainly by laying it out for us in:

> ***Ephesians 4:12*** *For the equipping of the saints for the work of ministry, for the edifying of the body of Christ,*
>
> *13 till we all come to the unity of the faith and of the knowledge of the Son of God, to a perfect man, to the measure of the stature of the fullness of Christ;*
>
> *14 that we should no longer be children, tossed to and fro and carried about with every wind of doctrine, by the trickery of men, in the cunning craftiness of deceitful plotting,*
>
> *15 but, speaking the truth in love, may grow up in all things into Him who is the head – Christ –*
>
> *16 from whom the whole body, joined and knit together by what every joint supplies, according to the effective working by which every part does its share, causes growth of the body for the edifying of itself in love.*

1. Equipping the Saints – Teaching, Training and Instruction

> ***Ephesians 4:12*** *For the equipping of the saints,*

When I was a child, we were so poor my folks could not always afford all the stationary I needed to do my schoolwork with. When I did get silly things like pencils, pens and rulers, I held onto them like crazy, because we did not know when we could afford more again.

It is so much easier if you have everything you need to get a job done. Once you get that out of the way you can really put your head down to learning the good stuff. Is it not like that in many things in life? When you have the right tools, the job is so much easier.

Well how about the church? The Lord has called us to walk in His love. He calls us to have patience and to walk in the spirit. He promises us that all our needs can be met in Him. You go through the scriptures and there are thousands of things that the Lord has given us to do.

But here is the tricky part… HOW do you do them? How do you walk in the spirit? How do you resist temptations? What rules do you live by? Doing what God wants to do as a believer is a lot easier to do if you have the right tools.

Unfortunately, though some believers are spiritually impoverished and as much as I had to scrounge to get my homework done without pens and pencils, they also battle along trying to please the Lord, but feeling like they keep failing miserably.

That is why your first purpose as a minister is to give the church those tools! They need to know how to face their problems every day.

> ***2 Timothy 3:16*** *All Scripture is given by inspiration of God, and is profitable for doctrine, for reproof, for correction, for instruction in righteousness,*
>
> *17 that the man of God may be complete, thoroughly equipped for every good work.*

This looks very similar to the passage I quoted in Eph 4, isn't it? How will you equip the church? It is simple - through teaching and training! Not only has God called you to instruct the church through teaching, but to get involved.

To train, mentor and to impart to others what you have. Now sure, this is not an easy job sometimes. If the Lord calls you to be a spiritual parent, it is going to take time to train someone in the right way. It takes time to mentor and get into people's lives.

How else though will you equip the saints? Jesus sure had the pattern. Take a look at everything He did with His disciples. He taught them and trained them. He said to them. "Come and see where I live!" He gave them all the tools that they needed to start an international movement!

How can you expect more of the church when it does not have the tools it needs to become more? It is time that God's ministers step forward now and take up that challenge.

Part and parcel of your purpose as a minister is to teach, instruct and to train. It is not given to the select few but for every single one of us to fulfill. When you do your job, do you know what happens? 2 Timothy 3:17 happens! Every man of God is made complete and is able to carry out good works of every kind.

Are you expecting those around you to walk in love? Well are you teaching them how to love? Are you trying to get everyone to walk in the spirit instead of falling into sin all of the time? Are you teaching them how to walk in the spirit? Are you training them, by giving them the tools to do it?

If I showed up to a class to write a test without any pens and pencils, could the teacher expect me to pass the test? No, not until I had the tools I needed. I might have the desire and passion. I might even have the skill, but if I was not equipped, I would fail.

In the same way many in the church are failing and simply because they are not equipped. They have the fire. They have the potential and would even have the spiritual gifts. However, until someone steps forward to equip them, those gifts will lay dormant and they will never become that mature man that God has called them to be.

2. The Work of the Ministry

> ***Ephesians 4:12*** *...for the work of ministry, ...*

The first thing I tell anyone who wants to go into ministry is this, "Do you know what the word ministry means in the scriptures? It means servant."

With all the lofty titles floating around these days, it is easy to forget this vital little fact. You have yet to come to a full comprehension of the power of the Holy Spirit until you have come to embrace the fullness of true servanthood.

Apostle Paul walked in power and mighty revelation, yet he announces himself as,

> ***Romans 1:1*** *Paul, a bondservant of Jesus Christ, called to be an apostle, separated to the gospel of God.*

He knew the power of servanthood and considered it a higher calling than that of his apostleship. When you understand the concept of true ministry, you will walk in a spiritual authority that you never knew before.

This is because being a servant means being emptied. Remember the parable of the servant who goes out into the field all day and returns to serve his master? Only when his master is happy, does he sit down to eat. This is servanthood and when you are so emptied that nothing of you remains, you will find the power of the Holy Spirit come on you and transform your life.

It is in fact this power that will equip you to do everything else you need to do. With a heart like this, you will have the knowledge to equip the church. With a heart like this, you will have the right motivation to reach out and flow in any anointing that God needs you to.

You see, a master dictates, but a servant follows orders. If you remain in a position of servanthood, you will always be following orders and when those orders belong to the Heavenly Father, you can rest assured that those orders come with His power to do them.

So a vital purpose of being a minister is the nitty gritty stuff. The scripture does not say that we should do the fun of the ministry it says that we should do the work of the ministry. It means to labor, to press through and to serve.

So when will you need to do the work of the ministry? The answer to that is simple – when there is a need. Whether the need is a spiritual or emotional one, God requires you to meet that need in the church.

It means laboring long with God's people. It means reaching out to them when they are facing hard times in their lives. It means speaking into their situation or healing to their bodies. It means to have compassion and to love them even when they do not deserve it.

Reaching Out

Think about it like this. Do you remember the last time you felt really sick? Perhaps you caught the flu and you were cuddled up under your covers feeling really sorry for yourself. Every time you turned around, your head pounded as if a jackhammer was playing out a tune on your forehead.

The last thing you felt like doing was getting up and cooking food or doing anything for that matter. It was harder still to believe the Lord for healing! It is at times like this when you need ministry the most. This is when you need someone to come and lay hands on you and to speak healing.

This is your primary function in the church. To reach out when there is a need. It is difficult to have faith for finances when you are poor. It is tough to have hope in your marriage when it is failing.

However, when you are on top spiritually, you have enough faith to go around. You have all the faith in the world to believe for someone else's finances and that is exactly what the Lord will call on you to do!

As you reach out and meet the needs of those around you, something miraculous is going to happen. You are going to find that new gifts will be manifesting in your life. When your focus starts to become more about meeting the needs of God's people and less about your position in the church, the anointing that always seemed to escape you will be given to you with a double portion.

3. Building up By Producing Faith, Hope and Love

> ***Ephesians 3:12*** *... for the edifying of the body of Christ:*

When you come with a message of faith, hope and love it will look like a brightly colored wrapped gift with a bright red ribbon on the top. No one is going to turn that away!

They will want what you have. The problem is that you often look at all the negatives that you do not take the time to see the good things that the Lord has in store. If you look at all the letters that Apostle Paul wrote, you will notice that in each one that he grades that church on their level of faith, hope and love.

When you build these three things up in a person, what you have is some powerful maturity! Unfortunately, this is not the message we are always seeing in the church is it? Nope, we have our doomsday prophets saying how God is going to destroy everyone and our brimstone and fire preachers saying how everyone will burn in hell for their sin.

Where is the faith, hope and love in that? People should leave a meeting a step closer to the Lord. Their faith should be so motivated, that they know their Heavenly Father hears their prayers.

Their hope should be so sparked that they can see clearly into their future and their love should be so filled up that they go out wanting to follow the Lord's commandments just because He is so special to them.

Producing Faith

It is for you to remind them that even though their earthly father might have fallen short, that their Heavenly Father sees all of their needs. You need to remind them that not a hair falls from their heads where He does not see it.

The Lord wants you to remind His church that they are the head and not the tail! That they only need to walk with boldness to their Father and that He will supply their needs according to His glory.

There are so many in the church that are in demonic bondage and oppression, but do not know how to break free. They need to know that they can stand on the name of Jesus and overcome every work of the enemy. They do not need to just accept sickness. They do not need to accept poverty. Can you not feel the faith in your own heart just soaring?

After a few more paragraphs like that, you want to pick up your sword, tell the enemy to take his hands off your life and you want to shake the very gates of hell! Well that is the purpose, is it not? It is for you to build faith!

Produce Hope

How many meetings have you attended where the people hung their heads low as they walked out the door? Instead of feeling His touch, they left feeling not good enough. They look at their lives and they do not match up and they feel powerless to try and overcome.

The Lord has called you to give God's people hope! He is calling on you to tell them that He will not leave nor forsake them. He wants them to know that He has good plans for them and not for evil.

He wants them to look forward to the future with expectation. He does not want them to feel that they have to try and earn His favor or His love and it is for you to make that message loud and clear. The Lord has a good plan for every one of His children, but not many of them know it.

Do not be afraid to stand up and to share that plan with them. Show them from the Word that He has called them to be a city on a hill. Stand and share your revelations that show that He is in control and is working things out on their behalf.

Give them a picture of the good future that God has planned. As they hold onto that picture and work towards it, they will be walking exactly where God wants them to!

Produce Love

When my son was first born he had no clue what love was. I would say, "I love you" and he would smile. After some time, he would say, "I love you" but I knew that he was only copying what I said.

But then a day came when he looked me straight in the eye and said, "Mommy, I love you" and I knew for the first time that he was starting to get the concept of love. He was starting to grow up. The ultimate yardstick for maturity is the level of your love.

Just read through 1 Corinthians 13 and you will see what I am talking about. Paul goes through all the gifts in the previous chapter and ends with, "But I will show you a better way" and then goes on to talk all about love.

When we were children we played around and did what we wanted, but when we grew up we put those things away. What else would drive a man to work long hours if it was not the love he had for his family?

What is it that inspires a mother to wake every two hours for her child and to press through with him, ignoring her own pain and weariness? It is the power of love!

When I was a little girl, I would play with my dolls and would pretend to be a mommy. However, when I got tired of playing, I would throw them down and run off. When I grew up and became a mother, things changed.

I did not get bored. I did not just run away. My love for my babies kept me going. In that moment, I realized I was no longer a child, I had grown up.

Now if you can give the Church a knowledge of Jesus and if you can teach them to walk in faith, hope and love, you will bring them to maturity.

What Spiritual Maturity Is

> ***Ephesians 4: 13*** *..., to a perfect man, to the measure of the stature of the fullness of Christ;*

Being mature is not about knowing what is right and wrong. Even a toddler knows it is wrong to sneak into his sister's room and to eat up her entire stash of fancy chocolates. No, maturity is knowing what is right and wrong and then making a choice to do what is right.

Not making that choice out of fear, but out of love and a keen sense of responsibility. How will we ever make the Church without spot and wrinkle? How will we bring Her to the place where She is irresistible to Her Groom?

Easy, we get Her to fall in love with Him! True love is true maturity. Only when you love the Lord do you listen to His commandments. Only when you love your brothers and sisters in Christ, do you work through your conflicts.

It is only when you love your neighbor as Christ loved you, that you have patience. It is only when you love your wife as Christ loved the church that you will win her heart.

It is only when you submit to your husband as unto the Lord, through love, that you will save your marriage. Love is the key to maturity and through it everything else falls into place. It is the center beam of our salvation and what keeps everything else in place.

Has the Lord challenged you again and again on walking in love? If so, then he is only preparing you for your purpose in the church. He is preparing you to bring her to maturity!

No matter how hard our parents tried, there is no way that they could give us all the love we needed. Only Jesus is able to do that. Unfortunately, so many believers are afraid to come to Him. They fear that He will reject them or they feel they must earn His love first.

It is crazy how at salvation a person will run into the tender arms of Jesus by faith alone and then continue to try and walk with Him for the rest of their lives trying to convince Him of their place.

The same love that Jesus received a sinner with at salvation is the same love that empowers us to walk in the spirit. Jesus said that if we love Him, we will fulfill His commandments. It is only through the power of love that we will see a spotless bride.

You can point out sin and failure all you like, but until that person knows the love of the Lord, they have no reason to change. What is the purpose of our salvation? Is it not to give the Lord the glory? The greatest sin we can commit is choosing something else in our lives other than the Lord.

When I consider that my sin separates me from Jesus, this breaks my heart. Knowing that it is "wrong" is just not good enough. True love is the greatest motivation to overcome sin and until you realize this, the church will continue to perform instead of just obeying the Lord through love.

4. Bringing Unity

> ***Ephesians 4:13*** *till we all come to the unity of the faith…*

There is a saying that goes, "Life would be so easy if it was just not for other people." Well that is a pretty tough break if you are a Christian, because not only does the Lord require us to work with other people, but He has knitted us into a single body.

Now not all body parts work together at the same time and not all of them have the same function, but unless we can learn to walk in some kind of unity, the body will trip over its own feet.

God is not in the business of going around and destroying relationships, but you would not say that looking at the lives of God's people hey? There are marriages that are being destroyed and families that are being torn apart. There is conflict and strife instead of unity. And so we have satan laughing all the way to the bank.

It is for you to bring unity back into the Church. To turn the hearts of the sons back to the fathers. To restore marriages and to rebuild the broken walls in the lives of God's people. Now it does not mean that we will always walk the same road, but we need to take the strife out of the Body.

In the book of Acts, it tells us that when the believers stood together in unity, that the very earth shook beneath their feet. This is the kind of unity that I am talking about. We must bring unity in our faith in Jesus Christ and His power in our lives. So often we allow the enemy into our lives to bring his little barbs and thorns.

Dealing With Conflict

People get upset or rub one another up the wrong way. Yet instead of working out those conflicts, they simply run away from them. Well it is for you to stop them from running! It is just too easy to run away from a conflict or a difficult situation. It is just too easy to leave and to try and sort the problem out by yourself.

But this is not what the Lord requires of us. It is time that the church faces its conflicts and overcomes them. Do you think that there were no fights in the early church? Think again! The Lord has often brought conflict at times to separate the paths of two people.

Consider Paul and Barnabas that separated in disagreement over Mark. Yet look again at what they accomplished! Through that, they covered twice the ground and in the end the Body universal was edified and brought together.

Not only that, but we see later on that Paul calls for Mark and says that he is "useful to him for the work of the ministry." They were able to work together because they both operated in the same spirit – the spirit of Christ! They had unity, perhaps not always in their views and doctrines, but they certainly had unity in their faith.

They worked through their conflict and the Lord brought something better out of it in the end. If you are working with your team or in a church, are you quick to take the back door, or do you have the courage to see a conflict through?

To push through with that situation until there is unity? Sure, we will always make each other angry. There will also be prophets around to "put their foot into it" or evangelists that will ruffle some feathers. But does this mean we just walk away?

An Example

We had a prophetic seminar once where included in the curriculum was a teaching on dreams. A couple attended who had never really "fitted in" with any church. After a few meetings, we began to see why!

During one of the workshops they shared a dream and the others in the group gave their interpretation.

They disagreed outright. Not only that, but when they offered their interpretations to others, they were quite off in their revelation. The leader of the group had to step in and try to bring peace. He tried to instruct and teach, but the couple would not have it.

They stormed out of the meeting and never returned. They lost out on such a blessing. The Lord was offering them something new and they could have worked through that conflict to receive what God had brought them there for. Unfortunately, they left without anything.

I am sure that as I speak others jump to your mind. Do you want to see the church grow up? Then it is time you start teaching them to confront and overcome the conflicts and work their way to unity!

5. A Knowledge of Jesus

> ***Ephesians 4: 13*** *...and of the knowledge of the Son of God, to a perfect man, to the measure of the stature of the fullness of Christ;*

Ok, now we are coming to my personal hobby horse. There are so many principles and so much good teaching out there, that you can often make the mistake of forgetting the purpose of learning all that stuff.

What is the purpose of preaching, working, dying to the flesh and going through the fire? It is to come into a greater knowledge of Jesus! Why? Why is that so important to the Lord? It is because when you come to a greater knowledge of Jesus, you come into a greater experience of His power.

It is in Jesus where you will find your ministry calling, the anointing, and where you will find the revelation and the power to overcome. The more you know Jesus, the more you are empowered.

It might sound a bit silly, but the way some folks act, you would think that the anointing and gifts are separate to Jesus. I say this because I see many seeking out the Gifts of the Spirit instead of the one who died to give them to us.

Don't you realize that when you find Jesus, you find everything you could ever need to do the work? When you find Jesus, you find salvation in every area of your life! There are many believers crying out to God for healing.

They are crying out to God to save their relationships or to give them a spouse. They do not realize that every single one of these things is found in the face of Jesus Christ.

It does not matter what you need from the Lord today, whatever it is, I can promise that it is found in Jesus Christ. When you come into a face to face relationship with Jesus, every need is met in Him.

By Colette Toach

There is no anointing or need that can be met outside of the Lord. He is our Mediator and He is the One that holds the power in this earth. He is the One that has been given the name above all names.

Now when you get a little closer to the Name you start getting a little closer to the power that the Name holds.

It is like having a rich Dad who is also strong and muscular. If you are walking down the street next to that strong Dad and someone walks up to you and tries to rob you, they are in for trouble! Your Dad will sort them out in no time.

However, what would happen if you ran away from that strong Dad and took a walk on a dark road where you could not see him? When those bullies came, you would be in trouble! Why? You moved away from Him!

In the same way, as you draw closer to the Lord, He draws closer to you. He covers you under His wings and protects you. The more you gain knowledge of Jesus, the tighter you become. Then as you walk through the streets of life there is no enemy that can get you down.

Where are you at right now? Is the enemy getting into your life? Are you under attack or suffering loss? Have you had some bouts of depression? Well then, tell me this, how good is your knowledge of Jesus right now?

How close are you sticking to "your Dad"? The closer you get to Him - the stronger you become. The church needs to be shown who Jesus is.

How Exactly?

This is the million-dollar question, isn't it? How do you bring the church into this kind of knowledge? You might not like the answer. To bring them to this knowledge they need to see an image of what Christ is really like.

This means that you need to become the image of Christ. The scripture says that we are to be transformed into His image. Why do you think that is? Well, how else would they know Jesus? Not every believer knows what Jesus looks like and it is for you to show them!

If I wanted to tell my friend about my husband, I could try to explain what he is like, or I could send her a home video. Which do you think would give her a real picture of his nature? It would be the video. She could see and not just understand.

Yet so many go around trying to explain to the Church what Jesus did for them and to tell them what He is like instead of showing them! You will bring the Church into a knowledge of Jesus by becoming the image of Jesus in this earth.

When people look at you, do they see the love of Jesus? Is His grace reflected in your face? You can preach and teach and train, but to transform this church, show her what Jesus is like. Let her see His love in action. Only then will we see the church rise up and take its place in this world.

6. To Warn and Protect

> ***Ephesians 4:14*** *that we should no longer be children, tossed to and fro and carried about with every wind of doctrine, by the trickery of men, in the cunning craftiness of deceitful plotting,*

Now I am not talking about the kind of warning that says, "If you do not do what God says, He is going to take your church or your business away from you."

If you get the urge to give such a warning, then I would check my flesh out first if I were you.

No, I am talking about the kind of warning where you are praying for someone and in the spirit you see them coming to a fork in the road. You know very well that if they take the wrong road that they will be in trouble.

A woman might come to you and share that there is someone she wants to marry, but has some doubts and needs direction from the Lord.

Do not be afraid to seek the Lord on their behalf and to share wisdom with them. If you tend to function more from the Word, then you can ask the person some questions. Questions such as, "Is this person born again?"

Clearly if they are not, you need to be bold enough to say what the Word of God says. You would be obligated to tell them that if they choose to go ahead and marry someone who is not saved that they are headed for trouble and that the Lord is against such a marriage.

Are you being cruel? No, your warning is saving their souls. Just as a shepherd would snatch a lamb from the mouth of the lion, sometimes in pieces, so also is the Lord calling you to snatch His people from the fire. It is not always easy or pleasant, but it is to save their lives.

The Lord is not in the business of running around saying, "If you sin, God is going to destroy you." That is not the warning I am speaking of.

A father will warn his child against putting his hand into an open flame to protect his child. The point of the warning is not for God's benefit, but for the Church's benefit! What benefit is it to a father to correct a child that is reaching out for the blade of a sharp knife?

He can see the child grabbing for the knife and knows he will not reach him in time, so he shouts angrily across the room, "Don't you DARE touch that! Move away right now!"

Is the father shouting for his own purpose? No, he wants to save his child the pain that he knows he is headed for. This is the purpose of correction and of giving warning in the church.

If you see someone who has chosen a road that you know will lead to destruction, the Lord will use you to call them back. Why? Is it because God is angry and He wants to strike them down? Not at all. He wants to call them back, because He knows the pain that they will have to go through if they go down that road. He is trying to protect them.

And so the Lord will use you as that protection. No scripture says it better than this:

> **Hebrews 12:10** *For they indeed for a few days chastened us as seemed best to them, but He for our profit, that we may be partakers of His holiness.*

How Do You Know It Worked?

You will see faith, hope and love developing in a person. Even though you might be warning them, you will see them take what you say with conviction. So do not be afraid to be bold in what you feel that God is telling you.

However, when you do stand up to give those warnings, make sure that you do them using the Word of God and not the words of your own good ideas.

7. Helping People Find Their Place – Fitting the Joints Together

> **Ephesians 4:16** *From whom the whole body, joined and knit together by what every joint supplies, according to the effective working by*

> *which every part does its share, causes growth of the body for the edifying of itself in love.*

Depending on your calling, there are times when the Lord is going to call on you to help God's people to identify their gifts and ministries (1 Cor 12:8-10).

They might not know exactly what it is yet, but they are just thrilled that the Lord has not forsaken them. They feel the love of the Lord knowing that He took the time to give them something. Often you do not even need to give a major word of revelation; often all that a person needs is a confirmation of what they already feel in their hearts.

That is why we have taken such time to put teachings together to help you identify the signs of each of the Fivefold Ministry. It takes a combination of flowing in the Gifts of the Spirit as well as just some common sense to help someone out.

Perhaps you flow in the Gifts of the Spirit and you feel that someone has a prophetic calling. However, when they talk to you they say, "You know I am so tired of heresy in the church! It just burns in me to teach the Word as it is and to put some solid doctrine in the hearts of God's people!"

Use a bit of common sense. What this person is sharing does not sound like a prophetic orientation to me! Now I am not saying that the Lord does not want to move this person into a more prophetic orientation at a later stage, but as things stand, they look more like a teacher.

Remember that the Gifts of the Spirit are there for you to confirm what is already in someone's heart.

In fact, sometimes the greatest ministry I have ever given has been a one liner. I can be talking to someone and I can see that they are definitely prophetic or teaching in orientation. All I need to say is, "Do you realize that you show clear signs of a teaching calling?"

Their eyes will go wide and they will say, "You know I always desired that! I always felt like the Lord was leading me in that direction, but I just thought it was my own idea."

Do not run around saying to the Lord, "Please Lord, give me a word of wisdom. Lord, please give me a word of knowledge."

No! Rather say to the Lord, "Lord, please give me what I need to help this person. They are struggling and they do not know their place. Lord if there is any way that I can encourage them, please use me as your vessel to do that."

When you pray with that heart, the Holy Spirit will rush to your side to give you exactly what that person needs right now. When you do this, you fulfill a powerful purpose as a minister.

You equip the church by showing them first where they belong, by confirming which part of the Body they are already in. When they realize this, they are ready to be built up and to mature in the Lord.

Where Prophetic Decree is Needed

Now the prophet will be used in this way even more so. This is needed especially when it comes to putting believers into their place in the church. It is not good enough to just get revelation as to what their place is - they need to be released into it as well.

The Lord has used me many times in this capacity and while there are some prophets that function in it more than others, if God needs you at any time to do it, then do not be afraid to step up.

The Lord uses the prophet to release someone into a ministry training or office. He might use that prophet to close or open doors in the person's life. He will also use the prophet to release Gifts of the Spirit into a person so that they can be equipped to do their calling.

This is another subject all together that I teach in detail in our prophetic school, so if you are a prophet start with this book and then move onto there!

A Word about Impartation

I have not included impartation here, because this relates only to the apostle. In the New Testament you will see that only the Apostles imparted spiritual gifts through the laying on of hands, Paul imparting to Timothy being our prime example.

I do not believe that any of the other ministries have the authority to impart into someone through the laying on of hands. That does not mean you cannot release things on their behalf though.

Every believer has the authority in the name of Jesus to command every knee to bow. Every believer has the authority to go to the Throne Room of God and to intercede and pray for His help. As a minister this is a vital function.

The Seven Purposes of Ministry

To bring it all together for you, here are the seven purposes that you should be fulfilling as a minister.

1. To Equip the Church with tools.

This is accomplished by both teaching and training God's people.

2. To do the work of the ministry and meet the needs of God's people.

This is a servanthood function and when you fulfill it, you are truly doing the "stuff" of the ministry.

3. To build up the Church bringing it to maturity using faith, hope and love.

Bring every single believer to maturity of knowing right from wrong and choosing right! This is done through the agency of building faith, hope and love into God's people.

4. To bring unity in the lives of God's people.

You do this by teaching them to work through and overcome conflicts. Not everyone will have agreement of the same doctrine, but the Holy Spirit and our faith in Jesus Christ is what holds us together.

5. To come to a full knowledge of Jesus.

Without this relationship there is no maturity. Until every believer knows Jesus, they cannot be without spot and wrinkle.

6. To warn and protect. This also includes correction.

You do this by guarding against the enemy and also warning them when someone is going the wrong way. To do so with a motivation of love and not judgment will bring the church to maturity.

7. To help people find their place in the church and then to release them into it.

This gives God's people a purpose and something to hold on to. Every believer has a calling and a destiny to fulfill in the Kingdom of God. Help them find their place and they will mature.

Become Empowered

As you look through the list, you start to wonder how you will ever be able to accomplish all of these things. Well that is why in a few passages above, the Word says that it is the Lord Jesus that gave the ministries to the church.

If you could fulfill this purpose all by yourself, what would you need the Lord for? Do you think that the Lord picked you out because you were capable of fulfilling this purpose? No, the Lord picked you out because you were weak and foolish.

He picked you out because He saw something He loved in you. He saw Himself! He saw that you had submitted to Him and were willing to be used. And so He has called you and picked you up.

Now tell me, if He called you and picked you up, don't you think that He can empower you as well? He did not call you only to leave you stranded.

Not only will the Lord give you the tools that you need to do this job, but He will also give you the wisdom, anointing and any other gifts you need as well.

An Unending Supply

He will not leave you stranded. He has an unending supply of anointing. He has an unending supply of revelations. I promise that He will never run out and for as long as you remain submitted to Him, He will keep pouring them out to you.

For as long as you are prepared to be emptied and to be a servant, He will keep filling you up again and again. When Jesus spoke to the woman at the well He told her about a well of water that never ran dry.

You have that well right inside of you. You do not need to go on a big search to find His power. You do not need to keep striving to flow in revelation. You have a well of water right inside of you that will never run dry.

It will be like the oil and flour that never ran out for the widow in the time of Elijah. The more you use, the more He will just keep topping you up. If only you depend on Jesus alone and not on yourself, the well of water inside of you will fill up again and again.

PART 02 - PERSONAL MINISTRY

CHAPTER 02

How to Hear God's Voice for Yourself

Part 02 – Personal Ministry

Chapter 02 – How to Hear God's Voice for Yourself

Do you know what I hated the most about dating? It was that you had to try and snatch your moments of time together. Do you remember what it was to be in love for the first time? You wanted to spend every possible minute with that person.

Unfortunately, though all you got were these snatches. For many of us, we were still living with our parents and of course there were curfews and annoying things like school or work that got in the way. So, what you did was try to snatch as much time as you could with the person you loved.

Craig and I were no different when we were dating. We would go late into the night sharing our hearts, pushing the boundaries until we had spent every last minute we could together. He would drop me off at home and then we would stand outside the front door talking until we really had to go our separate ways.

The most incredible thing about being married was that you could spend the whole night and day together. No more limitations!

This is the same progress your relationship takes as you get to know the Lord. As you first start to hear the voice of the Lord for yourself, it is like grabbing little snatches of His time. You learn to hear His voice through impressions in your spirit or through the Word. However, grabbing those snatches and really living with Him are two separate things all together.

As you come to pouring out to others and ministering to them, your relationship with the Lord is going to go up a notch. So in this chapter I want to teach you how to do just that. I want to take you past grabbing just snatches of time with the Lord and to walking in a full love relationship with Him.

Many folks think that hearing the voice of the Lord is a special event whereby you have to wait until He graces you with a Word. You could not be further from the truth! The Lord is talking to you all the time and just because you cannot hear Him, does not mean that He is silent.

Moving Beyond the Courting Stage

Now as you come to minister to others, you will need to hear the Lord more than ever. Those snatches you have had with Him before just do not cut it. Now you might be new in your walk with the Lord or you might have walked with Him for years. Either way, I am calling you into a deeper revelation of the Lord.

As the Lord uses you more in ministry, you need to be able to hear His voice more. You need to be sure of the revelation that you receive. This can only come with a more intimate relationship with the Lord. It is time to move beyond the courting stage and onto a closer intimacy with the Lord.

You cannot try to tell God's people how to hear His voice for themselves, if you cannot hear it for yourself first!

That would be a bit like a mechanic sending his own car to another mechanic to be fixed. How can you introduce the church to a Groom that you do not know for yourself?

Not only should you be able to hear His voice, but you should come to a place of rest knowing that He will always be there to speak to you when you minister. You should never feel that ministry is a "hit and miss" event where God could speak or God could be silent.

Expecting to Hear His Voice

When you know the Lord intimately, you can rest assured that He will be there every time to use you. His anointing will always show up. His revelation and wisdom will always flow out.

That would be like me lying in bed at night wondering, "Is my husband going to speak to me tonight? I wonder if he will notice me lying here." Of course I can expect to hear my husband's voice. We have a covenant relationship and I expect to communicate openly with him.

Should it be any different with the Lord? You should come to the place in your spiritual walk, where you no longer wonder, "Is the Lord going to speak to me or not? Oh, I hope He notices me." Rather you should be at a place of rest knowing that He is speaking all of the time and expecting to hear Him when you need Him most.

If a husband in the natural can fulfill this simple expectation - how much more our Heavenly Bridegroom?

So let me break it down for you again and give you some simple pointers in taking your relationship with the Lord Jesus up a notch.

Using the Urim and Thummim

There were two stones in the breastplate of the high priest. So if someone wanted to hear a clear "YES" or "NO" from the Lord, they would go to the priest. The priest would then use the "Urim and Thummim" to get their answer.

This is the same Urim and Thummim used in the day of Ezra to determine if a priest was given the "yes or no" to confirm his genealogy.

> ***Ezra 2:63*** *And the governor said to them that they should not eat of the most holy things till a priest could consult with the Urim and Thummim.*

So you could go to the priest and say, "Lord, should I marry this woman?" And the Lord would answer yes or no.

Wouldn't it be handy to have a Urim and Thummim in today's day and age? Well, I have some good news for you – you do! It is called the indwelling of the Holy Spirit and He has been giving you signals for some time now.

Think over the last week or so and the different situations you faced. Were you in a situation where you just felt a hunch? A feeling that said, "DO NOT do this". Or perhaps you had a feeling in your spirit that said, "Yes! Go for it!" The "gut feel" that comes from deep down in your spirit is the same as the Urim and Thummim of the priesthood.

If you would only listen to that prompting, you would find things going a lot easier for you. You see, the Lord is speaking to you all of the time and giving you direction, you have just not been aware of it. Now it does not matter what your ministry calling is, every believer has the ability to hear God in this way.

Simply learn to listen to your spirit and not to ignore those inner promptings. When you feel a check in your spirit, it is time to stop and not push through. However, when you feel that go ahead, you can walk forward with complete confidence.

Learning to listen to your spirit can transform your day. We do not always have the opportunity to run away for a quiet time with the Lord to hear Him more clearly. In the middle of ministry or when a situation comes up, this is the time for you to listen to the promptings coming from deep within your spirit.

The more you take that moment to listen, the easier it will be to follow the leading of the Holy Spirit. It is easy to shut off and hear the Lord when you are alone, but not so easy when someone knocks at your door and needs ministry right now. This is the time to listen to what the Lord is saying through your spirit.

When the Lord is giving you a "thummim" you might have a feeling of dread or uncertainty. A thought perhaps came to you that said, "I need to take things easy here and wait for a bit." Or perhaps you felt, "I wonder if I should tell this person about..."

Think back on times when you felt that prompting and you did not obey it. Afterwards you could have kicked yourself! Well, do not make that same mistake again. Make the effort to pay attention to what is coming from your spirit instead of hopping on a track and just going with it.

The First Impression is Right!

When someone comes for ministry, you need to be sensitive to what your spirit is saying. When someone asks a question, pay attention to the first impression that you feel in your spirit. Often you push that first impression aside and try to make sense of their problem with your mind.

You ignore the promptings in your spirit and go straight to figuring out the problem with your mind. Armed with tons of great principles, you try to analyze the person and the situation instead of listening to what God is saying first.

However, in my experience that first impression was the right one! The moment you heard their question, what is the first thing you felt? Did you feel positive or negative in the spirit?

So before you even minister or try to get revelation for someone, listen to your spirit! The Urim and Thummim is like a step in the door.

Knowing With the Spirit

When Craig and I were dating I could never tell when he was upset with me. He was always just an amiable nice-guy and had a smile on his face. He did not like to tell me when something bothered him.

After a little while of marriage though, I knew him well enough to just glance in his direction and know, "uh oh… I put my foot in it again! I said something I should not have!"

Learning to develop this way of hearing the Lord matures as your relationship progresses with Him. You go from trying to guess what God is saying to you, to sensing clearly in your spirit if something is of Him or not.

You do not always need to get a clear word of direction from the Lord with a full map and compass. More often than not, you get promptings that are like little lights along a garden path, lighting up one after the other. If you follow them, you will reach your destination.

You do not always need a full prophetic word and revelation to get your feet moving. If my husband always had to tell me, word by word, every single thought he had, our marriage would be in a sad state of affairs. I should know him well enough to follow his lead without him always having to give me full directions.

Not only should I trust him, but I should also know him well enough to know what is on his mind. Well it is the same with the Lord. You need to develop your relationship with him to the point where you can sense a step at a time where He is leading you. Then, you will know with the spirit and so walk alongside the Lord as He leads.

Now when you hear that prompting from your spirit, you have a choice to make. You can decide to follow that prompting or ignore it and do your own thing.

Now I am not saying that you should base your entire spiritual life on this one principle, but it certainly starts leading you in the right direction. From here you can learn to communicate more with the Lord and get clearer revelation.

By learning to be aware of His voice all through the day, you will be in a better position to flow in some of the other ways.

Flowing in Visions

In many circles visions are regarded as such a spiritual experience that they do not realize that flowing in visions should be part of the daily life of every believer. You should be able to hear the Lord all of the time. Now I am not going to delve into how to flow in visions, because I put a lot of effort into that in my *Way of Dreams and Visions* book.

Instead, I want you to bring experiencing visions to the place where you are using them to hear the Lord for yourself. You should be using visions in your personal prayer time all of the time. If you took the time to flow in visions in your personal prayer times with the Lord, flowing out in ministry becomes an extension of what you do all of the time.

Now, not only prophets can flow in visions! Any believer and the Fivefold Ministry can. Combined with what I have already shared, you will feel comfortable ministering to someone.

If you want to get to know the Lord, it is going to mean listening to Him in the quiet. It means getting revelation for your life in your private prayer times.

One on One Time

When Craig and I were dating, we were always around a lot of people. Even though we had a good time with the group, we only got to know each other after everyone had gone home and we were alone long enough to talk. We did not base our relationship on the interaction we had in the group, but rather on our private times.

Well it is the same with the Lord. When you stand up to minister or you are counseling someone, you are interacting with the Lord in a group. You are ministering, but you are not developing your personal relationship with Him.

I want you to remember that point, because it is so easy to forget when you start getting really busy in ministry. You think that pouring out is the same as intimacy, but it is not true at all. True intimacy comes when you are alone. It is the times when you are in the secret place, listening to your spirit, journaling and flowing in visions that God gives to you, that you really get to know Him.

You will start to feel comfortable with the sound of the Lord's voice. Then when you are in the middle of a crisis or someone needs urgent ministry, you will be able to discern the Lord's voice above all of the noise around you.

No Doubt – Ministry is Simple

With this kind of relationship, you will not have to doubt if what you hear was His voice or not. When you are ministering and He speaks into your spirit, you will not need to panic and say, "Lord was that you? Lord, please confirm what you are saying. I am not sure!"

You will be sure, because you would have heard Him enough in your private times to know that He is speaking to you and through you right now.

If you do this, then next time you stand up to minister, you will have so much more to pour out. You will no longer teach or minister from principles alone, but from principles that you experienced in your day-to-day walk with Jesus.

This is true ministry! This is what it means to represent Christ to His Church.

When you minister to others, you are flowing out of what you already have in the Lord. This brings such a peace. You no longer have to strive so hard to get the revelations or the answer. You can minister out of confidence and rest.

Journaling

As you develop your relationship with the Lord you can also use journaling to converse with Him. The great thing about journaling is that you can document all direction and revelation that He gives to you. I am not going to give you full teaching on that here again, because we have taught it in so many other places.

When you know that you have to meet with someone for the purpose of ministry, then journaling will put everything into perspective for you. I use this myself all the time, especially when I need to speak or attend a seminar.

I do not take a step forward until I have journaled and written down what God wants to say. It is so easy to get carried away with the things that you see in the natural, that you can overlook what God wants to do.

If you are about to give someone marital counsel it is so easy to look at their problem from the outside and make your own assessment. If you have studied up on a lot of principles, then you need to journal even more!

You need the Lord to cut through all of your knowledge and to pull out the one gem and direction that you need to use. Learning to journal before jumping ahead of the Lord will help you learn to flow in that kind of wisdom.

I have found that the Lord has a way of exposing a problem that I never considered before. He knows the heart of the person you are going to minister to. He knows the exact thing that will reach them. So take the time to journal and to hear what He is telling you.

The great thing about this is that when you do step behind the pulpit or have the person in front of you,

you feel confident, because God has spoken. This means you will also flow more in the anointing, because you are not trying so hard to minister, but rather just pouring out what God has already given to you.

Coming To a Place of Rest

As you learn to develop your relationship with the Lord, you will become comfortable with His voice. You will sense the changes in the spirit. You will get impressions and visions and this will give you security.

You will no longer fear that God might not show up. You can trust in Him. Why? Because you know Him! You read of all the ministry greats and how well they could hear from God and often it can make you feel a bit inferior.

You can feel that you have not yet "arrived" to be able to be used in the same way. Child of God, this is a lie from the pit of hell! Jesus does not play favorites. Not only can you hear His voice, but you can also rest assured that His anointing is ready and waiting for you.

You do not need to earn it or struggle to find it. It is right within your spirit. All you need to do is learn to get it out. You do this through a relationship with Jesus. This is the same relationship that Peter had when he reached out to the crippled man and said, "Silver and gold I do not have - but what I have, I give you. In the name of Jesus Christ of Nazareth rise up and walk."

That spirit was inside of him and he knew Jesus well enough to know that Jesus wanted that man healed! All he did was act on what Jesus wanted.

You too can know what Jesus wants. Ministry is simply flowing out from that. All of the anointing and power that you could desire is wrapped up in knowing His voice. You never have to fear Him deserting you in a difficult moment.

You can rest assured that the next time you stand up to preach or minister, that He is right there alongside you, speaking into your spirit and giving you the power you need to reach His people.

CHAPTER **03**

Using Visions in Personal Ministry

Chapter 03 - Using Visions in Personal Ministry

There is something that you do not see around much these days. Perhaps I am showing my age here, but when I was younger there was a place we used to visit called a Drive-In Theater. It is a place where you would take your car to watch a movie.

It looked like a huge parking lot and right at the front was a huge white screen where the movie was shown using a projector mounted in a building at the rear of the lot. Now, I remember the very first time I ever went to the Drive-In.

It was quite the rage when I was a kid and at the time I was about 11 years old. We went with a whole group of friends one summer's evening. It was warm, so instead of sitting in the car, we sat outside on blankets.

You know even though that happened years ago, I can still remember the movie. I can still recall the images on that screen.

There is something about us that is very visual and that is why visions are such a powerful tool in the hand of the Lord. Why is that? It is because we remember pictures more than anything else. We will remember pictures above a prophetic word or a revelation you received in scripture.

You will remember the pictures in your mind for years to come. When you realize this, you realize the power there is in flowing in visions. What are visions? They are simply pictures that are filled with a message from the Lord.

They are in essence, the language of the Lord. Each time that you receive a vision, you are hearing the Lord's voice. They are a guide stick and when it comes to preaching prophetically, there is no way that you can deliver a word without visions!

Now, I am not going to delve into the subject of how to receive visions, instead I am going to take you deeper into this subject and teach you here how to use visions in personal and public ministry.

Types and Shadows

It does not matter what your calling is, every believer can function in visions and every minister should see them as a ministry tool in their tool belt. I personally live and breathe visions. Since the beginning of time the Lord spoke in types and shadows and He has not changed.

I need a picture and a direction as I minister and visions are by far one of the easiest ways to get that direction. For many folks, they consider flowing in visions a random event. As a minister, not only should you be flowing in visions all the time but you also need to realize how vital they are to being effective in ministry.

This is one of the basic ways to hear the voice of the Lord outside of hearing Him through dreams or Urim and Thummim.

The Spirit of Wisdom and Revelation

> *Ephesians 1:17 That the God of our Lord Jesus Christ, the Father of glory, may give to you the spirit of wisdom and revelation in the knowledge of Him,*
>
> *18 the eyes of your understanding being enlightened; that you may know what is the hope of His calling, what are the riches of the glory of His inheritance in the saints,*
>
> *19 and what is the exceeding greatness of His power toward us who believe, according to the working of His mighty power*

Rule #1 Visions Received in Context

One of the most vital points to remember when flowing in visions is that you will receive that vision in context of what you are praying for. Just as this scripture says, the spirit of revelation and wisdom comes through knowledge of the Lord.

It is when you come and reach out to Him, that He will open the eyes of your understanding and show you the riches of His glory.

So what does it mean to flow in the spirit of wisdom and revelation? It means that you will flow and get revelation according to how you are ministering. Sometimes people get some strange ideas. They have this idea that as you are walking along your merry way... BAM a vision falls out of heaven.

It does not happen that way. So rest assured that if you have not had a cosmic experience like this it does not make you a second-rate Christian. In fact, you are just like the rest of us. We only receive visions in prayer or when we are seeking God for direction.

You know the only person who had an experience like that was the Apostle Paul. What he had was not a regular vision but an actual visitation from Jesus on the road to Damascus. We look at Peter praying on the rooftop where he received a vision of a cloth being lowered carrying unclean animals.

At the time of this vision, he was seeking the Lord. He was in a time of prayer and received that revelation that would affect the future of the entire church. Peter was not walking casually along the road, when suddenly the heavens opened and a huge cloth of weird animals dropped at his feet.

You will read of Apostle Paul saying often how they were in prayer and how the Lord showed them various things. Your revelation will come when you are seeking the Lord.

The Lord does not bang on your door, trying to push revelation down your throat, when you did not ask for it. You need to put yourself in a position to receive the direction He has for you. This can happen in different situations.

You might be in your prayer closet or in praise and worship. You might even be ministering to someone that has come to you with a need. So say for example you go to prayer with a personal need, whatever revelation you get during that prayer relates directly to that need.

God Answers Directly

Imagine that you picked up the phone to ask a good friend of yours a direct question. It would be very rude of that friend to ignore your question and to answer a question you did not ask. The Lord is no different.

He is not going to be rude and ignore what you are talking about to answer something you did not ask! If you ask the Lord about something specific, the revelation you receive will be in direct answer to that question.

The problem of course is that not everyone likes the answer that they get. You go to the Lord with a personal problem and He gives you a vision. However, the vision indicates something negative and instead of accepting that vision for yourself, you try to interpret it for someone else.

You will face this more times than you can count, as you minister to people, so get ready for it!

What is fantastic about knowing this truth is that it takes the mystery out of the revelation you are receiving. If you are ministering to a person, then the vision you receive is clearly for them. All you need to do then is share it with them.

You do not need to spend a good part of an hour trying to figure out "whom this vision is for".

So if you are praying before a meeting or before a ministry appointment, the visions you receive during that prayer are related to that meeting. Just knowing that gives you most of the interpretation.

Consider the last time you were in prayer and received a vision - what were you praying about? Were you praying for someone specific? Perhaps you were in intercession and you came to the Lord, ready to be used.

You did not come with a prayer list, but go to get a prayer list. While you submit yourself to the Lord and ask what to pray, you might see someone you know in a vision. If this is the case, then clearly the Lord is telling you to pray for that person.

I know that this sounds pretty simplistic, but you would be surprised how many people do not grasp this basic point.

The Lord is Not Rude

The Lord is not like some people who always want to talk about themselves. Do you know the kind I mean?

They are the kind of people that, no matter what you try to share, they always find a way to talk about what interests them and not you.

My youngest daughter had a phase of doing that. At one time she was really praying hard for a puppy. It did not matter what we were talking about, she somehow managed to squeeze her "puppy talk" into the conversation.

The Lord is not like that. He is not going to interrupt your prayer rudely. He is going to answer you according to what you have been waiting on Him for. So if there is something you need to know from the Lord, take the time to ask Him!

He is not going to force His revelation on you. Rather He is going to wait for you to come to Him and then He will share everything with you that you need to know for the moment.

Asking the Unasked

Now there will be times in your life where you are simply too afraid to ask the Lord about something. It might have something to do with a direction that you are unsure of. It might have something to do with a personal sin that you are struggling with.

Instead of asking the Lord about it though, you think to yourself, "If the Lord wanted to give me direction on that, He would have told me already."

Did you ask Him for direction? Did you ask Him for an answer? The Lord is not going to impose His revelation or answer on you. He is not going to tell you to go left or right if you did not ask Him for directions.

You are hoping that the Lord is going to interrupt your life to give you His will, but that is how the enemy works, not the Lord. It is the enemy that pushes you and forces you in a direction. The Lord Jesus leads, because He is the Good Shepherd.

Rule #2 Visions Come With Interpretation

Every couple or family has their own kind of language. You can see it if you sit around a dinner table, or perhaps you have this with your own family. There are things that you say to one another that only you understand.

There are mannerisms and sayings that only you would get. You have a host of inside jokes that only you laugh at. When you are involved in an intimate conversation with your spouse or close family member, you understand one another! You speak the same language.

The Lord is very much the same. However, there are many who think that when the Lord shares a vision that He is suddenly begins talking in a foreign language. This could not be further from the truth.

When the Lord talks to you, He speaks in a language that He expects you to understand. No husband would expect his wife to try and decipher his every word. No, if he is a good husband, he will communicate in a way that his wife understands.

Well, our heavenly Bridegroom is even more considerate! He will always talk your language! The Lord is not trying to give you a great mystery to hide the truth from you.

The reason why He speaks in types and shadows is to hide the truth from the enemy, not from you! He expects you to understand what He is saying.

So when you receive a vision from the Lord, He expects you to understand the vision. Now perhaps some of the symbols in the vision will not be fully clear to you because you are not so familiar with the Word.

So the best thing to do when you receive a vision or revelation is to look the symbols up in the Scripture. Find yourself a searchable bible online or for the computer and do a search.

The Impression in Your Spirit

When you receive a vision from the Lord, you will receive with it, an impression in your spirit. Very often this impression is easy to overlook, because the Lord speaks in a still small voice. He does not shout at you.

You might not receive the full interpretation the minute you get the vision, but you will receive an impression to begin with. For example, if I see a vision of a dark cloud building up, I would get an impression in my spirit at the same time whether that cloud is a good or a bad thing.

In the scripture a cloud can speak of a sign of blessing, or it can also speak of the principalities in the air – a work of the enemy. So the impression I receive in my spirit at the time of having that vision will affect its interpretation directly.

If I see a flood in the spirit, is that a flood of blessing I am seeing or the enemy coming in like a flood? Everything depends on what I sense in my spirit at the time of having the vision.

Only you, the person receiving the vision will be able to discern that. You cannot ask someone else to decide whether that vision is positive or negative, because the Lord gave it to you. You need to identify that very first impression that you received.

You have the opportunity here to mature in receiving and using revelation in ministry. Stop for long enough to get an impression in your spirit. Once you add to that the context of what you were praying for at the time, everything falls into place rather quickly.

Now there are times when you will see things in the spirit where you will not get the full interpretation right away. This is true of Peter again with the vision of the unclean animals. He only got the full understanding of it afterwards when he got a knock at his door.

This happened to me as well when my dad saw a jewel encrusted key in the spirit during one of our prayer times. He felt it related to my ministry, but was not sure in what capacity. So he released it. From that moment on my life turned upside down!

Only much later did we realize that what he saw was the Key of David spoken of in the book of Revelation and it was directly related to my apostolic calling. Without realizing it, he had released me into apostolic training. It took us a full three years to understand the fullness of that vision.

Even though we did not have the full interpretation, he received a clear impression in his spirit. He knew that the key was positive and related directly to my calling. The rest unfolded in time.

The important thing was not just the vision he received, but the fact that he applied it to my life and released me into what God had planned.

Rule #3 The Symbols in Visions Based on the Word

Whatever your vision is, you will find your interpretation in the Word. No matter what your vision is, ask yourself this question, "Can I find this symbol in the Word?"

It is true that the Lord will use things that are common to your culture, such as Peter with the unclean animals. Unclean animals had a clear meaning in the Old Testament.

Even when the Lord uses symbols that are characteristic of your culture, you will be able to back your interpretation of that symbol in the Word.

The Word of God is a universal language that every believer can talk and it is our foundation. A good indicator to use is this:

If you cannot use scripture in explaining the interpretation of your vision, then something is wrong.

If you cannot apply your revelation using the Word, then I suggest that you wait on it until you get a confirmation.

Unfortunately, there are many believers that base their entire lives on visions without applying them correctly.

Say for example you see a vision of someone bound up in chains. Can you think of any scriptures that you could use to minister? How about, "He who the son sets free, is free indeed"? If you have a vision of someone being blind, think back on what Jesus did in a situation like that.

He quickly reached out His hand and opened those blind eyes. Applying that vision is so simple. You speak to their eyes whether natural or spiritual and you tell them to be opened. Visions are a means to an end - they are not a means in themselves.

A Means to an End

Visions are just one of the tools that the Lord will use in your ministry to get His message across to you. The idea is not to concentrate on just getting visions all the time, but rather to receive those visions so that you can apply the healing or deliverance that the person needs.

For every revelation or vision you receive, you should be able to apply it using the Word of God. This is one of the reasons why I encourage my students to learn to visualize the Word. If every believer took the time to visualize the scriptures and see the pictures that God has already painted for us, receiving revelation would be so simple.

Each time you find yourself in a situation, when you have already pushed the Word into your spirit, the right picture will come out of your spirit for the right circumstance.

The greatest part about using the Word to apply your revelation is that it covers you. It is not something that you just made up by yourself. People can question your revelation, but they cannot question the Word.

There are times when you might miss the Lord. There will be times when you might interpret a dream incorrectly or apply a vision incorrectly. You can never miss the Word of God though. The Word stands as your foundation.

If you use the Word to minister to someone, it does not matter if they fight you or try to blow holes into your revelation. You might be fallible, but the Word of God is not. It is your protection. Stand on the Word and let it keep you steady.

No matter what vision you get, you should be able to quote at least one scripture with your revelation. If you cannot do that, then get some help. Speak to someone to get some confirmation. By applying that principle, it will help keep you clear of deception.

Not only that, but when you are on the receiving end of ministry, it will help you discern if the revelation you are given is of the Lord or not.

NOTE: The symbols in your vision might be culture based, but the interpretation should always be applied using the Word.

Rule #4 Application

Receiving a vision is just the first step in ministry. The real work begins when you apply it! Say for example you are praying concerning a financial need in your life and you see a vision of a mountain in your road.

The message is clear. There is a spiritual blockage that is preventing your financial release. So what are you going to do about it? The reason why the Lord gave you the vision was so that you could tell that mountain to be removed in the spirit!

If you are ministering to a person and you see them at a certain age or you have a vision of them in a prison, this is not just for your interest. The reason why the Lord showed you that vision was so that you could share it with them and help them get free.

There are people who are still holding onto the visions that they received years ago. Well, what are you doing with that vision? You see chains in the spirit, what does that mean? It means that the person in question is in bondage.

Why did the Lord show that to you? So that you could break that bondage in the spirit and so you could expose what is keeping that person bound up by the enemy.

Just receiving a vision is not good enough! It only becomes effective when it is applied. You see, this is how you set the captives free. Not just by getting revelation, but by applying that revelation whether in a vision or directly from the Word.

Flowing in Visions in Personal Ministry

As you learn to apply each vision that the Lord gives you, the next one will follow and so the Lord will take you a step at a time. The full revelation that He has for the person you are ministering to will unfold like a jigsaw puzzle falling into place.

When you first come to the Lord, He might give you just one vision or impression in your spirit. Perhaps you are praying for a spiritual breakthrough for someone and you see dark clouds in the spirit. As you come against that you see birds in the spirit pulling at the person. After you come against that, you see the person cut open and hurt.

The Lord is indicating that this person needs healing for the hurts they have received through all of these attacks through their life. But you see, it does not all come at the same time.

The visions will come one after the other. When the time of ministry is over, the visions will stop.

You do not need to feel that you must have the full revelation up front. No, it will unfold as you follow the Lord. It can be a bit daunting at first, because all of us feel more secure if everything is laid out nicely.

When you come to flowing with the Lord like this, you will learn to be dependent on Him and not on your own understanding.

Just Share It! Simple.

When it comes to ministering personally to someone, it is common to receive a vision that you might not know the full interpretation to. Do not be concerned about this, but just share what you see. The person you are ministering to will know what the vision means.

As ministers, sometimes we are just too keen to jump in and give our own opinions! The rules change in personal ministry though. Do not forget that this vision is for the person. If that is the case, then they will also understand it.

So if you receive a vision in personal ministry, before adding what you feel it says, just share the vision with them plainly. If they cannot relate, then you are welcome to share what you sense. More often than not though, what you share will spark them off and will make sense to them.

No Pressure

I want to add some balance here before we move on. As you learn to flow in the gifts of revelation in ministry, you will soon come to an experience where you suddenly do not get anything. When this happens to you, you might feel that you have messed up. You will wonder why you are not getting a vision.

I want you to remember here that it is the Holy Spirit that is the one who manifests the gifts and if He is not talking, neither should you.

Do not feel under pressure to get revelation or wisdom. If nothing comes, it might just be that the person in question is not ready for what God has to say. They might not have faith for their need or the Lord is busy doing something in their lives.

There is no shame in saying, "I do not get anything right now." Do not allow yourself to get under pressure to get revelation, but rather wait on the Lord for just one vision. As you receive the first vision, apply it and flow on from there.

On the other hand, if you do not receive anything, then rest and wait. Do not try to push out a revelation that is simply not there.

Bringing It Together

When you consider this final point, all of the principles come together beautifully.

> **1.** Firstly, you will only receive a revelation in the context of what you are ministering or praying.
>
> **2.** Secondly, only you can determine the first impression that you receive in your spirit.
>
> **3.** Thirdly, that vision's symbols will always be based on the Word.
>
> **4.** Then finally, that vision needs to be applied using the Word!

CHAPTER 04

The Five Golden Rules

Chapter 04 – The Five Golden Rules

Have you ever stumbled onto a programming website, or had the terrible misfortune of being stuck in a room of complete intellectuals?

When you find yourself in the middle of such a group you are pretty sure that they are speaking English. You are pretty sure that you should "get" what they are saying. However, no matter how hard you try, you cannot understand a word of it!

You just wish that someone there in that room, could speak your language! This rings true for ministry a lot of the time. Get yourself sandwiched between two theologians and you begin to wonder if you ever understood what salvation meant!

I guess that is why I became such a "step 1... 2... 3" kind of person. When it came to ministry I hungered for someone to talk my language and to say it straight without all the jargon in between.

So that is exactly what I am going to do for you here. Using practical illustrations, I am going to take your hand and show you how to jump right into ministering effectively every time.

Rule #1 Never Give Ministry Unless It is Asked For.

> ***Revelation 3:20*** *Behold, I stand at the door and knock. If anyone hears My voice and opens the*

door, I will come in to him and dine with him, and he with Me.

The way I have seen some folks minister, you would swear that the passage above reads, "Behold I kick in the door and bash it down!"

Even the Lord Jesus knocks on the door of our hearts and waits for us to open before He comes in and does His rearranging. This should be the pattern for your ministry as well. That is why the first rule of all ministry is to wait for the person to open that door before you can go in and "fellowship."

Just because someone is sharing their intimate secrets with you does not mean that they want help! I am sure you can identify already. There are so many people ready to come to you and tell you all of their troubles. Listening to them you feel compassion. You think to yourself, "Shame that is really tough. They must be having such a hard time. Let me help this person out."

You are all poised to gift them with your precious pearls of wisdom only to find that they only wanted someone to dump all of their rubbish on!

So do not give ministry or counsel to someone that did not ask for it. Make sure, before you open your mouth that this is someone that is ready to receive.

If you try to jump in ahead of time without knowing this first rule, you are headed for rejection! Not only that, but if you start getting into the realm of the demonic, you are headed for some backlashes in the spirit.

Have you ever tried to minister to a person only to have them fight with you about everything you shared? Perhaps after ministering to someone you left and things suddenly started to go wrong in your life. You got into a fight with your spouse or your car broke down on the way home.

What happened here? You ministered un-led. That person you tried to reach did not really want ministry - they wanted sympathy.

So, Rule #1 – Minister only when invited.

Practical Example

You are at a social gathering with other believers and someone comes up and starts sharing their heart with you. They share the conflicts they are facing at the moment. Perhaps they heard from others that you are a "dream expert" and they rush over to you with their dream.

They say to you, "Do you know what it means?" This is your foot in the door. You have just been given the go ahead to share.

It could be that after sharing their struggles in their marriage they say, "What do you think I should do?"

Wait for that invitation before leaping forward. Sometimes that invitation might not be clear. I find it easier to just jump straight to the point in a situation like that. After someone shares like that, you can ask gently, "Would you like to know what I feel?" or "I have an idea what the problem might be… "

Leave it open and allow the person to respond to your invitation. If they run right over you and do not stop to take you up on your offer, listen politely and move on. Do not force your ministry but rather wait until they are ready to receive.

After you are sure they want you involved, do not be afraid to step out and share what is in your heart.

Now that you have your foot poised to leap into the fray of ministry, before you start running, let me lead you to Rule #2.

Rule #2 Do Not Overfeed the Cow

There was a small farming town pastor faithful to minister to his little congregation each Sunday. The meetings were small and the people simple, but he delighted in serving the Lord.

One Sunday morning though as he drove up to the church only one man had shown up for the meeting. Discouraged the Pastor patted the man on the back and thanked him for coming with a, "Well, I guess there will not be any meeting today."

The man replied, "You know Pastor I am a cattle farmer and if at the end of the day just one of my cows comes in to eat, I still take the time to feed it."

The Pastor was both convicted and enthused. Taking the man up on the invitation he opened the church doors and stood behind the pulpit with great gusto. He preached with all the fire he could muster. He taught, he shared, he inspired and he dug deep.

After his sermon and feeling rather chuffed with himself, he walked the farmer to the door.

"Did you enjoy the meeting today?" He asked with enthusiasm.

The farmer replied, "You know Pastor at the end of the day if only one cow comes to be fed, I give him his portion. I do not give him the haystack meant for the whole herd!

When someone comes to you with a need, it is so tempting to jump in right away with all your grand knowledge and superior advice.

You have a bucket full of principles that you are just dying to try out and you cannot wait for the next "victim" to come along. So before the Lord gets a chance to speak, you are analyzing, determining and giving that person a good dose of what you think.

However, how much of what you are sharing is what God thinks?

Here is a Good Guideline to Keep in Mind:

Question: Why did the person come to you for ministry?

Answer: To hear what God has to say.

So this person grabbed you after church and has shared a dream with you. After listening it is clear to you that they have a demonic bondage in their lives that they need to deal with. Now knowing a bit about this sort of thing, you jump in right away. You start addressing and exposing and telling them exactly what to do.

There is just one little problem with this scenario. That is not what they asked for. They did not ask you to perform deliverance at the entrance of the church foyer. They asked you to interpret their dream.

Now, I understand where you are coming from. When you see people in bondage to a lie, you want to see them set free. It is hard to hold back sometimes. But do not forget, they did not ask you for your opinion.

They did not ask you for your counsel. All they asked you was what their dream meant. Now if you have already read the *Way of Dreams and Visions*, you probably have all those principles buzzing in your head. The temptation you have to avoid is trying to fit every last principle into that single dream interpretation.

The same holds true for any kind of ministry. Just because you have been on a marital counsel course does not mean that everyone that comes to you for marital counsel should get the full barrel load of your newly found knowledge.

Here is What You Should Do

As the person shares, tell them what God is saying. Do not tell them what you are saying or what you think. If you receive an impression in your spirit or see clearly from the Word where their failure is, then share that.

Consider when Joseph went to Pharaoh - how did he handle the situation? He knew right away what that dream meant, but he did not open his mouth with his good advice. No, he started out by sharing the interpretation and telling that man exactly what God had to say.

Only after the interpretation was given did he follow it up with his own advice. The ministry comes first. What God has to say comes ahead of any advice you feel to give. Leave your opinion and advice for later and you cannot go wrong.

So the bottom-line here? Do not give people ministry or advice that they never asked for. In the end, it will only discourage you when that ministry is not received or taken up the wrong way.

Back to our illustration of the dream interpretation - that person shares their dream and the interpretation goes something like this,

"Your dream indicates that the enemy has an open door in your life and as a result you are struggling to hear the voice of the Lord correctly."

Bam! You just served them a fastball. It is now for them to decide what to do with it. Do not pick it up just yet. Leave it there. Leave it hanging. Resist the temptation to jump in right away and tell them what to do about it.

Allow the person to accept or reject your interpretation. If they receive it, they will let you know. They will ask you what to do or how to deal with this open door.

Once they hit the ball back to you, you can take it from there. Only then can you step in and minister and tell them what you feel that open door is.

It is a basic principle, but it will revolutionize your ministry. Do you find that after someone has asked you for ministry that they never return?

Do people avoid you at the door?

Could it be that they feel like you just bowled a fastball at their heads and they found themselves diving to get out of the way? Give people a chance to respond.

Toss the revelation or what you feel God is saying to them and see if they hit it back. If they turn and run, do not run after them. Pray and let the Holy Spirit handle it from there.

Consider your own experiences. Have you ever met one of those "pushy prophetic types" that insist you must receive their revelation? It does not even matter if they are right or not, they are just so pushy you do not want to hear what they have to say.

Do not fall into this category yourself.

You must lead someone when it comes to ministry. Not push them from behind.

Rule # 3 Use Tact

What is tact? To use a common expression,

"Tact is telling someone that they are going to Hell in such a way that they are looking forward to the trip."

It can be tough sometimes and certainly in my ministry there are times people share things with me where I think to myself, "Well buddy, I do not know what you have been into lately, but you have some serious issues!"

Because one of the things we do is train the prophets, there are many that come to us with revelations that are way out in left field. Not only are those revelations demonic, but there is no doubt in my mind that the person sharing is completely demonized as well.

What is the right way to handle someone like this? I can tell you now that the worst thing I could say is,

"You are way into deception, you are demonized and I sincerely doubt your salvation!"

Oh yes, I can see them running to me right now saying, "Wow thank you for that, please can you slap me some more?"

If you have had people running away from you instead of toward you for ministry, could it be that it is not the revelation that you are sharing with them, but simply the way that you are presenting it?

Stop the pouncing! We know that there are things that must be uncovered, but there is a better way to do it than by jumping on their sin and exposing them to the point where they want to crawl under the carpet and go home.

Perhaps the reason why some folks look frantically at their watches and find a quick excuse to fly out the door is not because they did not like what you had to say. Perhaps the problem is the way that you said it.

So learn to use these words,

"Perhaps"

"Could it be?"

"What if... "

"I would like to suggest… "

These are simple little words, but please… memorize them! If folks keep running away from you after you minister, then it is likely that these words do not exist in your vocabulary.

Is it true that the person you are ministering to is demonized? Yes, it is.

Is it true that this person's revelation is a deception? Yes, it is.

Is it true that there are some deep sins that need addressing? Yes, there are!

There is a way of telling them those truths in such a way that they will be open to hear the truth.

"Could it be… that there is witchcraft in your generations?"

"Could it be… that there is an open door to the enemy, because I sense something wrong in the spirit as you are sharing?"

"Perhaps you do not know this, but that pushy feeling that you have inside of you is not the Lord, but something demonic from the enemy."

Doesn't that sound more inviting? It sure sounds a lot easier to swallow than, "You are demonized and need deliverance."

The idea of ministry is to get people to open their hearts to you. If you cannot even get your foot in the door, how will they get to hear the rest of the truth?

Now, I am not telling you to compromise the truth. Anyone that knows me knows how blunt and direct I can be at times. In fact, I am hardly sugar coating it for you right now am I?

There is a big difference though. You picked up this book to get taught. You asked for what I am sharing with you. You are a minister and you are ready to hear the truth without the fluff.

Not every believer is at that place yet and it is important that you meet them where they are. You will get those that can take the truth straight up. There will be others that you will have to ease into it.

You could say, "Your revelation is outright deception."

Or you could say, "I feel that there are some aspects to what you are sharing that does not line up with the Word of God. I would be cautious about this revelation if I were you and consider that it is not of the Lord."

Allow the Person a Way to Escape

Sure, it might sound a bit like adding some fluff, but what this does, is give the person the opportunity to back out if they want to, without closing the door on you for keeps. Give them a "way to escape."

My dad taught me this principle very early in my ministry. He said to me, "When you are sharing a vision with someone, do not be dogmatic when you share it and say, 'this is what the vision means!' Instead say, 'This is the vision I see, can you identify at all with it?'

Then if the person feels threatened and not ready to open their heart, they can back out."

By handling it this way, you cover yourself as well. This is especially true when you are not 100% sure of what you are sensing in the spirit. If you come out with it and insist on being dogmatic with your interpretation, you might be missing the point completely.

When you get a vision for someone when you are ministering, it is likely that they have an idea of what it means. Give them the opportunity to identify that revelation for themselves first and then you can add to it what you sense.

This covers you and it also gives that person the chance to receive a true conviction from the Holy Spirit. After all, what brings the greatest conviction of all?

When someone from the outside tells you a truth, or when you suddenly see that truth for yourself?

Give people a chance to get a conviction of their own. Present the truth to them with tact and give them the chance to take you up on that truth. This will bring more conviction and make your ministry more successful.

By Colette Toach

PLEASE NOTE: Personal vs. Public Ministry

I want to make a comment here quickly and say that what I am sharing here relates to personal ministry only. I am going to delve into public ministry in more detail later but I want to touch on this briefly.

When you stand up to present your ministry publically, the rules change completely. When you stand up to prophesy or to preach the Word, there is no time for fluff. The truth is the truth.

Jesus confronted the Pharisees publically and said in front of the crowds exactly what He thought of them. When Nicodemus came to Him in the night, He showed patience and asked the man questions.

He said to Nicodemus, "Are you not a teacher, yet you do not know these things?" He did not say, "You are an idiot and you should know better!"

No, Jesus used wisdom in teaching Nicodemus and history tells us that Nicodemus followed on to become a believer. This illustration is truly the best in making my point. Jesus made a statement and Nicodemus would follow it with a question.

Jesus did not land him with all the truth in one mouthful. Rather He led Nicodemus to the truth a step at a time.

Using tact will turn your ministry around. The Word says,

> ***1 Corinthians 10:13*** *No temptation has overtaken you except such as is common to man; but God is faithful, who will not allow you to be tempted beyond what you are able, but with the temptation will also make the way of escape, that you may be able to bear it.*

If the Lord Himself gives us a way to escape in our own temptations, then surely you too can give the person coming to you for ministry a way to escape as well.

If they are not ready to face this sin, or simply feel embarrassed about it, perhaps they feel insecure right now and are ashamed that you know the truth. Let them save face! Isn't that the true love of the Lord?

If you show them that much grace, when they are truly ready to deal with that problem, they will come back to you. You would have showed yourself a friend and trustworthy. There is a reason that sinners such as prostitutes and thieves felt comfortable enough to run towards Jesus.

There is a reason why the woman at the well fell and worshipped Him. He knew her sin, but did not condemn her. Rather He gave her an open door and she had a choice to make. She could receive His ministry or reject it. Jesus only told her the truth and then left the choice up to her.

If you come at them without any tact and insist on forcing your ministry on them, then I am afraid that you are in for some tough ministry experiences. You will not understand why so many people reject you or no longer want to share their thoughts with you.

The problem is that for many up and coming ministers, they think that this is a good thing. You think that the reason people are avoiding you is because of the anointing on your life. You think that people are just being "convicted" by you and that is why you are rejected.

No, they are not convicted by your presence. The truth is... they just do not like you! The reality is that people are simply afraid. They are not convicted, because the conviction of the Lord is never repented of. It is the sorrow of the world that brings this kind of fear and death. (2 Corinthians 7:10)

If people keep rejecting your ministry, then perhaps the reason that people do not like you is because of your approach to ministry and not your revelation or counsel.

Rule #4 Faith, Hope and Love

Revelation should always be shared in faith, hope and love and when you share without tact and with all of your own ideas, you are not allowing that person to sense the heart of the Lord.

Think about your own relationship with Jesus. When you think about the times that you have heard His voice for yourself, when was the last time He said to you, "You are a filthy rotten sinner and I want nothing to do with you?"

The Lord Jesus has never spoken to me like that and He never will. Sure there have been times when He has corrected me through my journals or even through the Word, however each time He did, His words struck my heart. They came with such a force of love that the very love brought me to my knees.

When you come into the presence of the Lord Jesus, you always feel His love. Even when you have failed completely and do not deserve to be used of Him, when you do go to Him, you do not feel condemnation. No, instead you feel His tenderness and His love.

It is this love that brought you to salvation and it is this love that keeps you. It is this same agape love that will melt any heart that you minister to. When you put aside your sword of the flesh and use His love, you will find it a powerfully destructive weapon to melt the hardest heart.

That does not mean that the Lord lets you get away with your sin and failures. When you come into His presence with your sin, He does not condemn you, but rather He says, "Yes, I know that you failed, but here, let me help you. Let me teach you how to overcome that struggle."

He does not spend an hour outlining your every failure and why you are not worthy of His love. Consider how many times you let Him down again and again. Did He give up on you? No, He continued to run after you and to catch you.

He continued to give you further revelations and even send people your way to speak on His behalf. Sometimes you got His message right away, other times it took a while to get it through your head. This is a failure of our flesh and our human nature.

If you consider how many times God had to speak at times before you surrendered to Him, you will have that same patience with others as well.

So let us have the same grace and see past the oppression, sin and failure of God's people. Let us look at them through the eyes of the Lord Jesus and see the potential there.

When you see the potential, you will reach past all the junk on the outside. You will do something that no one else has probably done their entire lives. You will touch their hearts with the love of Jesus.

When you can give people grace, you show them the face of Jesus Christ.

Faith, Hope and Love

These three words are the foundation of any ministry. It might not be very obvious to a lot of folks, but faith, hope and love blended together is the cornerstone for everything you do for the Lord.

Every revelation or counsel you share should contain at least one of these spiritual forces. If someone leaves a time of ministry with you feeling weighed down with guilt or fear, then you can know outright that you failed your ministry objective.

You will come to learn that fear, guilt and condemnation are not gifts from the Lord. The purpose of ministry is to bring the church to maturity.

Apostle Paul knew this and if you read any of his epistles you will see that he used this as a yardstick for the condition of each church. To some he said, "I have heard of your faith, but you have left your first love." To another he said, "I have heard of your love."

If you are looking for a yardstick that the Lord uses today to judge your success in ministry, you will find those same three words making up the core of it. Faith, hope and love.

What is faith?

Faith is based on a person.

Once you have ministered to someone, do they leave you trusting the Lord more than they did before?

On the other hand, did they leave having more faith in you and feeling more dependent on you?

That is why you have to share what God has to say and not what you have to say. It is for you to point them to the Lord and to build up their faith in Him, not in you.

They should leave knowing that the Lord is there for them and is listening to them. They should leave having faith in the one that will never let them down.

By building this faith in each believer, you are maturing the body of Christ. (Eph 4:11-13)

How do You Increase Hope?

You do that by allowing them to see a picture of the future. The Lord will often use you to bring conviction and to expose sin, but it should still bring hope!

How is this possible? When you expose something wrong in a person, their eyes are open to a future that is free from that bondage.

Do not be afraid to tell them the truth in love. On the other hand, do not give them such a bleak outlook on life that they want to crawl away and die.

What kind of ministry are you giving? You should be saying, "Look, I know that you are not there right now but this is the picture that God has for you."

They will leave with a clear picture and this produces hope.

How do You Produce Love?

You do this by allowing them to experience the love of the Lord. You do not produce love by bringing division and strife in the church.

Unfortunately, there are many who are guilty of this failure. I cannot tell you the number of people that have come to me and shared that they are going through a divorce because, "someone prophesied it over them."

Since when was a prophetic word an excuse for divorce?

This word did not bring love, but it brought strife and division. Your ministry should leave someone with a better understanding of the love of the Lord.

How is this possible? By showing them the image of Christ through your actions and love. It is one thing to tell them about it, but it is another to walk in it.

True love does not rejoice in unrighteousness. On the other hand, true love suffers the wrongs and labors long. It is this very balance that I am trying to build into you through each page here.

I want you to have the courage to tell the truth. On the other hand, I want you to tell that truth in love and with wisdom so that you might win them for Jesus.

As you look at other leaders in the church, perhaps you feel a bit insecure. Perhaps you feel that you do not have as much as they have. What is really important here? How well you do it, or the heart that you do it with?

When your heart is to bring someone into a relationship with Jesus or to bring healing, you do not need to worry about the rest of the stuff.

They just want to hear from God. So what if your revelation was a bit off? Did they hear from God? Did you build faith into them? Do they have hope for the future again? If so, then you have done your job well and you have pleased the heart of the Father.

Rule #5: Perfection is Over-rated

God Does Not Demand Perfection

This might shock you, but God does not expect perfection from you. If you were perfect, then He would not have had to send Jesus to the cross in the first place! You are not perfect, that is why you needed a Savior.

All He expects from you is to have a heart for His people and to love them. He expects you to have faith and hope for them. That is His level of perfection. If you can make this motivation your own, then it will become more about what the Lord wants to do in His people and less about you always trying to save face.

For the first time you will start to see change in the people you minister to. You can work with someone and minister to them, but then one day you will see how they have started to overcome. When that day comes, this journey will be worth it.

The rejections and the tough times make it all worthwhile.

Because of your own love for the Lord, I know how desperately you want to get everything right. You want to make sure that you share what God has given to you. You want to make sure that you are really ministering the truth.

What do you think pleases the heart of the Father more? That you got the principles right, or that the motivation of your heart was right?

You want to make sure that you apply each and every principle correctly. At the end of the day though, why are you doing this? To nail every principle head-on or just to touch the hearts of God's people?

As you learn through our courses, you can get quite hung up on principles. Let me tell you though, that it is not about giving the most perfect revelation.

Ministry is not about getting a 100% accurate vision or revelation.

Ministry is not about having a doctorate in doctrine.

Ministry is not about being able to quote everyone from Moses to Spurgeon.

Ministry is about producing faith, hope and love in the heart of God's people. It is about bringing maturity and making that Bride beautiful for Her Groom.

By Colette Toach

To do this takes a force of the spirit, not just principles.

So it is good that you are gaining knowledge, but I hope that through these pages, you pick up a lot more than that. I pray that you pick up the anointing to minister, because then you will truly be accomplishing what God has called you to do.

Stir It Up

I want to stir up the fire in you for ministry. I want to give you the kind of motivation that will keep you getting up again and again each morning. If your motivation for ministry is about pressing your own revelation or teaching, then you will burn yourself out rather quickly.

If your motivation is to heal the broken, set the captives free and give sight to the blind, then the Lord can work with you! I know that when you are fired up, you will minister correctly.

When the motivation is correct, you will not crumble when you are rejected, but you will have the grace to press on.

Remember, if you mess up with a principle, but you continued walking in faith, hope and love, then it is not a failure at all.

The Final Conclusion

When all is said and done and the anointing lifts, as you see the person walk away from you, ask yourself this question:

"How did my ministry draw this person closer to the Lord?"

If you can see that what you did drew them closer to the Lord, then you accomplished your responsibility before the Lord. You are fulfilling your calling and the Lord can now entrust you with more.

Before you know it, you are going to be busier than ever. Enjoy this season in your life. Enjoy even your failures and mistakes. As you have gone through these rules with me and seen how you have failed, do not be discouraged.

Rather thank the Lord that He is giving you the opportunity to learn. Next time when you step out, you are going to do so with a new heart. You will do it with the heart of Christ and it is this love that will revolutionize your ministry forever.

Summary of Rules:

Rule 1: Minister Only When Invited To.

Rule 2: Do not Overfeed the Cow!

Rule 3: Use Tact!

By Colette Toach

Rule 4: Faith, Hope and Love

Rule 5: Perfection is Over-Rated

CHAPTER 05

Counseling: The Rules of Engagement

Chapter 05 – Counseling: The Rules of Engagement

The world is not short of good advice. You get it from the busy body at the local market, the teller at the store and your annoying mother-in-law. Just have a kid and even more "good advice" will start crawling out the woodwork from every direction!

The biggest mistake that anyone can make when trying to counsel someone, is to confuse advice and counsel. So what is the difference?

Advice is My Idea. Counsel is God's Idea.

Advice is based on your own experiences and conclusions of life and no one in this world is obligated to listen to that advice. Counsel on the other hand is squarely based on the Word of God and they are obligated to obey it.

Can you see the difference? When you do, you will also understand the weighty responsibility that rests on your shoulders when someone comes to you for counsel. To get back to one of our earlier points, do not forget that this person came to you to hear from God. They do not need your good advice. They need the Word of God to set them straight.

This covers you and them. Firstly, when you base your counsel on the Word, they have to listen. Secondly, they cannot just say that you are putting your own ideas in there. The word is unyielding and a foundation of power.

Is it any surprise that the scriptures speak of the Word as a sword? It is sharp and it can convict. Check out another of my favorite passages here:

> **2 Timothy 3:16** *All Scripture is given by inspiration of God, and is profitable for doctrine, for reproof, for correction, for instruction in righteousness.*

The Word is your answer and even before you can think of ministering in the Spirit, start first with the Word. When you can learn to counsel using both the Word and the Spirit, you have the perfect combination.

It is fantastic to get revelation with regards to someone's problem, but your starting point is the Word. The Word will help you assess if their problem relates to their own sin or something that is coming against them from without.

The Word is also full of practical direction. It is the only way to give them something to do to overcome their problem. Revelation will tell you where the problem lies, but the Word will give them the solution to overcoming that problem.

So I am going to pass on some good counseling advice. I am going to give you some of my own experience and also some of what the Word teaches directly.

Of course you cannot take this one chapter as a full understanding of counseling as a whole. What I am going to do though is give you the bottom line. I am going to pass on the secrets and what you need to remember when counseling.

Wisdom Makes Knowledge Work

For the principles, I suggest you get your hands on the "The Crucified Life Series". What you will learn as you step out though is that wisdom has the ability to take your knowledge and to apply it.

Cramming your head full of knowledge and hoping that will make you a good counselor is like saying that stuffing your fridge with lots of food makes you a world-class chef. It just does not work that way. The knowledge is but the ingredient, but it takes a good chef to make that ingredient into a delicacy.

In the same way, your knowledge is just an ingredient. It takes wisdom to apply that knowledge in a way that it is effective in the life of someone else. So I hope to pass on some of that wisdom to you. It is more than a bunch of principles, but an anointing.

The Lord is standing by and ready to give you all of the wisdom you need, but reading and remembering these points is certainly a good start. Bookmark this chapter, because I promise you will be back to read it again and again.

Counseling 101

I could not have survived my first encounters with counseling had my dad not taught me these basic principles. They were my light in the darkness when I was not sure what to do next. Remember each point and be sure that you apply them diligently!

1. No Solo Acts - In the Mouths of Two or Three Witnesses

Do not run into a counseling session alone. This is to cover your back. Jesus sent His disciples out two by two telling them to be as innocent as doves, but crafty as serpents. Take this good counsel from the Lord.

The person who is the best to join you is your spouse if you are married. If not, a fellow minister is also good. That way you can confirm one another and also be a support if sensitive subjects come up.

This is especially important when counseling someone of the opposite sex. Do not give the enemy any leeway here. People are very vulnerable when they are going through tough times and are opening their hearts to you.

Rather counsel with someone who can support you. Craig and I always counsel together and the Lord will use us both differently. If I am flowing as a teacher, then the Lord will use Craig as a prophet and he will get revelation by the spirit.

This is the perfect relationship when it comes to counseling. If he is functioning as the pastor-teacher, then the Lord will usually give me spiritual revelation. That way we cover all our bases.

2. Do Not Take Sins Into Confidence About Someone Else.

When someone comes to you with their problem it is between you, them and God. Do not allow anyone to tell you secrets or sins that involve someone else. You cannot counsel someone that is not there and you do not want to be put in a situation where you know something you should not.

Make it clear from the beginning, that you do not want to know anything about someone else that they would not be happy to tell you themselves. You can let the person know that if they insist on telling you things that relate to someone else, that you are then obligated to bring that person into the counseling session.

3. Keep That Person's Problem to Yourself

This is especially important in a church or a small ministry. Do not take the personal problems that people have shared with you and advertise it to anyone without their permission. That is why it is also important to include your spouse in on counseling sessions.

I do not suggest keeping anything from your spouse and this is something that anyone you counsel should know. They should know from the beginning that you would keep everything that they share with you confidential, with one exception – your spouse will be informed.

This will avert any attack of the enemy and again cover your back. The Lord has given your spouse to stand with you, so do not overlook that!

4. It's All About Them

You cannot counsel someone that did not ask for it! When someone comes to you for counsel, you can only address their problem not someone else's problem. Even if it appears that the main source of the problem is someone else, you have to address them.

This is the biggest mistake I see in marital counsel. The counselor is quick to try and pull out the spouse's problem even though they are not present. Naturally it is great if a couple comes to you together, but this will not always happen.

No matter how innocent the person in front of you might seem, you have to give them the counsel and address any of their shortcomings. If they apply your counsel, this will be an open door for the other person to come to you as well.

5. Confronting Conflicts With Others

If someone brings conflict situations to you that involve someone else, you are obligated to bring that person into the counseling session. When the disciples were arguing about who would be seated at his right hand, He addressed them all.

Even though it was the mother of James and John that caused the ruckus, Jesus addressed everyone involved. Follow this example and do not be afraid to involve people that are in the conflict.

The Word says to walk in the light as He is in the light. In the same way, do not walk in darkness. Do not take words in confidence about someone else's sin and very importantly – pull someone into the session if they are involved in the conflict.

Naturally the other party might not want to join, so you will need to use wisdom. This might mean going to meet with that person or giving them a personal call.

6. I Understand

Memorize these two words until they can roll off your tongue without a problem. You might not agree with a lot of what people share with you, but you should try to understand.

You want to be the kind of person that they want to open their heart to. Before you start attacking them with "good advice" say "I understand" and watch their heart open up.

Once they have finished sharing and you are all out of "I understands", it is your turn to start talking... with the sword of the Word in your hand.

7. There is No Such Thing as a Victim

Underline that header. Circle it. Highlight it. Memorize it! Do not get caught in a situation where you only see a victim in front of you.

The cause of all problems is sin. Never forget it. Even in a case of abuse, if you only look at what happened to them, you will never help them to break free.

Yes, always show love. Always understand, but do not get so wound up in seeing the victim that you do not apply the sword. At the end of the day, the hurts of the past have remained because they have held on to bitterness and are holding onto that hurt.

For you to help them be free will often mean lancing that deep wound to allow all of the pus out. Not a pretty picture is it? The problem though is when someone comes with some horrific experiences; you cannot help but feel sorry for them.

There is nothing wrong with that. Please, show compassion! As a counselor it is your most important asset. However, if you have true love, you will not stop with just understanding, but you will follow through with the sword.

You will come to learn that you can only apply healing to the hurts of the past when they are ready to let that hurt and anger go. This is another flaw that I see in many that go for counseling.

Instead of their sin being addressed so that they can break free, they are given excuses for their sin. The person feels justified in their bitterness because of what was done to them. This does not bring freedom and all of your "compassion" was nothing but a natural response.

No - true love takes a whip and lashes to the moneychangers. True love is the Father sending His only son to the cross. True love is helping people get free by pointing them back to their sin.

8. Do Not Over Identify

This is a biggie and a tough one to notice. It is devastating to any counseling session though, so be on your toes ok?

When someone comes to you with a problem that sounds a lot like one you have gone through yourself, you are tempted to think that they feel the same way as you. Before you know it, you are identifying with their hurt so much, that you overlook their sin.

Here is the truth though – they are not you! You cannot allow your own experiences of the past to color your counsel. This is especially true in marital counsel.

If you have had problems in your marriage and someone else comes with a similar problem, it is tempting to over identify and see yourself in their conflict. This is a dangerous place to be! You will not help them by excusing their sin.

Chapter 06

Counseling by the Word

Chapter 06 – Counseling by the Word

From here you are going to start seeing a lot of headers and points as I summarize the basics. To help you along, I suggest you think back on a recent counseling experience you had. If you cannot think of any, think about someone that does have a problem and how you would use these principles below to counsel them.

First Step: Ask These Three Questions

It is difficult to give anyone counsel if you do not know what their problem is in the first place. Very often people are so overwhelmed with their feelings that they have not stopped and wondered what the real problem is.

More than ever though they think that their problem is a person or a situation, but you as a counselor need to point it back to them. Consider yourself a mirror. No matter what the person shares, you point it back at them.

NOTE: Get ready for it... you are about to get involved. Do you know those pictures of someone sitting on a couch while they pour out all their woes to the counselor? Scratch that image. Smash it, because that is not what you are going to do. You are about to get your hands dirty just like Jesus did each time He reached out to someone who needed help.

1. What is Your Problem?

This might seem like a simple question, but it will make the person stop and think. If they do not know what their problem is (or what they think their problem is) you do not have a starting point. Before you start giving any direction at all ask the person what they feel their problem is.

2. What Have You Done About It?

This will tell you right away if they have been getting counsel from anyone else or taken on some good advice from Aunty "so-and-so". It will also tell you if they mean business or whether they are coming to you for a magic wand.

The Magic Wand

Do not assume that everyone who comes to you for counsel really wants help. Pay attention to this point right now, because it will save you hours of time. Very often the person is struggling with the consequences of their sin and do not really want to change.

Someone struggling with smoking for example just wants you to pray to "make it go away" and is not willing to look at their sin.

You are not there to wave a magic wand and to make problems go away. You are a counselor and it is for you to apply the Word to problems. If the person is not prepared to do anything about their problem, you will find yourself up against a wall with no results.

3. What Would You Like Me to Do About It?

This follows on from my last point. Do not assume that they have come to you so that you can tell them to change. More often than not, they want you to make the person or their problem go away. Sometimes in the case of marital counsel, they want you to deal with their spouse and not their real problem.

So get your facts straight. Once you have received the answer to these three questions, you have a starting point. Do not proceed without knowing this first! It will let you know if you can start helping them or refer them to a teaching so that they come back later when they are ready for real help.

Step 1: The Problem

I have already covered this step for you. Ask those three questions to identify what the problem is that you are facing. Get the person to describe the problem for you, what they have done about it and what they want you to do about it.

More often than not though the real problem is not what they think it is. The Pharisees kept seeing Jesus as the problem to their conflicts but that was not the truth was it? No, Jesus was not the problem. The truth is that their pride was the problem.

Killing Jesus did not make their problem go away. The great thing about realizing that the root of all problems is sin is that you can give hope. You cannot change other people, but you can certainly deal with your own sin.

Often you will get people coming to you who seem to get rejection everywhere they go. It feels as if the whole world is against them. Well can the whole world change? It is hard for them to imagine that the reason they keep being rejected is because of them.

It is your job to point that out to them. The problem is not the whole world... the problem is you.

Step 2: The Root Cause

Like I said before, the root cause for every problem is sin. There might be a lot of symptoms and emotions flying around, but there are only three roots of the flesh that you need to look at.

The roots of bitterness, lust and temporal values are found at the base of all problems. The root of bitterness being the taproot that the others lead into. Look at what James says here:

> **James 5:9** *Do not grumble against one another, brethren, lest you be condemned. Behold, the Judge is standing at the door.*

Just before this verse he speaks about having good fruit and being patient. Afterwards he goes on to explain how to deal with sickness. Bitterness destroys your relationship with the Lord, messes with your emotions and makes your body sick!

It does not matter what happened to a person, if they are not willing to look at their sin first, they will not break free. You can understand all you like, but healing will not come unless they allow it to come.

Consider someone who has a terrible illness caused by a festering wound in their body. The wound was caused by someone that struck them with a stick. They are afraid of doctors, so they do not get it treated.

So instead of getting healing, they go around showing everyone how someone hurt and struck them. They show their festering wound and go on to say how bad it feels. The longer they wait the worse it gets and by the time they come to you, you can bet that there is a lot of infection in there that hurts!

However, in order to bring healing to the original hurt, you need to get to it first! That wound may need to be cut open so that you can cleanse it. That is how it will feel when you address people's problems.

I will tell you this now – until you address and bring conviction to their sin, healing will never come.

Step 3: Applying the Sword for Conviction

It is the Holy Spirit that convicts and not you. Do not think that you can argue your way to a conviction. You must understand that the person you are ministering to is bound! They do not see the truth and your great explanations will not help.

No they need the Word and the Holy Spirit. The Word is very clear. It tells us to love our enemies. It tells husbands to love their wives. It tells us that bitterness is never an option. It does not give any loopholes.

It does not say, "If a person was really mean to you, you do not need to forgive them." No, the Word goes so far as to tell us to turn our cheeks for a second beating after getting the first blow.

This is your standard and never be moved from it. Until the person is willing to look at their bitterness, lust or root of temporal values (lust for things), they will not break free.

Very often, the Lord will even use conflict situations to expose that sin in our lives. So do not even think of moving onto the next point until the person you are ministering to is ready to repent.

Step 4: Healing and Deliverance

When they see their sin and are ready to hold it up to the Lord, the rest goes quickly. I will speak more on inner healing in the next chapters because it is a powerful transforming process.

Again, it is the Holy Spirit that heals and all you need to do is pray. Now before I carry on with that, I need to bring the demonic realm to your attention.

You can guarantee that if there has been sin, that the enemy was only too quick to jump in there. You will almost always find something demonic to deal with.

So before you lay hands to bring healing, you can bet that you have a demon to deal with. In one of the later chapters I teach you on how to deal with demons, but remember that now is the time you will deal with it.

When you are dealing with drug addiction, the sin is obvious and when the person has a conviction, then you need to deal with the demon associated with it. It is during this step that you will deal with generational curses and spiritual links to others.

Once the demons are dealt with, speak healing. It is during this time that you will feel the anointing and the presence of the Lord Jesus. This is truly the good part and all you need to do is pray and ask the Lord to do the healing.

Step 5: Get Practical

Now just before you think that you are done… think again! It is one thing to bring conviction and another to change the bad habit.

This person has lived with this problem for a long time and although they see their sin, they are going to need some help in rearranging their lives. Do not just lay hands and leave it to that.

You need to follow through with something practical to do. Send them to a book and get them to report back on it. Give them specific verses to memorize.

In the case of marital counsel, give them something specific to do for their spouse. In a conflict situation where both parties are aware of the conflict, get the person to go and ask forgiveness of the other party.

Then when they get back to you, you will be able to give them further counsel.

Watch for Backlashes

Before I finish this section, let me warn you quickly of something we have experienced often in our own ministry. If you fail to follow through and deal with the demonic bondage that someone has, it is likely that you will experience a backlash.

You have probably had something like this already. You pour your heart out to someone only to toss and turn with bad dreams all night! You pray for someone with a sickness and end up having the same thing.

You pray for someone regarding finances and yours take a dive. Sound familiar? All that you are experiencing here is a backlash. It is a sure sign that you did not follow through to victory and the person you prayed for did not break free.

The demonic bondage that was on them is now attacking you. If this is happening, do not panic! Simply break spiritual links and ask the Lord for wisdom on ministering to them effectively.

Case Scenarios

I have given you a lot of pointers here, but let's make them even more practical by giving some help for specific situations. Like I said, please do not take these guidelines as the "beginning and end" for all counseling.

They are simply a skeleton to hang the other counseling principles on.

Marital Problems

There is a very simple rule when it comes to marital counsel and it lies in this passage:

> **Ephesians 5:22** *Wives, submit to your own husbands, as to the Lord.*
>
> *23 For the husband is head of the wife, as also Christ is head of the church; and He is the Savior of the body.*
>
> *24 Therefore, just as the church is subject to Christ, so let the wives be to their own husbands in everything.*
>
> *25 Husbands, love your wives, just as Christ also loved the church and gave Himself for her,*

If there is a conflict in a marriage, then you can be sure that the failure is one of two things (or both)

1. Wives submit to your husbands.

2. Husbands love your wives.

If a couple is struggling, then they have overlooked these simple guidelines laid out for us. Now depending on who is sitting in front of you will depend on the counsel.

It does not even matter if the other party is wrong - you always address the person in front of you. Someone asked me once how I dealt with my kids when they were little and got into a fight.

My answer was simple – I disciplined them both. I did not care who started the fight, because neither of them acted properly.

I disciplined the instigator for starting it, but I also disciplined the retaliator because they did not turn the other cheek. Just because someone else does a wrong, it does not mean we have license to sin.

Because a wife does not submit, does not justify a husband to withhold love. On the other hand, just because a husband does not love, does not mean the wife has license to avoid submitting.

No matter who is at fault in a conflict, it is your responsibility to address both sides equally. If only the wife comes to you, then you must address the wife. You cannot address the husband without him being there.

Never find yourself caught in a situation where you are "ganging up" on who you feel the guilty party is. No, we are all responsible before God to walk out our own call with fear and trembling.

You address the person sitting in front of you. Deal with their sin and their failure.

Here is the Secret

When a wife truly submits, she comes under her husband. This means that for the Lord to meet her need, the Lord has to go through her covering.

You cannot imagine the power of a submitted wife. Having lived this in my own experience I can only say… *do it*! So often women think that to submit is to "suck it in" and bare it. This could not be further from the truth.

There is power in vulnerability and submission. True submission not only melts a man, but it brings the hand of God on him as well. If a wife wants to see change in her husband, then follow the rules. Submit and watch God work!

The same holds true for a husband who shows love. There is no greater force than love in this world. The Word says that a man should love his wife as Christ loved the church. How did Christ love the Church?

Well He loved the Church enough to die for Her! Imagine it. What power! A man whose wife has gone astray might want to hold back his love, but what he does not realize is that it is this love that will change her.

Love is not just a good idea - it is a force of the spirit. It is an atom bomb of power and if a man can love his wife as Christ, he will see the hand of God come on her. The key is to love with the love of Christ. We are all limited and none of us can submit or love in ourselves.

As believers we do not need to do it alone though. We can reach out and ask Jesus to love through us. When you give this kind of direction, you are giving hope. There is suddenly something that they can do in their situation.

If you sit and listen to their story and agree about how terrible their spouse is, you will never bring change. Worse than that, you might end up bringing the actual conflict that you are trying to avoid.

So the bottom-line here? Address the person in front of you. Address each person equally pointing out the sin of each.

Let's Get Practical

A friend named Susan comes to you frustrated with her husband. She is weary of him always letting her down. Whether it is in the work of the ministry or just around the house. It feels to her as if he is more interested in his work than in her or the needs of the family.

She tells you that she often has to call him at work to ask when he will come home. She is frustrated and cannot seem to get a good response out of him. What must she do?

Now using the principles I have taught you so far, you ask her the three questions:

1. What is her problem?
2. What has she done about it?
3. What would she like you to do about it?

Hopefully if Susan is honest, she needs to see that the problem is not her husband, but a breakdown in communication and relationship with her husband. She has likely nagged and tried to force her husband to do things her way. She might have prayed.

In the end, she is hoping that you will give advice, challenge her husband or maybe tell you that it is ok for her to leave him!

Do you remember the five steps I gave you on counseling by the Word? Let me use them here to show you what I would do in this kind of situation.

1. The Problem

If you look at the basic principles of marriage here, you see that both have failed. The husband has failed to love the wife, but the wife has also failed to submit – trying to coerce the husband into what she wants. Now because only the wife is in front of you, you cannot deal with the man's sin. You must deal with hers.

The problem here is a breakdown in communication and also not fulfilling their covenant vows. The problem is also an expectation that Susan has on her husband. She might not know exactly what he is facing at work. She is only aware of her own conflicts and is not seeing what he might also be facing. She is not seeing both sides of the coin.

2. The Root Cause

The root of all problems is always sin and failure to do things God's way. Just off the top of my head a couple of scriptures come to mind:

> *1 Peter 3:1 Wives, likewise, be submissive to your own husbands, that even if some do not obey the word, they, without a word, may be won by the conduct of their wives;*

> *1 John 4:18 There is no fear in love; but perfect love casts out fear, because fear involves torment. But he who fears has not been made perfect in love.*

> *1 Corinthians 11:7 For a man indeed ought not to cover his head, since he is the image and glory of God; but woman is the glory of man.*

> *Proverbs 21:19 Better to dwell in the wilderness, than with a contentious and angry woman.*

I love the last scripture the most. There is no man who wants to be around a nagging and contentious woman. Could it be that her husband would rather be at work than at home, because at least there he feels his needs are met?

There is a good question that I ask married couples to think about. I ask them, *"How does your spouse feel about themselves when they are around you?"*

This is a pretty loaded question but it hits home. Susan has the misconception that her husband owes that love to her and that she will reciprocate when she feels that love. The Word is clear though. It does not say to submit or to love when she is first loved. It only says... to love!

3. Apply the Sword

I just love using the Word in counseling because there is never a way for escape. No matter what Susan's husband has done in their marriage, has she fulfilled her terms of that covenant? It is easy to see the failures of others, but what about hers?

The incredible truth is, when she deals with her own sin and attitude, it releases the power of God to work on her husband as well. A good place to start though might be to make the home a place that is nice to return to.

Solomon knew a lot about women, being Mr. Lover boy that he was. He said in a few places that a nagging woman was like the rain dripping on the roof. You know the picture. Here you are trying to sleep and in the darkness a sudden "drip" echoes through the roof. Then again, drip… drip… drip. It drives you crazy. You want to pull the plumbing apart to fix it.

That is the same reaction a nagging woman will get. Her husband will delay coming home and find other things to do. Does Susan really want her husband to return home out of obligation or does she want him to return because he loves her?

Then the ball is in her court. That is exactly what I would share with her. Of course being a woman I must say that I have a unique perspective on this and having lived it myself can speak with a hint more of authority backed by experience.

"Susan, the reality? It is very possible that your husband is not in a rush to come home, because he does not feel comfortable there. What have you done to make coming home a pleasant experience?"

I would go on to share the scriptures above and if she was open dig a little deeper. I would ask her, "Is there any special effort that you have made for lovemaking and intimacy?"

"Is there something special that your husband likes to eat?"

"Are there particular kinds of clothing that he likes or a way that he likes your hair?"

"What are you doing in your marriage right now to be the glory of your husband? What are you doing to show that you submit and respect him?"

4. Healing

As you share and as Susan opens up, you might find that this is not a new thing for her. It is likely that even growing up, her father treated her the same way. She has never seemed to find success in her relationships.

It is at this point that you can expose any bitterness still from her father and also any hurts left there. Once identified, praying with Susan is a natural process. Later on I share about the process of inner healing, so I will not go into that now.

This is also where having someone who flows prophetically is invaluable. As you go to prayer, they will get revelation that you can then follow through using the Word. This is often how Craig and I will operate. I will usually bring the person to this point and then he will get revelation on where this hurt first began.

Together we will bring healing and deliverance if necessary. In the next chapter I share more detail on how to flow in this way.

In most cases when someone comes to you with a problem like this, the root ends up tracing right back to parental or first love experiences. This does not excuse their sin though and until you address their failure, you will never be able to get to the root of the problem.

5. Practical Project

Once you have allowed Susan to see her own failures and she has asked the Lord for forgiveness of her sin, you can pray for healing for the hurts of the past.

When you have a good breakthrough, the change is very quick. In situations like that I have seen a physical change in the person I am ministering to. Their face will seem lighter and you can see the joy coming through.

Do not leave it at that though. The final step is vital to make sure that everything you did in this session sticks.

As you identified, the problem here is communication and also that Susan has not been fulfilling her part in this marriage. So give her something practical to do.

Here are some fun ideas I like to give the ladies that come to me. Perhaps after reading them, you will come up with a few ideas for yourself.

1. Stop the nagging! This week try as much as possible not to question or tear down anything your husband says. Learn to really listen to him without coming back with all "your big ideas." Simply listen and take time to respect him as a man.

2. Take time to prepare a meal each day that you know is your husband's favorite. Silly things like a cooked meal and socks in the drawer go a long way to making a man feel special.

3. Make an effort with your wardrobe! Invest in some lingerie and some new clothing items that make you look good. Pick out something especially sexy for a "private meal for two" at home when he is ready.

4. This is the most important one of all. Lift your husband up daily to the Lord and speak blessing on him. Whenever you think of him during the day, speak blessing and ask the Lord to give him wisdom. Speak the love and blessing of the Lord on him as he sleeps.

Get Susan to report back to you after a week to tell you how things worked out. If other problems arose, you can work through them again together. The point is, she is now active in the changing process. She is giving God license in her marriage and you have just been used of God to bring healing and change to His people!

Not only that, but it opens the door for her husband to want counsel as well. When he starts to see the change in his wife, he is more likely to trust you for counsel as well.

Abuse and Sexual Problems

There are hundreds of books written on this subject, but I am going to give you a few pointers to keep in mind.

Luke 6:35 But love your enemies, do good, and lend, hoping for nothing in return; and your reward will be great, and you will be sons of the Most High. For He is kind to the unthankful and evil.

36 Therefore be merciful, just as your Father also is merciful.

37 Judge not, and you shall not be judged. Condemn not, and you shall not be condemned. Forgive, and you will be forgiven.

You cannot bring healing to the hurt until the judgment and sin has been dealt with in the person. It stands to reason that anyone that has faced any kind of abuse is angry. While you can understand this, the Lord Jesus cannot reach in to heal until they let that go.

This is where the Word of God is your sword. Stand on the truth and make it clear what God says. This is not your idea. This is God's idea.

So you are counseling someone and they start questioning you, the conversation should look a bit like this:

Person: "So you expect me to forgive that man that hurt me all these years?"

You: "Yes"

Person: "Well why should I?"

You: "Because the Word of God says so. The Word tells us to forgive our enemies and for good reason. Don't you realize that while you hold onto this anger that you hold onto the hurt and this person as well?

For as long as you hold onto your judgment you are carrying this person around with you. On the one hand you want to put the past behind you, but yet you still hold onto this person.

Are you ready to let that person go now once and for all? You can only do that when you forgive them."

You see what most people do not understand is that while they hold onto their bitterness and judgment that they hold onto the person that hurt them. They deliberately hold onto the hurt. While they are bitter they are still linked with that person in the spirit.

They have to decide if they love their bitterness more than the freedom that they want. Until you can bring the person to this conviction, healing cannot come.

I understand that this is not easy as a counselor. Some of the things that people will share with you will blow your mind. However, you cannot allow what you would do in such a situation to hold you back.

Firstly, say that you understand and show love. Then start to point at the bitterness and let them know that if they want healing that it begins there.

Spirit of Lust

You will find that such a person also struggles with lust and if they had sexual abuse as a child they grew up and became promiscuous. They will not be able to bind that spirit of lust until they forgive the original offender.

They can try to push down their feelings or hide away from it, but sooner or later it will come to the surface again.

If you have someone that comes to you with a problem with lust, you can be sure that there was always an open door. It might surprise you to know that very often if a man has had a problem with lust his whole life, that very often the original open door is bitterness towards his father.

Remember how I shared that bitterness is a taproot? Check out the *Crucified Life Series* for more teaching on that.

No demon can walk up to anyone and make them a victim. Always keep in mind that they gave it license. If someone who has been abused has been promiscuous, they cannot blame the abuser for their own sin.

Sin is still sin and they chose at one time or another to step out of God's will and sin deliberately for themselves. They must repent of this before they can be free. It is just too easy to say that "someone did it to me" as an excuse for sin.

It might take the pressure off the sin, but it does not bring victory. They will continue to walk in broken relationships and wrestle with the flesh until they are willing to look at their sin. Will power is just not enough – true conviction is needed.

Again, as a counselor, point them to their sin. Point them to their bitterness towards the abuser and their own choice to sin willfully.

Once they are ready to repent, you are ready to bring healing and to bind the spirit of lust in their lives. Until you reach that first point, you will not get victory.

Insecurity Problems

Remember how I shared that no one is a victim? Let me take this point even further to tell you a secret about people who are insecure.

Did you know that insecure people are the most selfish people in the world? Think about it. When someone is insecure all they can think about is what other people think about them.

They walk around looking at others thinking all of the time, "I wonder how that person sees me? I wonder what they are thinking about me?"

It is very possible that no one is even noticing them, but still they are looking inwards. It is all about "Me, Me, and Me!"

> **John 3:16** *For God so loved the world that He gave His only begotten Son ...*

The most powerful force in this world is love and as we see in John 3:16 when God loved the world, He gave. When someone is insecure they wonder all the time what others can do for them.

However, the Word tells us that we should be salt and light. The Word tells us to pour out the love of Christ. When an insecure person realizes that, they have a place to start. If they can only see their selfishness, then they can start on their way to healing.

More than anything what they need is healing from hurts of the past and then to develop a relationship with Jesus. This kind of learning takes time, but your first step is pointing them towards this important fact.

They need to have an other-orientation and instead of always wondering what they can get from others, to start wondering how they can pour out and give.

As they allow the Lord Jesus to minister through them, healing will come to their own hearts. It is only in a face-to-face relationship that true healing can take place.

I had this in my own experience. I struggled so much with insecurity that I felt lost in a group. As Jesus took me aside into a face-to-face relationship with Him, I started to change. I did not even realize I had changed until I woke up one day and noticed the fear was gone!

Sometimes you have to shock people into reality before they are ready to deal with their problem. Remember… no one is a victim. Keep that principle in mind, armed with the sword and walk in love and you will bring real healing.

CHAPTER 07

Ministering by the Spirit

Chapter 07 – Ministering by the Spirit

Counseling and ministering by the spirit are two of the most exciting forms of ministry that I can think of. Sure, it does not put you behind the pulpit, but it is here that you will see people change before your very eyes.

As a minister myself, there is always one thing that goes through my mind after I have shared everything the Lord has given to me and it is, "Did I bring real change?" You never want to feel as if your words fell on bad soil or that you wasted your time.

After you have gone through so many of your own struggles and experienced the truth, when you share that with others, you want them to experience the same breakthroughs. You want to think that all of the investment that you are giving to the kingdom of God is bearing some fruit.

You want to feel that you left something real behind you that will last for years to come. It is in personal ministry where you are most likely to experience that kind fruit.

By now you might have noticed how much I enjoy breaking things down for you into point form. I like you to walk away from a chapter holding onto the main points of what I am sharing.

By Colette Toach

This chapter is no different! This time I will be leaving you with just two very clear steps to follow.

Step 1: Receiving the Revelation

So often you can walk around with a problem where you feel depressed and discouraged and not even know why. Have you had an experience in your spiritual walk where it feels like the Lord has disappeared? It feels like all hell has been let loose against you.

Your finances suddenly die, you get sick, the dog dies and your taxes are due.

You wonder what is going on! No matter how much you pray or try to deal with any curses, you still feel stuck.

This pretty much describes a hefty portion of the body of Christ at one time or another. Do you know how fantastic it is when you can go to someone for prayer and say, "I am feeling so stuck right now, everything is going wrong, please can you pray for me and help me see what is going on?"

There is often no greater relief than knowing where the problem is. Say for example you slip and your arm hurts like crazy. The first thing you think is, "I wonder if it is broken?" Sometimes the greatest medicine is going to the doctor and hearing him say, "Do not worry. It is not broken. It's only a sprain and should heal up in a week or so."

Even though you still need to heal, relief is the best medicine in the world.

It is the same for God's people when they are facing a conflict in their lives. There are many that know enough about their spiritual walk to deal with their problems. What they struggle with though is finding the problem in the first place.

That is the hard part. How often have you hit a wall yourself and just wished you knew where to go from here?

That is what you need to be helping others with. It is for you to minister by helping identify their problems.

What is Keeping me Bound?

When you are struggling under a load, it is hard to hear from the Lord for yourself. That is why you are needed in the church. They want to know the answer to this simple question, "What is keeping me bound?"

It only takes a moment to listen and to pray to get a revelation from the Lord. Being able to flow in visions plays a huge part in this kind of ministry.

Example

Your friend, Eric is having a tough time in his life. Something goes very wrong and he ends up having a car accident that trashes the car. Before that, he had a huge fight with his wife.

He feels so far from the Lord and is struggling to hear His voice. He has prayed and fasted, but still there is no sign of things coming right. Eric comes to you and says, "Please can you pray for me?"

What are You Going to Do?

The worst thing that you can do is jump in with all your principles. "Have you fasted and prayed? Have you tithed? Have you asked for forgiveness?" Wrong move!

The next incorrect response would be to just lay hands on Eric and pray any old blessing in the hope that it helps him out.

After you have heard all of the facts about the situation and need, here is what you need to remember. Do not open your big mouth until you get revelation!

The First Thing to Say

"Let's take this to the Lord."

You need to get into the Lord's presence and ask Him what is going on. There is such a temptation to try and use all of your knowledge and learning to give an answer. However, Eric is not coming for advice - he is coming for a miracle.

Analyzing the problem instead of looking for the source of it would be like taking a good look at a bruised and broken arm and giving a full description of how bad the arm really looks.

You might be outlining how truly bad the situation is, but you are no closer to bringing healing until you can identify the main source of the problem and a course of action to take.

You will only exhaust yourself trying to figure things out for hours, what will only take a minute in His presence to get the simple answer to.

Here is some of the best advice that I can give you when it comes to ministering to someone by the spirit:

Sit down, and hear God's voice!

You cannot jump in and start giving ministry until you have heard from the Boss. Otherwise you will be ministering from your mind. Do not assume that everyone's problems are the same. Once the Lord gives you direction, only then can you pass it on.

So sit Eric across the way from you and submit yourselves to the Lord. You can pray something very simple like,

"Lord Jesus we just submit ourselves to you. I bring Eric to you with the problem he is facing. You are the only one that has the answer to this and we ask you for revelation and that you would open our eyes so that we know what we need to pray and do."

At this point, do not forget that it is Eric's faith that has brought you to this point. As he is reaching out to the Lord, the Lord will give you what you need. It is his faith that will cause any of the Gifts of the Spirit to be manifest in you.

As you pray and commit Eric to the Lord, you may see a vision or feel an impression deep down in your spirit. A scripture might come to your mind or an event might suddenly come back to you.

You might see a vision of a chain wrapped around him or handcuffs on his hands. If you flow in the gift of discerning of spirits, you might even see a demonic bondage.

How to Handle the Revelation – Say It Like It Is

The easiest way to handle the revelation that the Lord gives you is simply to share it. Because the revelation is for Eric, the Lord will give you something that he should understand. You might see a vision of fiery darts coming against him and you sense that they speak of negative words spoken against him.

You would share that vision with Eric and say, "I see fiery darts in the spirit and feel that they are negative words being spoken against you. Have you had some opposition from anyone lately?"

The Lord might give you a word of knowledge that there is someone that he has come into contact with recently that is under a curse. Simply share that with your friend and then allow him to receive that revelation.

Give them the opportunity to get the revelation for themselves. Without realizing it, you might be delving into some very sensitive issues in their lives. So give them the chance to take what you say and to see how it fits into their lives.

Eric might respond with, "Yes, you know I bumped into an old girlfriend a few weeks back. She is not saved and was into some really strange stuff in the past, but we had a good talk and it reminded me of the time we were going out…"

It is so easy to step in from there. You could ask, "All these problems you have been having recently, would you say that they started round about the time you bumped into her?"

If he can confirm that, you have just identified the source of Eric's problem. Dealing with it is as easy as breaking that spiritual tie with that person and submitting himself to the Lord again.

You will not get that kind of revelation until you take a moment to pray. (The subject of curses is covered extensively in *The Strategies of War* book or in our many articles on our websites)

I have ministered in this way more times than I can count. Often people will come with what seems like a mountain of problems. When they first share it sounds so complicated and in the natural you feel like there could never be a simple solution.

I have experienced it a few times where a couple would come for prayer because everything was going wrong. No matter how much they sowed into the work of the Lord, their finances were always going from bad to worse.

As we would pray we saw them in a conference setting with someone laying hands on them. We would share the vision and say, "Is there someone that you received an impartation from?"

After they confirm that there was, they also identify that this problem with their finances started during that exact time! What looked like a mountain of problems was dealt with within a short time of seeking the Lord and renouncing that impartation.

I think that we just get too complicated sometimes and when people come to you with their long list of problems it is easy to get sidetracked. Try to avoid the temptation though and come to the Lord.

Allow Him to bring the right scripture or principle to mind. Allow Him to give you a vision or an impression in your spirit. When this happens, you have the real source of the problem and you can start helping that person break free.

Step 2: Applying the Revelation

This is where things can get a little tricky. The reason is because it is simple enough to get a revelation, but another to know how to apply it.

A prophet might see a vision, where a teacher might have a scripture come to their minds. At the end of the day, it does not really matter so much how you received your revelation. True change does not hinge on the revelation.

Instead, change hinges on how that revelation is applied!

You get so many extremes when it comes to this step. You get some prophets who see a vision and because they do not know how to apply it, they wrack their brains trying to think of every scripture they can quote that lines up with their revelation.

They bombard the poor person until both their heads are spinning. If you are a prophet, do not try to suddenly act like a teacher and vice versa. A teacher has the ability to take a single scripture and to bring it to life for a person.

The prophet flows more in the revelatory gifts and sometimes just one vision can be all you need, to speak healing into someone's life. Each of us has a part to play and it is not really important what part that is. What is important is that the person leaves that meeting having had a touch from God!

If that touch came through the Holy Spirit coming on them externally or a scripture speaking to them quietly, it does not really matter. There is only one thing that matters here - to set the captives free.

Using our example again of your friend Eric. Let's say that as you ministered you saw a cord in the spirit tying your friend to this ex-girlfriend of his.

Obviously you have found the source of the problem, but knowing that does not set him free. He opened a door to the enemy there and opened his heart to someone he should not have. Perhaps he even entertained some thoughts he should not have.

For him to be completely set free, he has to break that cord! This is where you need to step in and use the spiritual authority that God has given to you.

Once you know what the blockage is in Eric's life, you can then get them to pray and to ask the Lord to break that bond.

Only then can you step in and pray. Now it is time for you to apply your revelation. It is not about getting the words right, but about using your spiritual authority. Some people will pray long prayers, but you might be the "short and to the point" kind of person.

In this situation, if I were ministering, I would first get the person to pray and repent for opening their hearts. I would then get them to break the spiritual tie with that person. Then I would pray something like, "Lord as Eric has broken that tie, I just stand in agreement with him right now. I set him free in the name of Jesus!

I bind every work of darkness and I cut those ties that are holding him back! I come against that oppression now and set him free."

What Happens if Nothing Comes?

What do you do if someone comes to you for prayer and you do not get any revelation at all? It is very simple, if God does not say anything, you do not say anything!

I think that for anyone that can flow in the spirit, you get under a lot of pressure sometimes and think that the revelation is up to you. You start to think, "I must get revelation!" Then if you do not get anything, you feel like a second rate minister.

If you do not get a vision or any kind of revelation, then you feel like there is something wrong with you. Let me share something exciting with you. Do you know when all the Gifts of the Spirit will manifest the most in your ministry? It is when God's people desire it! The gifts will flow when God's people reach out to Him in faith.

Even Jesus Himself could not perform many miracles in His own town. Their faith was so low, that they did not expect anything of Him. When did God send Moses to the children of Israel? Was it not when they cried out for a deliverer?

God did not pick Moses up by the scruff of his neck one day and say, "THERE! Deliver them!" No, they had to ask for it first.

Now if you find yourself in a ministry situation where you do not get any spiritual revelation, relax! It is not up to you - it is up to the Holy Spirit and also that person to reach out to the Lord. Perhaps they are not ready to receive the revelation that the Lord really has for them.

Perhaps they are not ready for the truth of where the problem truly lies. It could be that they have to go through a few more circumstances before they are ready to face it. So do not push it! If you try to push out a revelation, you will get something all right... but it will not be the spirit of God!

So relax! The gifts are not dependent on you and that brings a relief in itself. It is a spiritual gift. It is the Holy Spirit speaking through your spirit and giving you that revelation. And so if He is not giving it, then you are not getting it! Simple.

If you push beyond what God intends, you will tap into a realm that is not of the Holy Spirit. You will end up in deception, so relax and do not come under pressure.

God's Ability to Reach You

What will make you effective is not your ability to hear God, but God's ability to get through to you! I promise that if the Lord places one of His hurting lambs in front of you and you are the only vessel that He can use, He will most certainly use you!

And if the Lord does not use you, then it is for a very good reason. I have experienced this so many times myself. There have been times in my spiritual walk where I have been going through a season of death. There was a time in my life when He was dealing with a deep root of bitterness.

I am sure you know what it is like when the Lord is dealing with things in your life. I was flat on my face before the Lord. I felt so horrible. I was in the grave and I did not even feel His presence. During this time someone came to me for ministry and I said, "Lord, you have got to be kidding me! I have got nothing here! I am so full of the flesh that I do not even want to be around myself right now!"

I felt that deep nudging and the Lord saying to me, "Just minister in your weakness." So I brought that person before the Lord and I had hardly begun to pray when suddenly the revelation started flowing. I received visions, a prophetic decree and the anointing just fell.

By His Grace

I thought, "Ok! What just happened there?" When this happens to you, you will also come to understand why I say often, "It is not dependent on you. Rather it depends on the Lord and the person across from you that needs to hear Him."

That person came to me crying out to the Lord for help. I was just the pot that He used. He picked me up, filled me up and poured me out again.

Of course, what you might also experience is that after the anointing leaves that you are still the rotten sinner that you were before you ministered. However, you go away with the knowledge of the power of His grace.

You leave understanding the love that He has for His Bride. Your place in the Church is simply to be an available vessel. And so if the Lord wants to put that vessel on the shelf for tonight, be content with that, because another time will come when He will pick you up and pour you out. You will realize that it is His hand that moves you. Not your own hand.

Not only does this set you free, but you also come to understand the true power and grace of the Lord. It is only when we know our own limitations that we can appreciate the limitless power of the Lord. Only then can you understand what it truly means to walk by His grace.

CHAPTER 08

The Ministry of Inner Healing

Chapter 08 – The Ministry of Inner Healing

Have you ever broken an arm or a leg? I know a few people that have and it does not look like a lot of fun. Not only do they suffer the actual accident, but the whole process of going to the doctor afterwards.

The discomfort of the horrible cast they have to use to set the bone again is probably a greater suffering in the end than the original break!

Isn't it amazing how in the medical world, doctors have learned what it takes to heal the human body? Whether it is a broken arm or leg that needs fixing or as something as dramatic as a heart transplant, it is incredible what medical science can do in our day and age.

However, no matter how advanced our society becomes, it might even come to the place of replacing entire limbs - it will never be able to heal the broken heart. That is where God needs us as ministers to step in.

We have something to offer God's people that the most expensive medical care cannot. We can offer healing to the broken and sight to the spiritually blind.

The Joy of Personal Ministry

There is nothing more fantastic than personal ministry. It is like someone coming to you with a broken arm and you apply some ointment and a cast to set it. Then in time you see how that arm heals to the point where they can use that arm again.

It is so satisfying to see this kind of change in a person. When you stand behind the pulpit, you send out the Word that God has given to you and you pray that it hits the mark. Perhaps someone will tell you after the meeting how much it blessed them.

It is another all together to work personally with someone and to see them go through a transformation. There is no greater gift than to have people come to you with their broken hearts and open wounds and to see God heal them.

To see that same broken person change the way they live and to become something beautiful for the Lord.

Inner Healing

I wish there were more of God's doctors around to heal God's people. The reality is though that there are not many around ready to speak healing to the hurts of the past.

What I am talking about here is something called inner healing and if the Lord ever uses you to counsel or to minister to an inner conflict, I guarantee that what they need more than anything is inner healing in their lives.

Miraculous Healing

One of the first things to understand regarding the ministry of inner healing is that this is as miraculous as a physical healing. With so much influence in our society from psychological teaching, it is hard to imagine sometimes that there is such a thing as real and miraculous change.

Having worked with many people though, I can tell you that the Holy Spirit can accomplish something in a person that a psychologist cannot give after 10 years of lying on the couch.

When you have a heartbreaking experience as a child, there is no doctor that you can go to that can fix it. There is no cast that you can apply that will set a bad experience straight. Sure, there are many psychologists that could explain why it hurts, but there are none that can reach in and take the hurt away.

I could look at someone with a broken leg and understand how they got it. I could show them x-rays on how exactly the broken bone is lying, but no amount of figuring out the injury will heal that bone. Nope, it needs to be set!

Doesn't it seem strange to you that this is obvious with something like a broken bone, but it is not obvious when it comes to a broken heart? People think that if they can understand why they got hurt or what caused their pain that this will help.

The Ministry of Inner Healing

Unfortunately, it does not help. They need healing and there is only one way that the healing is going to come and that is through the power of the Lord Jesus Christ.

When Jesus said what His mission was on this earth, in amongst healing the sick and giving sight to the blind, He also said, "...and to heal the broken hearted!" Isn't it something that along with these miraculous physical demonstrations of His power, that He lists the healing of the broken heart right alongside them?

It is a fact, inner healing is as miraculous and as important to God, as a physical healing in the body is.

Every one of us has had bad experiences in life. Perhaps you had a father that was not there or rejected you. It does not matter how much you have grown up or tried to shake off the rejection, the hurt remains and as you get on with your life, things happen that will suddenly dig that hurt up all over again.

When this happens, you know that something from your past is very much in your present. These hurts are what prevent you from rising up and coming into a relationship with the Lord.

What Hurts Do

One of the first things that hurts from the past can do is act as a blockage in your spiritual life.

Spiritual Blockage

As you try to develop a relationship with the Lord, you might feel blocked on every side. Your heart cries out for intimacy, but you cannot seem to get past this block.

It is as if the Lord is just not interested in you right now. No, it is not the Lord that is silent, but rather that hurt on the inside that is bringing a blockage. It is like a man that has a clot in his veins that is preventing the blood from reaching his heart. It is not the heart or the blood that is the problem here. Rather it is the blockage that is the problem!

Struggle with Relationships

Hurts from the past also prevent successful relationships in your family and in the church. Because hurts from the past are so real, they shape the way that you think. You see things from the wrong perspective and often you say things that you should not.

If you are always upsetting people and cannot seem to develop real relationships, then you need healing from the hurts of the past.

And so as you minister to people, this will come up again and again. They will come to you with struggles in their relationships, fears they cannot conquer, addictions they cannot overcome and spiritual blockages that prevent them from getting closer to the Lord.

In each case, you will discover that it is hurts from the past that are holding them back. Is this not what the Psalmist is saying here?

> **Psalms 147:3** *He heals the brokenhearted and binds up their wounds.*

Even though someone might know God the Father as a loving Dad, they still struggle to come into His presence. They fear Him. They fear His judgment. The worst part is, because they fear Him, they cannot come to Him for the healing that they need.

This is where you step in. It is for you to take them by the hand and bring healing to them so that they can run to their Heavenly Father and feel His approval of them.

Insecure Mouse

When I think back on when I first received my call to the ministry, I do not recognize myself. I was an insecure little mouse sitting in the corner. I was short, skinny and not exactly the most popular kid in the class.

Add to the fact that I was also a pastor's kid and you get a good picture of where I was coming from. God raised me up and put me in the place I am now, so that I can stand in confidence without all of those fears of the past.

If it had not been for the ministry of inner healing, I would still be that insecure mouse and not where I am today.

The ministry of inner healing is miraculous and can change the direction of someone's life completely.

Rewriting History Using Soul Surgery

Many believe that you cannot go back and rewrite history. Or can you? Let me tell you, with the ministry of inner healing you can!

You can go back into that painful past and bring healing. You can undo the effects of that event and put someone on a completely new road.

And so as the Lord calls on you to minister, He is calling on you to do some soul surgery! He is calling on you to heal the hearts of His people. First though it is going to take some "eye-opening" to prepare them.

> ***Matthew 13:15*** *For the hearts of this people have grown dull. their ears are hard of hearing, and their eyes they have closed, lest they should see with their eyes and hear with their ears, lest they should understand with their hearts and turn, so that I should heal them.*

Now the best way to function in inner healing is through the gift of visions and the word of knowledge. Now, I am assuming in this book that you already have some experience in ministry and also in flowing in some of the Gifts of the Spirit.

Regardless of your ministry calling, these gifts are available to you. In fact, when you start ministering, the Lord will give you what you need to step out. Have you desired to flow in visions or prophecy? Then put yourself in a position where these gifts are needed.

There is certainly no point in asking the Lord for a gift you never intend on using! And so if the Lord is going to use you to counsel, minister inner healing or give direction, you are going to flow in at least one of the revelatory gifts.

You will flow in visions or in the gift of knowledge. Again, I do cover these in so much detail in our other books, so I am going to spare you the repetition and get straight to the "nitty-gritty" of real time ministry!

Into the Deep End

And so I am throwing you into the deep end here. I am going to take your hand and teach you how to take the Gifts of the Spirit that you already flow in and to use them effectively in practical ministry.

> **Luke 4:18** *The Spirit of the Lord is upon Me, because He has anointed Me to preach the gospel to the poor; he has sent Me to heal the brokenhearted, to proclaim liberty to the captives and recovery of sight to the blind, to set at liberty those who are oppressed.*

If you love God's people, then this scripture burns in your heart as much as it burned in the heart of the Lord Jesus.

How many believers are walking around today, having been beaten down and discouraged? Look at those that have backslidden or walked away from their calling and you will find someone with hurts from the past that they never overcame.

Will Power is Not Good Enough!

Some people think that if they simply push through and try with their natural strength to serve God that they will get it right. They try to avoid sin and not fall back into the bad habits of the past.

It is like struggling within day and night, hoping and praying that you will overcome. However, until the hurts of the past are healed, those demons from your past will continue to come against you.

Getting Started

Often people will come to you with problems that seem to be unrelated to the subject of inner healing. Someone might come to you and say, "I do not know what is wrong with me. I just cannot seem to come into a relationship with the Lord. When I pray, it always feels like He is a million miles away."

What is the first thing you should do? Well, hold off on trying to think this through. Until you get revelation of the source of the problem, any counsel that you have will be ineffective.

Step #1 Get Into His Presence

After they have shared their problem with you, bring it to the Lord in prayer. This is where flowing in the revelation gifts are vital. Pray and hold the person up to the Lord.

NOTE: When counseling by the Word and the Spirit, you would already have identified the person's sin and brought them to conviction or identified where they got off track.

It is important now to take charge and to lead the person. If they are coming to you for ministry, then they need someone to follow. Do not stand back and assume that they know what is wrong with them. Make them feel comfortable by taking them by the hand and leading them into the Lord's presence.

So you need to pray first. "Lord I bring this person to you. Please Lord, can you show us where the problem is?"

As you pray, you might have a vision of this person at a certain age. You might not get a vision, but will receive a word of knowledge or an impression in your spirit instead. You might even get an impression or vision of particular circumstances surrounding them.

At this point, you might have some ideas of what your vision means, but for now, just share your vision or impression with the person. Give them the opportunity to open up and allow you to reach that painful part of their life.

You might see a child at a young age sitting in a corner crying alone. You would say, "I see a vision of a child around the age of 6 or so and they are sitting in a corner crying. They feel alone as if no one understands them. Can you relate to this at all?"

More often than not, if the person is willing to open up, they will say, "You know around that time of my life, my parents divorced… or I went through a really hard time…"

For example, they might share something like their parents divorced and their father left them behind. As they share, if there is any hurt or bitterness remaining, you will see it starting to come out. You would have identified the source of their problem.

Now I am not going into detail here, but this really does not take long at all. It takes as long as it needs for you to pray and ask the Lord for wisdom. Once you receive a revelation, the rest follows quite easily.

Some Helpful Hints

As the Holy Spirit gives you revelation, now is not the time to jump right in and tell them what you think. Rather say simply, "I see a vision of you at around 'this' age, did anything happen round about that time in your life?"

Or if you get an impression in your spirit you could say, "I sense that something happened to you around your teen years. I just feel a lot of conflict. Is there a particular event that took place during this era of your life?"

This opens the door. Do not get your revelation and say, "Clearly you had a bad experience as a teenager that made you bitter towards your father and now you have a spirit of lust that is destroying your marriage..."

I do not care if this is true. Show grace and lead that person to conviction. Never forget that the Holy Spirit is not dead. He is well able to come into this situation and bring conviction. Share what you see, let them share how they can relate and then you can take it from there.

How would you feel if someone just barged into your life and started digging up painful memories? How would it feel if they just dragged them all to the surface and left them all out in the open for the world to see?

Perhaps you might be mature enough to handle that, but for most people, they are not ready for that. They need healing - they do not need condemnation.

If you put someone in a corner and do not give them a "way for escape" you give them no choice but to react to your revelation. If they are ready to receive what

God is showing, that is wonderful, but if they are not, you will get one of two responses:

> **1.** They will smile sweetly, say thank you and run out the back door, not really getting the breakthrough they needed.

> **2.** They will react with anger and reject your revelation openly, bringing a rift in your personal relationship.

Do not think, "Well this is my revelation and if they do not want to receive it, then they can just go away!" The Lord Jesus is not like that with you. No one in this world is required by the Word or by law to bow down to your revelations.

Give God's people some of the same grace that Jesus has given you over the years.

They Must Let Go

Identify where the hurt is and only then as the Lord leads you, point out the sin or the anger that is keeping that hurt firmly in place. Just like I shared earlier in the counseling principles, until they are ready to let go of the anger and bitterness, there is no way that you can step forward.

You cannot bring healing to a hurt that is being used as a trophy or as an excuse for failure in life. If they want healing, then they must be prepared to forgive as God forgives. The Word is so clear on this one. When the

Disciples asked Jesus how often they should forgive an offense, Jesus told them "seventy times seven... or as often as you want the Lord to forgive you!"

Until they are prepared to forgive and acknowledge their own sin, the Lord Himself will not impose. Jesus never walked up to anyone who was broken and imposed His healing on them. They always came and asked. He offered and it was for them to take Him up on the offer.

In the same way, until that hurt is offered up to you and the bitterness left behind, you cannot bring healing.

Step #2 Deal with Demons

It is important to remember that sin is a wide open door for the enemy to walk through. The hidden secret of inner healing is not just the change it brings to the hurt, but also the deliverance it brings to the person. Through the years I have found again and again how hurts harbor demonic bondages in people.

Sure there are the obvious bondages when someone got involved in the occult or drugs and as a result are demonized. There is no dealing with that demon until they repent and tell it to leave. However, this does not hold true for most believers in the church.

For many of us, the bondage came through experiences of the past. Just spend time with someone who has suffered physical abuse or who had very difficult experiences through life and you will not find it hard to see the demonic bondage that goes along with it.

This is a fault that I often see in the mainstream "deliverance ministries." They are quick to cast out demons, without realizing that what God's people need is healing. You do not read of any demons being cast out of New Testament believers. Because we have the Holy Spirit dwelling within us, it changes things completely.

I will talk to you more in a later chapter on the subject of demons and how to address them, but here I want to cover how it relates to the ministry of inner healing specifically.

People often wonder what it is that keeps generational bondages in their lives. This is one of the biggest ties you will ever find! When a parent has hurt a child and they harbor any anger at all, the demonic bondage finds its roots in that hurt.

They can tell the demon to go away and they can try to break free, but until they let go of their anger and then get healing, that bondage will remain. I see this so often in ministry. I see people bound by poverty, sickness and a host of other curses that are experienced by everyone in their family lines.

When I get the opportunity to work with someone closely though I am always so excited to see these curses literally "drop" away as they let go of their anger and receive healing. It is so true when the Word tells us to "put off" our old man and to continually "put on" the new. It is when we walk in the newness of Christ that the curses fall away.

It is when we walk in the spirit that Christ can reign through us. Unfortunately, though when you walk in the old man and in the old hurts, Christ is not in control. Instead the enemy holds the deeds to that part of your life and he is quite happy to use them when he wills.

You would think that anyone who discovered they had a demonic bondage would be quick to want to deal with it. It comes with a price though. It means letting go of the very thing that gives the enemy that deed to their lives. It means revoking his license by letting go of that bitterness or of that need to be vindicated.

It means letting go of the jealousy or desperate need to prove themselves. It means letting go of trying to prove themselves and to put that into God's hand. This is where the gift of discerning of spirits is vital and if you do not flow in this, I suggest you seek the Lord in faith for it.

Practical Example

When I pray with someone for inner healing it is very common for me to see a demonic bondage involved. In one situation when I prayed with someone regarding sexual abuse experienced as a child I saw a clear spirit of lust that came from that time.

On the one hand there was a deep hurt that was created, but of course through that experience they took on that same spirit of lust that the perpetrator had. In turn they became promiscuous later on in life. Now, later on in their lives this was causing a major problem in their current relationship.

The first thing I had to do was to get them to let go of their bitterness against that abuser. This was the anchor holding that chain in their lives in place. After that, they then had to acknowledge their own sin in living the lifestyle that they did.

Although that hurt was terrible, it was not the perpetrator that went out and slept with so many people… no they did that out of their own will. They reinforced that bondage for themselves. Only then could they tell the enemy to leave.

The great thing is that sin always has a solution! At first it is not easy to look at. It was easier to blame the abuser for all their problems in life. It became their crutch. In their eyes, they could not develop meaningful relationships because of what happened to them.

They could not be a success in life because of what happened to them. They could not love others, because of what happened to them. If this was true, then the Word of God is false, because the Word tells us to love - to love even our enemies. It does not make a suggestion, but the Word in fact commands us to love.

Does this seem unfair? Not at all, because God knew what it would take to heal our broken hearts. It takes love to bring real mending. Only when you can let go and truly love through the eyes of Jesus will that huge tear in your heart suddenly heal up miraculously.

When you keep using abuse or things that happened in the past as a reason for your failure in life, then there is no hope for you. Your entire future is based then on your past and you will never rise up. However, if you stop and see things God's way, the view changes altogether.

If your failure in life is because of your choices to harbor bitterness, then we have a solution for that! You can be healed. You can let go of the things that hold you back!

It is only when I brought that person I was ministering to, to this conviction that they could finally break free. The demon they had struggled with for years suddenly left. That lust and compulsion left them. The unclean thoughts and dreams left them.

For the first time in their lives, they realized that they no longer had to be a victim. They could break free and overcome.

Like I said before, never get so caught up in the hurt of a person that you see a victim in front of you. As a believer they are victors in Christ. They are overcomers. Now you as the counselor must teach them to overcome.

Step #3 Apply the Healing

Now you are ready to lay hands on that person and speak healing to them. Just like you would cradle a small child and pray for the Lord to heal them of the flu or an upset stomach, you can lay your hands on a person's head and pray that the Lord would heal the hurts in their heart.

"Holy Spirit I ask you to come and heal this hurt from the past. Come Lord and cover up the wounds and the scars of the past. Bring restoration and give back all the good things that the enemy has stolen."

When you put yourself in a position to be used of God in this way, you will be standing in a place to flow in this kind of healing anointing. If you would only reach out with true love for someone and reach out in faith, you will start to see the Lord moving. You will see Him do the healing.

That is the best part of all, isn't it? It is not up to you to heal that person. It is up to the Lord to heal that person. All you can do is reach out your hand in love and ask God to use you. I promise that if there is someone with a need who is crying out to God, the Lord will give you what you need to minister to them with!

Some Personal Experience as Spiritual Parents

Craig and I have been working personally with people like this since 1999 and the change that we have seen has been incredible. We have also seen how the Lord has brought healing to people in layers. If the Lord has given you the opportunity to mentor someone or be his or her spiritual parent, get used to doing this kind of ministry.

There is so much potential in every believer, but the hurts and bondages hold that potential back. To release the full potential in someone has often just taken some time in the presence of the Lord to deal with those hurts from the past.

There have been times when the people the Lord sent to us were so demonized that I doubted if I had heard Him right. As a trainer by nature, I only saw what needed to be fixed. I wondered if we would have demonic manifestations and how many sessions of "deliverance" needed to take place.

I have come to find though that this kind of drama really does not need to be the norm. As we worked through the experiences and hurts from the past, the person seemed to just get lighter and lighter. As the Lord healed them and as they let go of their sin and anger, the enemy had no foothold any longer.

All you need is to cut down the tree and the birds have nowhere to rest. It is the roots of your sin that give this tree its roots. It is the hurts of your past and the pains that you carry that continue to water those roots.

When you can let go of your sin and offer up your hurts to the Lord, that tree is cut down and the healing is permanent! Just like when a bone is set, does not suddenly "undo" one day, so also is a broken heart healed for good.

It might feel tiresome sometimes working with someone again and again. Often you will deal with the same hurt, but from different angles. Do not "grow weary in doing good" because you are making more progress than you realize.

I am always amazed at the transformations that God has taken each of my team and spiritual children through. There is no bondage too big for God. There is no hurt so deep that it cannot be healed and there is no demon too strong that it cannot be shaken out of its tree!

This is ministry in its raw form. My prayer is that God will raise up true ministers who are prepared to follow through with God's people like this. My prayer is that God will transform the "man for the hour" into someone who is there every minute of the day for God's people.

Having read this, I have now given you a tremendous responsibility. I have let you know some of what God expects of you as a minister. You are called to mature the Church and to do as Jesus did. You are called to give sight to the blind, to heal the sick and to mend the brokenhearted.

CHAPTER 09

Dealing with Demons and Deception

Chapter 09 – Dealing with Demons and Deception

Nobody likes to talk about deception and out of all the Fivefold Ministry - prophets are about the worst! I have found that a prophet (especially in training) would rather die than admit that his revelation was not from the Lord.

I do not know what the hang up is about. Sure deception is not very pleasant, but it is a vital part of the training God takes His ministers through. In fact, it is so vital that you will not be able to pass through your ministry training properly without going through the "deception phase."

This is no different with someone called to the teaching ministry. It is only when they have tried to get revelation in the flesh and failed, that they will recognize truth when it really comes. It is only when you have failed and fallen for the honeyed words of the enemy can you be armed with a true understanding of heresy and how it can come about in the first place.

All of us have moments of the flesh and I am here to reassure you by saying that it is part of the process. In fact, it is vital to the process of being able to identify deception and the work of the enemy in others.

As in all things, you have to live it for yourself first before qualifying to point it out in others later.

By Colette Toach

It takes someone who has matured in the Lord to say, "I missed it!" As I have worked with many leaders, I get so many different kinds of people at different places in their training.

However, when I come across someone who is not afraid to say, "Oops! I missed it! I failed there!" I know that I am working with someone who has matured in the Lord.

So I am going to ask something strangely ridiculous of you. I am going to ask you to get excited about the subject of deception. Now before you think I am crazy, hear me out for a bit. When you finally stand up and speak God's word and you can do so with confidence, knowing that you are speaking exactly what you should, it brings such a rest.

Let us not be naïve and think, "All my revelations are pure and come directly from the Throne Room of God and should be taken word for word as such."

My advice? Grow up a little bit. Let's be honest, we are not perfect. We can mess things up. Now if you can be humble and admit that you are able to be deceived you will have a good chance of not being deceived.

If you think that you cannot get into deception, then you already are!

A good place to be is admitting that you can fail and get into deception. From there, you can realize that it is all right to fail! If you have been in deception in the past, I would never condemn you for it. I would judge you however if you did get into deception and you are not prepared to face and deal with it.

Play it Safe

So here are some good points to help you to clear up what is deception and what is not. While I point these out to you, it's just you and these pages, so be open. Do not read through the points and say to yourself, "Yup! I can think of a few people who need to read this!"

Instead point a good straight finger at yourself and face your fears right here and now. If you are prepared to do that here in the quiet of your room, then you will not have to face the humiliation of any startling discoveries of deception later in public!

I cannot think of anything more devastating than a prophet that refuses to look at the truth when it comes to deception. They would rather hold onto their false revelation because of the recognition they get, than to know the reality of Jesus Christ.

Why settle for second best? So let's look at this subject openly. No holds barred. You are welcome to pull out some of your revelations from the past and have a good, honest look at where you stand. No one is condemning or judging you. This is solely between you and the Lord.

The Spirit of Divination

You will find this kind of deception referenced to a lot in both the New and Old Testaments. You would be shocked if you knew how much of this is rampant in the Church right now.

It is not uncommon for someone to come to us, interested in our prophetic training saying, "You know ever since I was a child I used to dream of bad things happening and then they would come to pass. Now I realize I was just a prophet all along!

I thought I was strange back then, but now I realize I had a prophetic gift and that it was God showing me these things!"

I look at them and think, "No… it was not because of a prophetic calling, you are in fact demonized!"

That is not how the Holy Spirit works, that is the work of a demon.

It is no different to the fortuneteller that ran after Paul saying, "Listen to them, because they have been sent by the most high." We all know how Paul handled that, don't we? He turned around and rebuked that demon and told it to leave her.

After that she did not do any fortune telling. That is what the spirit of divination looks like. I find people who have this kind of bondage the hardest to deal with.

The reason is because they think that the voice that they are hearing and the visions that they are receiving are really from the Lord.

A True Story

There was a Christian woman that wrote in to me once. She said that she had certain experiences where she would experience things before they happened. She told me one of her experiences where she heard a voice tell her that her father was going to die and then it went on to even give the date and time.

And so she lived in constant fear as she approached this date. As the time came closer the fateful day arrived and in the morning everything seemed all right. However, that evening they got a knock at the door saying that her father had disappeared and that they did not know where he had gone.

So she prayed and suddenly she got a revelation and knew exactly where he was. So they rushed to him and found him trying to commit suicide. She grabbed him and he seemed to be suddenly shaken As if coming out of a dream, he looked at her and said, "You know, I do not know what came over me, I just suddenly wanted to commit suicide."

That is not the work of the Holy Spirit! The worst part is that she sent this as a testimony saying, "I must be a prophet because I knew that before it happened." No, she did not "know" that this was going to happen.

The sad truth is that she released it by believing that demonic word. She gave satan license to do exactly what he wanted to do. The difficult truth is that she could have brought about the death of her father. That is scary, but it is the cold truth about the spirit of divination.

If the enemy can get a hold in your life and through his spirit of divination give you revelations, as you speak them out and have faith in them, you release them to come to pass in the earth. You give satan the exact license that he wanted to work out his own plan.

That is why the spirit of divination is deadly. So do not think that just because you knew something was going to happen and it did, that it was God speaking. We do not serve a Savior of strife, fear and condemnation.

The Lord does not go around telling you that people will be murdered and destroyed. If you know Jesus as I know Jesus, you will know that He does not operate in that way. You would know that Jesus brings faith, hope and love through everything He tells us.

His words do not produce fear or condemnation.

I consider the passage where Jesus spoke to Peter about the way he would die. He told Peter that when he was an old man, that he would be led to a place he did not want to go. (John 21:18) This revelation did not bring fear to Peter.

In fact, some time later Peter was bound and put in prison. There was talk of death and punishment, yet when the angel came to save him, he had to give Peter a kick to wake him up. Could you fall into a nice comfy sleep knowing that this could be your last night on earth?

You see, Peter knew that this was not his last night on earth. In fact, he knew that he would be a nice old man before he would have to die, so he could sleep peacefully. This revelation gave Peter hope. It did not bring fear and it also did not come with graphic detail. It only gave an indication.

This is another big difference I see with a spirit of divination. The images are usually very vivid and clear, whereas the Lord always speaks in types and shadows. History tells us that Peter was crucified upside down, but this is not what Jesus told him.

Instead He said to him, "Another will dress you and lead you to a place you do not want to go… "Can you see the difference here between this and the encounter I shared before it?

All is Not Lost

Now as you read this and you suspect that you have had similar experiences that hint towards a spirit of divination, I want to say that all is not lost. You can be set free and come to hear the voice of the Lord clearly.

I must be blatantly honest with you though and say that if you suspect a spirit of divination in your life, then there is a demon involved. There is something strongly demonic that is binding you and holding you back. It is blocking you from a face-to-face relationship with Jesus.

That horrible demon is destroying what God is trying to do in your life. In fact, it could well be that a lot of the problems and struggles you have been facing in life have not just been prophetic preparation. All those tough times might very well be the result of that bondage in your life.

Now if this is speaking to you, now is not the time to allow yourself to get under condemnation or to try and justify yourself. You need to rise up and shake this thing off!

You have authority in the name of Jesus to deal with this. It is best if you have someone who can stand in agreement with you, but if you do not, you can still take authority over it on your own.

Dealing With It

> ***James 4:7*** *Therefore submit to God. Resist the devil and he will flee from you.*

So the first thing that you need to do is acknowledge your sin. Satan did not jump in when you were not looking. He may have given you the deception, but you received and believed it. You took it into your heart.

So the first step is to ask the Lord for forgiveness for allowing that thing a hold in your life. This might even be something that has been passed down through your generations. You might see it in your family as well and you grew up with it your whole life. You still gave it license.

There was a time in your life when you gave it a place in your heart and you need to repent of that and submit yourself to the Lord once again.

I hope that what I am stirring up in you is a righteous anger, because you do not have to accept this deception. You do not need to take whatever the enemy dishes out. You can enter into a new relationship with Jesus!

Once you have submitted, then you can resist and tell that demon to take a hike. You can command it to stop its influence over you.

Understanding Strange Experiences

Perhaps as I have shared, you can identify with a few of these experiences, but it is not typically a habit in your life. What I want you to do is think back on these experiences and think about what was happening with you at the time.

Identify the circumstances you were in at the time this strange experience occurred. Perhaps you had a mentor or were going to a specific church at that time. Did you perhaps get involved in a new teaching or did someone lay hands on you and impart something to you?

The point is that during this time you opened your heart to something that was not of the Lord. You received something here that gave the enemy license in your life. Once you can identify it, you can quickly submit to the Lord and see the enemy for what he truly is.

You can turn around and tell the enemy that his number is up! You will not listen to his voice any longer. You have authority in the name of Jesus. You are not a victim and you can overcome this thing.

There is a Good Side

Although having to look at divination in your life does not sound like a lot of fun, there is a good side to it. Once you have overcome it, you will be able to identify it so much easier in others. So break free and then teach them to break free.

If you have not had these experiences for yourself, I promise that you will come across people that have and you better know how to minister to them. Do not mistake their "gift" for prophetic ministry. Above all do not feel insecure next to someone who has those strange experiences.

Do Not Feel Insecure!

When a person is under the influence of a spirit of divination, their "revelations" sound so out of this world. There is a temptation to feel insecure next to that. You think, "Well I just want to speak a word of encouragement so that I can bring people into a relationship with Jesus. I do not run around having out of body experiences."

You know what? You are the one that has the truth. Never feel insecure about that!

How Deception Comes

Deception is different to the spirit of divination. Divination is akin to witchcraft whereas deception is simply a revelation that was not from God.

It comes a bit like this:

You received this incredible revelation from the Lord for someone. So you rushed up to them and gushed all over them! Instead of being impressed, they look at you as if you just crawled out of a piece of cheese.

You wanted to crawl away. You thought to yourself, "What happened there? What was that?"

The answer: It was just deception.

You will identify deception by the pushiness that comes with it. Now here are a few things that you need to watch out for. Deception is identified in a word that brings fear to the hearer instead of love. It sounds a bit like,

"You better come right with God or He is going to take your son away from you."

"You better repent or God is going to destroy your business."

That is not the spirit of Christ. That is deception. It is a revelation that did not come from the Lord, but from the enemy. Once again (sorry to break it to you) but you are not a victim.

If you are receiving revelations that are a deception, then something is wrong. There could be a number of reasons why you missed it. It could be that you are not under spiritual authority.

Where Did It Come From?

If you suspect that you have fallen into deception, identifying where you opened the door to the enemy is a huge leap forward. Look for any strange teachings you got into, mentors that you received from in the past or perhaps others that spoke into your life that were in deception.

It could be that you received from someone that was not under any kind of authority or covering from a team themselves and some of their revelations and experiences felt a bit strange to you. Before opening up and just taking everything from someone, see if the spirit they are walking in is of the Lord.

You can identify the fruit of a prophet by the trail of disaster or the blessing that they leave behind. Now I am not saying that every revelation that we speak should be all pretty and nice.

Condemnation vs. Conviction

Sure, there are times when the Lord will call on you to speak a word of warning. There will be times when you will speak with a strong conviction and anointing. However, even though you might be issuing a correction or warning, that word should bring a conviction.

It should bring the person to their knees before the Lord. It should not leave them trembling in fear or guilt.

> ***2 Corinthians 7:10*** *For godly sorrow produces repentance leading to salvation, not to be regretted; but the sorrow of the world produces death.*

If you bring a word that produces condemnation, it only brings death. You leave the person thinking, "What is the point of going on any longer? I give up. What is the use of serving the Lord?"

This is the sorrow of the world - it is not conviction. When you speak a word of correction and they are pierced in their hearts and fall before the Lord, you can rest assured that you are speaking on behalf of the King of kings.

Their relationship with God is restored and when you see this happen, the short sorrow they might experience because of the correction is short lived. They do not regret it, because it did something wonderful in their lives. That is why it says that true godly sorrow comes without regret.

You never regret a good conviction. I personally love a good conviction. One of those when the Holy Spirit speaks so clearly and it cuts you straight to the heart. You feel so naked before the Lord and you fall flat on your face and cry before Him.

It is a good experience because you get up again feeling so cleansed and closer to the Lord. So do not confuse condemnation and conviction.

Do it NOW!

Many of us have experienced this one at one time or another. You are sitting in the meeting and you feel that you must give the word that God has given to you *right now*! If you do not give the word, then you have failed God and their blood is on your hands.

So you stand up and say, "The Lord is going to destroy this church because you refuse to repent." Then you sit down and you feel a sinking feeling in the pit of your stomach.

That pushiness you felt was not of the Lord. The Lord Jesus is a gentleman and He leads. He does not push and shove. The Scripture refers to the Holy Spirit as a dove and the Lord Jesus as a shepherd.

When last did you see a shepherd standing behind the sheep with a stick, whacking them from behind and telling them to move their fluffy little tails?

No, the Good Shepherd goes ahead of the sheep and leads them. Even when a sheep goes astray and He has to pull that sheep from the pit with his staff, it might be uncomfortable, but it is to save its life.

The worst with that pushy feeling is when you were not sure, so you did not stand up and give the word. Afterwards though you feel just terrible and you think you failed the Lord. The Lord will never make you feel guilty because you did not let Him use you.

There are many others that He can use. You do not hold the world in your hand, He does. He is well able to raise up many others to speak His word.

So do not allow yourself to come under that condemnation. If you think back and feel that horrible guilty feeling, then I want you to let it go right now. The Lord does not condemn you and the guilt is not from Him. That is the voice of the enemy accusing you.

By Colette Toach

Being Pushed Beyond What God Intends

I remember when I learned this lesson for myself. I learned that when the enemy cannot get away with deceiving you, then he will push you beyond what God intends. In other words, the enemy will take something that is real and he will push you to the point where you will start off with a real revelation and take it way beyond what you were meant to.

Example

Say for example you are attending a church where the pastor often uses tithing to keep the people in bondage. The deacons that have been appointed gave a lot of money to the church and you wonder how much of their appointment had to do with calling or the size of their check.

The ones who are promoted are the ones who give the most, while those who have a real anointing are not given a chance.

Your heart burns for change. And so as you are interceding the Lord gives you a revelation. He says that He is going to start leading the church in a new direction and do something that He has never done there before.

He is going to open doors that will change the way they have been going and that He is going to lead them to a new land.

This is a fantastic word, but unfortunately with all your frustration of "the system" in this church, instead of sharing it like that, you share it differently.

You stand up and say to the pastor, "God has seen what you are doing and He is going to bring about a change in this church. He is going to force you to go His way and not to follow your own way any longer.

And if you do not follow His way, He will break this foundation and break this church down that you have built."

What just happened here? You were just pushed beyond what God intended! That is not what the Lord meant, but because of your own anger, when that word came out of you it did not come as it should have.

This is something that you will have to watch out the most for as a minister.

Pre-conceived Ideas

It is just so easy to look at someone from the outside and to assess them, knowing that they have a problem in their lives. You might even know that they are bitter towards you.

As you are praying with them, you get a revelation and instead of "saying it like it is" you try to interpret it to deal with their bitterness against you. You will not minister to their need, but you will add to that revelation.

When you are aware of this in yourself, you will see it in others that stand up to minister. It is humbling when the Lord reveals this in you because you realize that although you had some zeal, you did not represent Christ.

Avoiding Deception

STOP!

When you are ministering to someone that you are struggling to love or you feel too much emotion regarding a church or person, it would do you good to stop and wait for a confirmation or to journal your revelation first.

Wait for your emotions to calm down and be sure that you are speaking in faith, hope and love. I have said this a hundred times before and will probably say it a hundred times more - Err on the side of speaking blessing.

You can never go wrong by speaking blessing. Speaking a blessing does not bring harm to anyone, however speaking a curse can bring about devastating results. So if the word you feel you must bring is one of correction or judgment, you better be pretty sure that the correction is coming from the Lord and not your own pre-conceived ideas.

If you come with the right attitude, it will bring conviction and there will be change. Make sure that when you stand up to minister, that the vision or word you share is of God, as well as the interpretation.

A Word to the Ladies

Women do not like me saying this, but I am going to say it anyway because I just so happen to be one myself, so I can get away with it. Ladies, you have to be under the submission of your husbands. The Scripture is clear. Adam came before Eve, because Eve missed it badly.

The Lord has given us our husbands to cover and protect us. Run to your husband and come under his protection. Do not run off on your own and try to run the ministry all by yourself. If you do that, you are begging to get into deception.

If you are an unmarried woman, then find yourself a spiritual father.

This is certainly the stand in our ministry. None of us are loners. We all work within a team so that we can cover one another. Even though Craig and I stand in apostolic office, we do not run off independently and do what we want, when we want. We cover one another's backs.

Two by Two

The enemy will certainly try to sneak in. Even Jesus sent His disciples out two by two. Even after Jesus was glorified, everyone traveled as a team.

Apostle Paul traveled with Luke, Timothy and Silas. Even Peter traveled with his wife doing the work of the ministry. If Jesus did it and the apostles did it, is this not our example to follow? No one is meant to be an island and to do things alone.

I do not like being negative, but have someone there to watch your back. If you try to head out into the great blue yonder all alone and you fall flat on your face, there is nothing worse than falling alone. Not only that, but if you have someone else there to cover you, you have less of a chance of hitting that big wall in front of you that reads, "NOT THIS WAY!"

So even if you are a man, realize that God has called you to work in a team setting. Do not run off and make major decisions without getting backing from your team. Learn to be a team player and this will help prevent you from getting into deception.

Know Your Limitations

It is good to know your weaknesses and limitations. I had to correct someone for an incorrect dream interpretation once and instead of being open enough to listen she said, "I only speak when God tells me to speak. I only prophesy what God tells me to prophesy.

This ministry is not of God and is a complete deception and I want nothing to do with you, because I only speak what God tells me to."

She then went on to slander us with some terrible insults that were not only personal, but also very incorrect!

I thought to myself, "Not only are you arrogant, but you are deceived to think that you only speak what God tells you, when right there, the voice coming from her was anything but the voice of the Lord Jesus Christ."

Be a little mature and be prepared to look at yourself and to admit that maybe... just maybe, not everything you speak is what God is really speaking.

If you have that kind of humility and you are open to correction, then the Holy Spirit can train you so much quicker. However, if you say, "I am only here to minister. I only give the words when God says and I press on forward and never give up. God can count on me because I am so humble. You have never seen anyone more humble than me."

That is so self-righteous and someone like that is like a hard rock that God has to smash before any real training can begin.

Rather say, "Ok Lord, I am open. Show me! Where did I miss it?"

By Colette Toach

Now you are ready! Now you are mature and the Lord can start working with you and training you. Sure, it is not so comfortable.

It is not fun to mess up! But you know I have greater respect for someone who messes up and then takes responsibility saying, "Yes! I failed." Than I do for someone who goes off on a tangent all the time and is never prepared to admit that maybe they are not perfect.

What can God do with such a person? I look at King David and he was so humble. You read his Psalms and you see how he was not afraid to speak out all of his failures and mistakes. He was not afraid to voice his fears, but yet he was the greatest king that Israel ever had.

Do Not be Afraid to be Humble

God can do something with someone who is prepared to be humble. Then with all of your failure and weakness, you will certainly rise up higher than those who put on the mask of superiority. I would rather hang out with someone who is real than with someone who wears a mask and that you cannot get close to.

Signs of Deception

We have covered this in many places, so I am going to make this easy for you and list just 5 clear signs of deception for you to remember and to weigh your revelations with.

Pull out some of your own revelations and compare them. Then look around at some of the revelations others are sharing and weigh them as well.

Sign 1: It Does Not Line Up With the Word

This might seem obvious to you, but you will still see many saying, "This is what God is telling you…" when the Word tells us the complete opposite.

I had a woman come to me confused and frustrated. She was going through a bad time in her marriage and she and her husband were in continual conflict. He was a Christian. She came and said that she had received a prophetic word that she was to divorce her husband and to move on.

Clearly this word is not from God. The Lord is not in the business of telling people to get divorced, without first following the clear guidelines in the Word.

Sign 2: The Word Brings Fear

The scripture says that the spirit that has been given is not of fear, but of a sound mind. If you are bringing fear that completely disables a person, something is wrong. Now I am not talking about a reverential fear of the Lord, but the kind of fear that brings death.

An example is a woman preacher who told two men who did not want to get saved that the Lord was going to kill them because of it. This is not the voice of the Lord Jesus. How do I know this? Because Jesus Himself said he did not come to the world to judge it, but to save it from its sins. Jesus died for us to save us. He did not come to save us... only to kill us later on down the line!

Sign 3: The Word Brings Guilt and Condemnation

This kind of word can bring a lot of confusion as well. Someone might come into a meeting feeling on top of the world, but they leave it under such guilt that they feel they cannot come to the Lord any longer.

They leave feeling as if they failed the Lord and are not worthy to come into His presence. They look as if they are walking under a load. This is the kind of thing that Jesus accused the Pharisees of all the time. He said that they weighed the people down with such a load and then never lifted a finger to help them carry it.

Sign 4: Watch the Pushiness!

If you feel that you have to "drop everything" and give the word immediately, then be careful. The Lord does not push - He leads. If you feel the sudden urge to run and force your revelation, wait on it for a bit.

You might be doing a chore in your house when suddenly a revelation comes out of nowhere and you feel the urge to drop everything and act on it right now! Wait on that word or impulse and give the Holy Spirit time to confirm it for you. I have found in personal experience that when you wait on the word a bit that if it was not of the Lord, the feeling often fades. However, the words that are truly from God are confirmed through others and through the Scriptures later on.

Sign 5: When the Word Exalts the Person

Unfortunately, we see this way too often. People leave a meeting saying, "Wow! That man was so amazing. He saw that great demon and then he spoke to that angel. Then, he had such an incredible revelation. He must be so close to God. Wow! I wish I was like him!"

People leave that meeting speaking about that man and how wonderful he is and the Lord Jesus is… where? Did this ministry bring the people closer to the Lord or did it bring the people closer to the prophet?

Watch out for that. Now I am not saying that God does not give great revelations, because He sure can. I am talking of people that walk in that all of the time, sharing their great experiences more than they share about our great God.

Is the point of ministry not to glorify the Lord? It is Christ in us that is the hope of glory and it is through our weakness where His strength is displayed.

When we stand up with this kind of attitude, it ministers Christ to the people and draws them into a relationship with Him.

No one should leave a meeting that you ministered at thinking that God forgot about them. They should not leave thinking that you are more important to God than what they are. They should leave with hope that they too can have a relationship with Jesus and that He cares about every part of their lives.

Hopefully by now you understand deception a little bit and that the mystery is gone. Everyone that has been in ministry has experienced one of these shortcomings at one time or another. So do not be discouraged if you too fell for one of the tricks of the enemy.

Rather submit yourself to the Lord, resist the devil and he will flee from you. (James 4:7). Then rise up once again in your authority, knowing that what the enemy sought for evil, God has the power to turn around for His good.

CHAPTER 10

Dealing with Demonic Manifestations

Chapter 10 – Dealing with Demonic Manifestations

No one ever forgets the first time that a demon manifests during their ministry. Suddenly all of the principles that you have learned seemed to fly out your head as you face the reality of dealing with a demon face to face.

The first times for Craig and I was just as startling. We were holding a home church meeting when during praise and worship, a woman started manifesting a demon and shouting at us. Her voice changed, her eyes changed and it was clear that when you looked at her face, she was no longer in control of her senses.

So we made the first mistake everyone usually makes. We told the demon to get out. It did not. We shouted. The demon shouted. We shouted louder. The demon shouted louder. Clearly we were not getting anywhere.

She was only getting more violent and for a moment she launched at me, stopping an inch from my face. In that moment I felt such a peace of the Lord come over me. I knew this enemy and I knew that he was defeated 2000 years ago. I looked the woman straight in the face and I called her by name.

I did not talk to the demon. He was really not worthy of my time. It was the woman I wanted to help out here and as I looked at her, I felt a deep compassion for her.

By Colette Toach

The demon stopped short, just staring at me with a bewildered look on its face.

Then I reached out, took the woman's hand and said, "Hey, I love you, the Lord Jesus loves you and we want to help you break free here."

The demon gave me one more confused look and then the woman's face changed as she returned to her senses. After that we could counsel her and get her to renounce the hold the enemy had on her.

We had another similar experience in a public meeting. As I was leading praise and worship a woman started manifesting a demon at the back of the meeting hall. Dressed from head to toe in a classy white suit, she was yelling and rolling on the dusty wooden floor from one end to the other.

Craig walked politely up to the woman, tapped her on the shoulder and said, "Could you come with us please." He did not argue and he did not try to "fight it out" with the demon right there. Instead he spoke to the woman.

Together with another minister he took her aside and they could minister to her and help her break free. She had experienced this manifestation for many years and thought that it was the power of the Holy Spirit throwing her all over the floor all these years.

Not only was this manifestation an interruption to the meeting every time the anointing began to flow, but it was a blockage in this woman's life. She always came so far in her walk with God and no further. She could not understand what that blockage was. Once they showed her in the Word the kind of gentleman Jesus was, she was ready to renounce that bondage.

No further demonic manifestations were needed. She submitted herself to God, repented of her sin and told the enemy to leave. The manifestations did not return and she made the first real steps forward in her spiritual growth.

Two Camps

The reason I have shared a few of our own examples is to bring some balance between two main camps in the church when it comes to demonic manifestations. You have some who are just "too afraid" to go there and avoid the demonic realm altogether.

Then on the other end of the pendulum you find "deliverance ministries" who see demons everywhere that they go.

Yes, demons are real. Yes, angels are real. However, never forget:

> **Philippians 2:10** *that at the name of Jesus every knee should bow, of those in heaven, and of those on earth, and of those under the earth.*

> **Luke 10:19** *Behold, I give you the authority to trample on serpents and scorpions, and over all the*

> *power of the enemy, and nothing shall by any means hurt you.*

I cover a lot of detail regarding the doctrine of demons and angels in *Prophetic Warrior*, but I will mention one point here that is poignant. If you do a study, you will notice that the Apostles did not go around casting demons out of believers.

You see the work of Jesus and He often cast demons out of people, but this was before he was crucified. These people were not born again and this kind of deliverance was not restricted to Israelites either. He cast demons out of Israelites (Mary) and He cast demons out of the Syrophenician's daughter.

However, in the New Testament even though it was clear that Simon the Sorcerer was demonized, Peter did not "do deliverance" on the man. Rather he said, "You do not know the spirit you are of! I sense bitterness in you. You need to repent." (Acts 8)

This comes back to the point I made earlier in our counseling section of this book. There are times when you will have demon manifestations that you have to deal with right away. Then there are instances where the demon has gained entrance through hurts from the past or bitterness that the person has held onto.

While this is an extensive subject, I am going to give you some simple steps to follow on how to handle both of these situations.

Demon Manifestations

1. Know Your Authority

I am going to let you in on a secret here. Demons are not walking around just "jumping" into people. If someone is demonized, then they gave that demon license. Is this not true of your salvation? The Lord says that He stands at the door and knocks.

When you were born again, the Holy Spirit did not just overpower you and enter into your spirit without your free will, did He? No, the Lord has set up this earth and our lives with clear rules and guidelines. It was for Eve to choose to obey satan or not.

The moment that she obeyed satan and ate the fruit that she was not supposed to, she gave him license into this world. As a result, a curse entered into the earth. Adam and Eve lost their freedom and instead of walking in the blessing that God had given, they lost it.

Satan stole it, because they gave him that license in this earth. When God placed Adam into the garden, He gave him authority to tend it. Adam had the reins. He had the keys to lock and unlock. Unfortunately, though when they fell into sin, they handed that license over to the enemy.

Suddenly sin became an issue and that nasty little "seed of sin" entered into the world. That is a doctrinal study all on its own, but the greatest part of all is that the Lord did not leave it there. Right at that point the

Lord said to them that He would send a Seed of His own through Eve that would crush the head of that serpent!

That seed was Jesus and through His blood we can now take back the authority that was lost to man in the Garden.

Not only does it make you appreciate your salvation all over again, but it also makes you realize that you have authority in the name of Jesus!

> ***John 1:5*** *And the light shineth in darkness, and the darkness comprehended it not. (KJV)*

I will never forget the look of confusion on that demon's face when I reached out to that woman in love. It is true that satan cannot understand love. It is completely contrary to his nature. It is as confusing as light is to darkness just like the scripture says above.

When your intent is to minister and help set someone free, you do not need to worry if you have the authority or the faith. This is a situation where your love will draw on the power of God to give you the gift of faith that you need.

2. Talk to the Person

It looks pretty awe-inspiring to see someone slithering around under demonic manifestation while the itinerant minister barks out commands and communicates with the demon.

Now let me ask you this question. If you were the person slithering around on the floor, how would you feel? When someone comes to me with an intimate problem, I counsel them privately and help them break free. As a counselor they trust me to bare their hearts and even share their sin so that I can help.

So how does this differ when it comes to demon manifestations? If someone does happen to manifest when you are ministering to them, you are not going to make any progress until you can get that person to be in agreement with you.

It is like I said before. If there is a demon, then that person gave it license through sin or direct demonic involvement. This could be through false religion, getting into heresy or even receiving an impartation from someone who was also bound.

This is when you take Peter's approach when dealing with Simon the Sorcerer. He spoke to Simon, not to the demon he obviously had. In the same way, if someone manifests, avoid the urge to struggle it out with the demon.

That demon has been given license in that person's life and he knows it. Your goal is to "cool down" that manifestation and to get that person in their right mind long enough to be able to help them break free.

Look at the person directly and call them by name. Ignore the demon and talk to the person sitting in front of you. Talk in love and wait for them to regain their control. Rest assured that even if the demon is going off like crazy that the person can hear you and that they can choose to take control again.

Never forget that they have the Holy Spirit inside of them and that they can break free.

NOTE: The only time this differs is if the person is an unbeliever. In the case of an unbeliever you can tell the demon to leave. When it leaves, it is important that you follow through with salvation or you stand the chance of them reverting once again.

Demons in Believers vs. Unbelievers

My dad shares an illustration between the difference of someone who is demonized who is a believer and someone who is not. He shares a story where a believer who was demonized had a standoff with a warlock.

While they both manifested a demon, there was one part of their experience that was decidedly different. The unbeliever could not remember everything that happened during the time the demon manifested. It was as if they had "blacked out".

The believer however could remember everything. They said that it was like standing and watching themselves say and do things, although they knew it was not really them doing it.

What makes the difference here is that a believer has the indwelling of the Holy Spirit. Remember the parable Jesus shared about the man who was set free of a demon? He said that the house is swept and made clean, but if that demon returns and finds it unoccupied, he brings back seven other demons and the man will be in a worse condition than before.

What Jesus was saying is, that it is not just good enough to go around casting out demons. The person also needs to get their "house" occupied. In other words, they need to get saved and have the Holy Spirit come and dwell inside of them.

When the Holy Spirit comes to dwell inside of you, He takes up permanent residence! Satan cannot control your spirit any longer. What he can do however is control your soul and this is what he will use in a believer. He will manipulate your mind, emotions and your will until he is told to leave.

When you understand these main points, you are ready to help set that person free.

3. Bring True Deliverance

Once the person has calmed down it is for you to bring conviction of sin. Just because someone manifested a demon does not mean they want to get rid of it. I just shared how satan takes control of the mind, emotions and will and this is where he plays his game.

Not only does he control this person, but he gives something to them as well. Perhaps the person in question is very insecure and unsure of themselves.

This demonic force may give them the boldness that they lack. So it is not always a case of "casting out demons."

If you have seen someone set free of a demonic bondage only to regress again, this is the main reason why. The enemy's license was not removed. That person liked his demon. It sounds crazy hey? You only have to be in ministry for a short time to see the truth of this point.

This is why the Word of God is vital in this situation. A conviction of sin must come and that means relying on the Holy Spirit to bring that conviction. It is for you to allow them to see that they have sinned against God and as a result satan has a hold on their lives.

No matter how much they are benefitting from this demon, it is stealing their ability to rise up. Only when they are ready to look at their sin, can you progress to the steps I have mentioned below.

Setting Someone Free

Step 1: Identify the Open Door

Like I said before demons do not go around just jumping into people. They have been given license through sin. Either that license came through family generations or through their own involvement. In many cases the open door will be clear.

If the person has used drugs or gotten involved in false religion, this is certainly a good place to start. In many countries witchcraft is a part of growing up. When ministering in places like this it can be really difficult.

We had a gentleman attend one of our conferences and ask for prayer. He had experienced out of body experiences since he was a child and he needed to know if these things were of God. God was starting to move him into the prophetic ministry and he was suddenly uncomfortable with all these strange experiences he kept having.

When we asked him when they started he said they were with him from birth. He went on to share that his parents were into voodoo and raised him in this until he got saved. That open door was pretty obvious. We told him that these manifestations were definitely not from the Holy Spirit. How could they be? He did not even have the indwelling of the Holy Spirit when he experienced it for the first time!

He was keen to deal with it and break free. No demon manifestations were necessary. He told it to leave and it left.

Some situations are not so clear. What does help is to ask the person when they first started experiencing these manifestations in their lives. It will usually come down to a specific time when they received something or got into something.

Once you know where the enemy got in, you are well on your way to victory.

Step 2: Repentance

James 4:7 says to submit yourself to God, resist the devil and he will flee. You cannot tell the enemy to go without submitting to God first. You disobeyed the Word of God through sin and you need to get right with God before you will have the authority to break free.

Jesus does not condemn you for your sin. He came to save you from it. However, the enemy is not as congenial. If he can take out a believer, he will use any means that he can.

So restore your relationship with the Lord first. The Word says that if our hearts do not condemn us, that we can approach the throne with boldness. You cannot break free if your heart condemns you. So lay the sin aside.

Repent of doing what you did or going where you went. In the case of generational bondages, break those generational links!

Daniel was a prime example of one who prayed on behalf of his people's sins. You can do the same regarding generational curses. You can repent for accepting whatever curse or bondage you allowed into your life. Once you have set things right with God, the most important thing is to tell the demon to leave.

Step 3: Deliverance

The scripture says that we have been given authority over serpents. Every believer has this authority, not just certain ministers. This means that the person in front of you has all the license and authority he needs to tell the demon to leave.

It was them who invited the demon through their sin - they have the same authority to take away that license. This is such a powerful step for anyone.

It is one thing to repent, but another to tell the devil to leave. When someone gets born again they make a choice to accept Jesus and to put off the old man so that he can put on the new. He takes the hand of Jesus and then deliberately chooses to tell the devil to get lost.

This is very much the same concept. Our words carry power! When you speak words into the earth, things happen! With every healing and miracle Jesus did, He said something. He did not nod or do a dance. He said something.

When he raised Lazarus from the dead, He said, "Come forth!" He did not just stand around praying to God. In the same way a person who has repented must say out loud, "I tell you to leave in the name of Jesus! The hold I have given to you I now take back. Get lost!"

Once they have prayed, you can step in and stand in agreement. If you flow in the gift of discerning of spirits, you might see the demon in the spirit you are dealing with and you will also be able to sense if the prayer was effective.

These are the same steps that you would follow if you are praying for inner healing or helping someone break free of the bondage that they got themselves into through a recent sin.

Step 4: Healing

Like I shared in the Ministry of Inner Healing chapter, very often a lot of bondage comes through the reactions of hurts in our lives. If the open door that you found relates to a situation where a hurt occurred, then you need to follow through with healing.

In cases such as witchcraft, deception or receiving contaminated impartations, then you will not need this step. However, if the open door came through abuse or any other kind of hurt, you need to ask the Holy Spirit to come and heal that hurt once and for all.

Some Signs of Demonic Bondage

Before ending off this chapter I would like to leave you with some points on what to look out for in someone that is in demonic bondage. Although you cannot use these as a "hard and fast" rule, they are some of what I have experienced in my own ministry and also what is clear in the Word.

1. Continual Lying

The Word says that satan is the father of lies. When someone has a habit of lying there is a good chance that they have a demonic bondage in their lives. Especially, when they cannot seem to control that lying.

2. Uncontrollable Anger

Someone who lashes out and cannot seem to control themselves shows a sign of demonic bondage. Remember how I shared that the enemy takes control of the mind, emotions and will? When those emotions are completely out of their control, then something is amiss.

3. No Control of Their Mind

This backs up what I shared in the previous point. This will especially manifest at times when you try to get into the Word or when the anointing begins to flow. It will seem that they suddenly do not understand anything and a "cloud of confusion" comes on them.

4. Spirit of Divination and Psychic Abilities

I think that this is pretty obvious and we sure know how Paul dealt with the "fortuneteller" that followed him around. He dealt with the demon in her and she no longer had this ability.

5. Spiritual Blockages

Although this one is not a hard and fast rule, I have often found that when someone has a strong spiritual blockage that something demonic is usually the problem. This is true of someone who just cannot seem to flow in the Gifts of the Spirit or goes so far and no further in their walk with the Lord.

That blockage is often demonic in nature and I have found that when we have dealt with it, that the person breaks free miraculously and flows in all of the Gifts of the Spirit.

6. Strange Physical Manifestations

I was a bit apprehensive about putting this point in, because it can be easily misunderstood. It is clear that when the Holy Spirit comes on us, that there are often physical manifestations. People will fall under the power of God. Some have been known to shake in His presence.

When Solomon dedicated the temple to God, the priests could not stand to minister. When the Early Church was spirit-filled, everyone thought they were drunk because of the way that they acted.

There are other manifestations though that are not of the Lord. This is especially true if these manifestations come when the anointing begins to flow and it interrupts the meeting - putting everyone's attention on them.

We had a couple once that had a strange manifestation. Every time the Holy Spirit came, their heads would shake violently. They had been told that this was something from the Holy Spirit. When we asked them when it started they said it started not long after they had all decided to set up a booth at a New Age fare.

After being involved there, everyone started having these manifestations. Obviously they had a backlash and by getting involved with everyone there, they picked up something that was counterfeit. What confirmed it for us as well is that they had no control of these manifestations. They prayed and renounced them. The manifestations stopped.

When you look at the manifestation ask yourself this question, "Does this line up with what I know about the Lord Jesus and His Word?"

When you know someone, you also know how they would act. You know what lines up with their nature. At the beginning of the book I shared a lot on getting to know the Lord for yourself. The more you get to know Him, the more you will know what is counterfeit.

Of course the gift of discerning of spirits is vital in helping anyone break free. Every believer should flow in this gift.

Final Note

Finally, the Lord has given you the authority in this earth to overcome any work of the enemy. Do not be afraid to stand in it. On the other hand, do not get so hung up on demons that you forget to notice that a blood bought Child of God is sitting in front of you.

The Lord has called you to mature His Bride and make Her beautiful. This part of ministry is the water that washes Her and prepares Her for the oil and perfume that will make Her lovely.

PART 03 – PUBLIC MINISTRY

CHAPTER 11

Taking Charge of the Public Meeting

Part 03 – Public Ministry

Chapter 11 – Taking Charge of the Public Meeting

Did you ever play "follow the Leader" as a kid? I remember playing this game for hours. There was a whole group of us, and usually the popular kid got to be the leader. Of course good old Colette here was the last one in the line, the shortest of them all, trying to keep up with the leader.

What was it with these leaders? It seemed that they tried to do the craziest things and see if everybody could follow.

There was this one guy. He would jump on top of a wall and stand up tall. And there I was... poor Colette just trying to climb the wall. I was barely getting my balance and he was running off doing something else.

I could never seem to keep up!

Depending on where you were, I am sure you have your own memories. Maybe you were the big, strong, tough guy up front, showing off all your fancy moves. Or perhaps you were like the rest of us... falling off the wall.

Now leading a meeting is like playing follow the leader, except this time you are the guy up front.

By Colette Toach

Taking Charge of the Public Meeting

There is one passage in the Bible that portrays this picture perfectly.

> ***Psalms 23:1** The Lord is my shepherd; I shall not want.*
>
> *2 He makes me to lie down in green pastures; He leads me beside the still waters.*
>
> *3 He restores my soul; He leads me in the paths of righteousness for His name's sake.*
>
> *4 Yea, though I walk through the valley of the shadow of death, I will fear no evil; for You are with me; Your rod and Your staff, they comfort me.*
>
> *5 You prepare a table before me in the presence of my enemies; You anoint my head with oil; my cup runs over.*
>
> *6 Surely goodness and mercy shall follow me all the days of my life; and I will dwell in the house of the Lord forever.*

Can you see the pictures? Can you see the shepherd as he goes by the still waters? You can imagine his little sheep running on behind him?

Now in this picture can you imagine the shepherd jumping on a wall and expecting the poor sheep to keep up?

Maybe some of the big sheep can try to scramble up and just make it. Unfortunately, though you have those short, little "Colette" sheep at the back and there is no way that they are going to get up on this big wall.

In contrast the passage says that He leads them to a resting place by the water. Then when things get a little scary and the sheep are in the shadow valley of death, the shepherd does not run off. Instead he goes at a nice steady pace and the sheep can see him and follow through. They are not afraid.

This is the picture on how to take charge of a meeting.

You are the leader up front and it's up to you to lead the sheep to green pastures.

The Main Problem

There is a major problem that many leaders starting out think though. They think that everybody else knows what to do.

You think, "It's obvious, we should stand up now. We should worship now."

The congregation thinks, "The leader knows what he is doing. We'll just follow him."

So in this case scenario... you are following the people and the people are following you. In the end you are going around in circles.

Never forget that you are the leader up front. You are the one that they are going to follow, so do not be afraid to stand up and be heard.

By Colette Toach

Taking Charge of the Public Meeting

There is nothing worse than coming into a meeting and it doesn't feel like anybody is in charge.

Usually everybody arrives five to three minutes before the meeting and then they still want to have a conversation about what happened during the week.

Even though they know that the meeting is about to start you have the usual hubbub of,

"Do you know what my mother-in-law said to me then?"

"...Can you believe it? My husband went and said... "

"You think that's bad? Do you know what my daughter did this week?"

"No! I cannot imagine..."

In the middle of the conversational hum, you walk up to the front of the hall in plain sight of everyone. Right away they take their seats with an attitude of, "Awesome! We are going to start! Let me take my seat and get ready to receive"

Not! Usually what happens is that everyone just carries right on doing what they were doing.

So you clear your throat, hoping to get some attention. The result? They talk louder because you are interrupting their conversation.

That did not work. Let's try the next tactic. You pick up the microphone and you tap it with the hope that a few raps through the sound system will help them notice that you are standing there.

Unfortunately, they think that you are just doing a sound check or something because instead of their rapt attention you hear somebody in the corner erupting in sudden laughter at a private joke. Next to that person a child starts screaming, so the mother jumps up and gives it a full lecture, which reminds another mother that she needs to take her child out of the meeting... leading to the door slamming in the back.

Let me give you a tip here. Clearing your throat into the microphone again is not going to save you.

So what are you doing wrong here?

Your problem is that you think the people know what to do. You think that when you stand up there, they are naturally going to know what you are thinking.

Let me save you the agony by letting you know outright - it's not going to happen. You are the leader. Until you give the people direction, they are going to do what they want to do. It's for you to take charge of the meeting.

Opening a Meeting

So, walk loudly up to the front. Deliberately show some presence. Stand up straight. Put your shoulders back. You grab that microphone, "Good afternoon everybody!" If that doesn't work, say it even louder.

"Can I have your attention please?" They can't help but notice you.

You have to break through their conversations. You must demand their attention.

If you go up there asking for their attention with a small mousy voice, do you know what they are going to answer with subconsciously?

"No you can't have my attention, because I am in a deep conversation here about the new mall that just opened up down the road and I can't imagine what you could say that would be more interesting.

So until you offer me something more interesting, I am going to talk about the sale that will be on, what I am going to buy – and every other unimportant detail that comes to mind."

No, you don't ask for their attention, you demand their attention, because you are the leader.

"Hey follow me!"

Jesus did this all the time in His ministry. He was not afraid to tell the Disciples to, "Put down your nets and follow me." You do not read of Him saying, "Umm guys, do you think you will be free for this afternoon? Maybe after you have had lunch, we could go for a walk and discuss some Kingdom dynamics…" No, He said, "Drop your nets and follow me!" He grabbed their attention.

Now perhaps you think that's being dominating. The opposite is true. This approach makes people feel comfortable because they are waiting for you to make the first move. When you have the confidence to make that move they, like sheep, will follow.

Something to Remember

Before you stand up front, know what you are going to say ahead of time. Taking charge of the meeting is not a prophetic function. Don't think you are going to stand up and from deep within, you are going to get the first words to speak and the rest will follow.

This isn't a prophetic word! This is opening a meeting. This means you are going to have to use some of your brain and you are going to have to put some effort into it.

So know what you are going to say before you step up to the front. Know clearly what you have to discuss.

Do you know what makes me uncomfortable? It is when you are in a meeting and the guy who opens stands up to try and introduce himself and says,

"Ummm, aah... I believe the children will be leaving right after the praise. So if you uh, have any children, umm... then ah... they can go out. Then we uh... "

In the middle of his sentence he looks to Pastor, tilting his head in an unsure gesture to confirm if he has it right before continuing.

"Yeah ok. Alright then next, we're going to uh... have some praise and worship... yeah... and that's our announcements."

You look at someone like that and think to yourself, "Are you sure? Because to me, he doesn't seem so sure."

You know it wouldn't be so funny if it didn't happen so much. If you stand up to talk like that people will not believe you. If you keep looking at the pastor or someone else for confirmation on everything you say, they will be looking to see where you are getting your information. "Who is he looking at? What is he going to say?"

Know what you are going to say and don't look around hoping that somebody is going to throw you a line. Come already prepared. Make notes if you have to. If there are announcements that need to be made, now is the time to make them.

When to do Announcements

There is another thing that always irritates me in a public meeting. You have a fantastic time in the presence of the Lord and you are ready to get into the word, hungry for the Lord.

In the middle of that somebody stands up and says "I would like to announce the new curriculum we have pinned at the back of the hall" and then proceeds to harass you with another bunch more announcements.

No. Get your announcements out of the way at the beginning of the meeting. Don't break the flow of the Spirit. There is a reason that the Holy Spirit is known as a dove. He is gentle and He is easily frightened away.

I can tell you as a minister that it makes it much more difficult to stand up and flow in the anointing once the Dove has flown. When the Holy Spirit is moving it is a good time to stand up and share the Word. Unfortunately though many churches seem to enjoy frightening the Dove and calling Him back all the time during a meeting.

Sure as a preacher I can get the anointing back, but it is a lot easier if He never had to leave in the first place. Save your announcement for the opening or closing of the meeting. That way, the Holy Spirit can do His job as you do yours.

It should be a perfect harmony. Jesus did not stop in the middle of preaching the beatitudes to give His itinerary. In fact, He would get so carried away that people would follow Him for miles before realizing that it was way past lunchtime.

When the Holy Spirit is given His place in a meeting then you can rest assured that you will see the miracles and the healing taking place that you have asked God for.

Know Who is in Charge of What.

If you are taking charge of the meeting this week, know who is in charge of the sound system. Know who is in charge of the bookshop materials. Know who is leading the worship and know who is bringing the Word.

Don't just get up there and wing it.

When a shepherd leads his sheep, he doesn't go half way down the road and say, "You know what, I've never gone this way before. In fact, it doesn't look familiar to me at all. Oh well, let's just give it a try."

The next thing you know he is falling down a steep hill, over the edge of a cliff - and there the sheep are, still following on behind him.

Know where you are going and it will make everybody feel secure.

The great thing is that you only need to get it right once to gain the confidence of the people. The next time you stand up there, they will know that they can trust you and they will even follow you down that cliff if that is where you are going.

Handing Over to the Worship Leader

You are doing well so far! You stand up. You greet the people loudly and boldly and the time comes where you have finished your list of announcements and then praise and worship will begin.

If you are not the worship leader, introduce the worship leader. Say something along the lines of, "We welcome Craig Toach today. He is going to be leading us in praise and worship, so let's stand up and get ready to praise the Lord."

What you are doing is leading them from one pasture to another.

Don't leave uncomfortable silences where people wonder what is happening next. If you do that, you will lose their attention and they will be back to talking about their day.

Make it easy for them and lead into it nice and gentle.

Introducing the Speaker

You won't believe how important this is.

This is something that we have experienced so many times, so hopefully this will save the next speaker that you need to introduce. Do you know how horrible it is to introduce yourself? Especially if you are speaking in

Taking Charge of the Public Meeting

a church for the first time and the people do not know you.

There are a hundred things that go through your mind when you stand in front of people you do not know. You don't know them. They don't know you. You are thinking, "What are they thinking?" And they are thinking, "What is she going to preach? Shall we trust this woman? Hmm she looks a little strange. Short. I don't know... looks a little strange... don't know whether we should trust her."

So you stand up to preach and you have all these faces staring back at you. They are not smiling. They are checking you out. The women are checking out your hair... the outfit you picked out, right down to your shoes. "Nice shoes!"

Or they are thinking, "She has no taste at all."

Women are merciless.

You feel like a goldfish in a fish bowl, naked before this whole group of people. They are checking you out and deciding, "Do we receive or not?"

Now depending on the first sentence that comes out of your mouth will determine whether they receive or not.

You elders are killing us here. Give us a break would you? We are jet lagged. We've had four hours sleep.

The food is strange. The people are strange. Introduce us nicely.

Don't you feel that way when a friend of the person you are with walks up to you? It's for your friend to introduce you. If they do it right, you can all get on and be good friends.

So don't miss this important step. Take a moment to introduce your speaker. You can face those first terrible moments for them and smooth things over. You will win the hearts of the people and you will win the deep gratitude of the rest of us.

The Point of the Introduction

The whole purpose of introducing the speaker is to get people to open their hearts, because if they open their hearts they are going to receive the word.

This is no time to be insecure and afraid that they will like the speaker more than you. In fact, the more they like the speaker the better for you because if they are a good speaker the people will say to you, "Hey that was a good idea of yours."

Unfortunately, some leaders are intimidated when a strong leader comes in to bring a message. They are afraid to lift him up too much in case the people like him better. There's no place for that in the kingdom of God and let me tell you, as the speaker, it can take a full half an hour before you get through to the hearts of the people.

Who loses out in the end? You? No, the people lose out because of your pride and arrogance.

So get yourself out of the way and be as Jesus was when He washed the feet of His disciples. Bend down and serve a little. By doing this you will raise yourself up in the eyes of the people. The speaker in turn will lift you up in the sight of the people. You can work as a team.

Some Pointers on What to Share

You want to share something personal about the speaker. Let's say for example, you are really blessed and you got an Apostle to come to your meeting. This is a rare moment in itself. You dragged him there and there he is in the meeting.

It is possible that there are a lot of people there that don't really know him. Depending on your relationship with the Apostle will depend upon how you introduce him.

Say for example that I had Apostle Les attend one of my seminars. I would introduce him by saying,

"I'm very proud to introduce my spiritual father to you today. I know that I have personally received a lot from his ministry. It has made me into what I am for the Lord.

I know that as he shares now, that if you could open up your hearts you will receive more in this next hour that will empower you, that will encourage you than you have received in the last year of your Christian walk.

I know from experience that Apostle Les doesn't share just what's in his head. What he's going to share with you today is something he has lived and he shares it with power. There are so many around the world today whose lives have been transformed through his ministry.

So it is an honor for me, to be able to sit in this meeting with you today to receive from him. It's a rare opportunity and I know you guys have been as excited as me!

So let's give him a really warm welcome, let him know how much we love him and let's get ready to receive."

After an introduction like that, you want me to move over and have Les take over now, don't you? You know he could probably just stand up there now and say, "Howdy" and the people would say, "I feel the anointing," because I've prepared their hearts.

From the minute he stands up, the people's hearts will be ready to receive, which means he is going to stand in a greater anointing. In turn this means they are going to be doubly blessed.

By doing this you are setting an example for them to follow. When it is your turn to stand up and speak, you can only hope that you will have somebody as good as you introducing yourself.

Who is Really in Charge?

As you are taking charge and leading your sheep through green meadows and having a good time, never forget who is really in charge.

Jesus is in charge. He is the one who has enabled you. Never forget that. I think sometimes you get so wound up with administration that you say "Look Holy Spirit, I've got my notes here for the announcements, so if you could move between points 3 and 4 that would be great."

No, you fit into the Lord's plan – not the other way around.

It is good to be prepared and to have a good message structured homiletically with your points neatly listed as A, B, C. There are times though when the Lord will decide half way through your structure that He wants to mess things up a bit.

I remember I had this perfect meeting planned for a conference we were invited to. I was proud of my notes. They were great notes. We had just got through the praise and worship and I had been introduced. I stood up to share and I ended up sharing prophetically. I thought, "Okay well that's good, but I sure hope I can get to my notes soon."

Nope... the Lord kept giving me prophetic revelation. After a while I thought, "Lord this is going a bit long now... I've got my notes!"

The Lord said, "Do you know what I think of your notes? I'll talk to you later about what I think about your notes…. Right now you minister to my people!"

I didn't get to preach that day, but I ended up ministering to a lot of people there. It was a great meeting and it was just what God wanted.

So come prepared. Find some balance there. You get these prophetic types that think, let's just dance through this whole meeting while everyone else wonders what is going on.

Then you've got those business types who strategize from point A to C. You need to find a bit of a way through the middle there.

Have your good structure, but don't be afraid to throw it out of the window if God says so.

The Failsafe Approach

Those notes are your ultimate failsafe. If it turns out to be a really bad meeting, you are terribly un-anointed and the speaker turns out to be the worst idea you ever had, we thank the Lord for the notes. At times like that, your notes are sometimes the only thing that will get you through to the end of the meeting.

And so I promise not to leave you hanging. In the next chapter I will tell you exactly how to put those notes together and how to preach them.

CHAPTER 12

Preparing & Presenting a Sermon

Chapter 12 – Preparing & Presenting a Sermon

I had one great fear when I stood up to preach for the first time. Now I know you should not fear when presenting the Word of God, but I challenge anyone not to feel butterflies the size of Volkswagens in your belly the first time you stand up to preach.

I sat under my father ever since I was old enough to throw my rattle out the crib, so I knew what good preaching was. I knew the principles and how to put my notes together. I had learned from the best, but even so, my greatest fear was that I would be boring.

Do not ask me where that fear came from. Perhaps it came from the time I attended a Methodist church and fell asleep with my friends during the early morning service. I swallowed hard imagining what it must feel like to have someone fall asleep while I preached. Thinking about that almost made me feel sorry for that Methodist preacher. Well... almost.

You see it is one thing to be anointed and another to be able to structure that anointing and release it in power. When someone makes a bomb, he does not just throw all the pieces together and hope that it works. In fact, some of the elements of a bomb are completely harmless by themselves.

No, to get the full destructive power out of a bomb, you need all the right elements and you need to put them together in a very specific way. Preparing and presenting the Word of God is very much like that.

You have the potential to set off a bomb with what God has given to you. You have all the elements for that bomb. You have the anointing, wisdom and knowledge. But do you know how to put that bomb together to make all that good stuff effective?

You Are a Bomb Waiting to Happen

Well that is what I am going to teach you in this chapter. I am going to teach you to ignite a bomb the next time you stand up to preach.

Preparing Your Notes Step 1... 2... 3

You know how I love to be the step 1... 2... 3 queen and I am going to give it my all in this chapter. Like I said before, having well-structured notes is a lifesaver. We would all like to think that every time we stand up that the anointing will be there and that everything will just "flow." The truth of the matter is though, that everyone has a bad day sooner or later.

There are times when you will be flowing powerfully in the anointing and then there will be a sudden phase of warfare that will cause you to lose your thought in mid-revelation.

What I am about to teach you falls under the doctrine of Homiletics and you might have already done a study of this on your own. To help you out here I am going to share with you how I prepare my own messages and at the end of this chapter I will include an example of one of my sermon notes for you to see for yourself.

Step 1: Your Topic

Someone asked a famous preacher once how long it took for him to prepare his notes. The person was expecting an answer such as "30 minutes" or "A few hours." Instead the preacher looked at the man and said, "Forty years."

No greater truth was ever spoken when it comes to preaching. When you stand up to preach, you are not just throwing some notes together. Rather you are sharing what you know through what you have lived in personal experience.

So when I come to presenting a sermon, the first thing I ask myself is, "What am I living right now?"

Apostle Paul was king on this one. Read through his Epistles and you will see how often he talks in present tense. He does not tell you about stuff he lived years ago. Rather he speaks about what is living and breathing.

Not only did he teach from his own experience, but he also spoke about what he was going through at that time. As a result, his teaching was relevant and just what the people needed right then.

Fresh Manna

When Craig and I were in Germany we had a chance to visit a famous castle there called Hohenschwangau. In one of the rooms they had a loaf of bread on display that had been a gift to one of the kings.

The bread was 200 years old and perfectly preserved. As perfect as it looked though, it was as hard as rock. It might have made a good meal "back in the day" but it had long since lost its nutritional value.

The same can be said of many preachers today. Still preaching the same message since they were first saved, their bread has long become stale. I have had the privilege to read over some of the old great works of mighty men of God. Spurgeon, Moody and Watchman Nee were all amazing men.

However, until I lived the principles they spoke of myself, all of that bread was stale in my hand. I could try to re-preach their stuff and it might even look like bread, but would it feed? No, that bread is stale unless it comes with fresh revelation.

You cannot pick out a sermon note from last year and think that it will feed the people in the same way now as it did back then. That is why when picking a sermon, you have to preach what you are living right now or have lived recently.

Preach a "Now" Word

When you do this, you will realize something quite startling. You will realize that you have been living just what the people needed to hear. When Apostle Paul preached his sermons, it was just what the people needed to hear.

Read the book of James and there will be no doubt in your mind that what he was speaking of was just what everyone was living at the time. You see the Lord is putting you up there because His people have a need. You are like Moses that has been called back to Egypt only because the people were crying out!

If this is the case, you can rest assured that everything you have been living right now is just what the people need to be taught on.

I experience this before every seminar we minister at. Suddenly a month or so before I am scheduled to preach at a seminar, I start living what I am going to teach. Have you ever wondered why you always "live" something when you read one of our books?

It is because we just lived it and as a result that very anointing is captured in it and you live it. Do you want to see real change in the church? Then preach a "now" word. You can only do that though if you have lived the "now" word for yourself.

Preparing & Presenting a Sermon — Page | 269

Picking Out Scriptures

Before you sit down to write your thoughts on paper, put together all the scriptures that are relevant to your topic. Make a nice long list and write them or type them out somewhere.

It is very unlikely that you will use these, but they are handy to have ahead of time as you put your notes together. If you have been living your topic, then you would already have some scriptures that God has been teaching you. Make a note of these.

If you feel that you need more, pick up a good bible program and do a little search on your topic. Pull out all the scriptures that catch your eye. Once you have done that, put them aside and forget about them for now. You will know which ones to pick out as you start putting your notes together.

Step 2: Putting Your Notes Together

There are three parts to a sermon note. These are the Introduction, Main Part and Conclusion. Begin by typing out those three words in a word processor document.

Just by putting those three large headings on your page, you are putting together a skeleton to hang your notes on. It immediately gives you a structure. In fact, why don't you do that right now?

Pull out a piece of paper and write the following three headings on it nice and clearly:

INTRODUCTION

MAIN PART

CONCLUSION

Setting Your Goal

Now even though it seems logical that you will start with your introduction, you need to start about thinking what you want to accomplish. Let us say for example that you have been learning lately about how to live by faith. If this is the case, what is the point of your message?

At the end of the message, you want your hearer to have an understanding of how to trust God in faith for every need in their lives. With this goal in sight, you now have a direction for the rest of your message.

Introduction

I am ruthless. If you do not catch my attention in the first five minutes of your message, you will begin to lose me. Others might be more forgiving (especially if they have no exits close to their seat and have no choice but to sit and listen).

I will say it to you straight though – if you do not catch the hearer's attention right away, you will find it hard to get it later. Jesus sure knew how to open up a sermon.

He walked into a temple. He opened up the Scripture and read from the book of Isaiah. He closed the Book.

Pregnant pause.

Everyone's eyes were glued to him. Looking back, He said, "This day the scripture is fulfilled in your ears" (Luke 4:21)

All right, we can hope that after presenting such a profound introduction that our congregation also doesn't want to throw us off a cliff, but you have to admit that Jesus sure had style. He got their attention and He caught it so well that we remember it a few thousand years later.

The Attention Getter

So for your introduction you want to open with something that will catch the hearer's attention. You can do this in a number of ways. I personally like to take one of these three approaches.

1. Say Something Dramatic

We already covered that with Jesus. His opening line was dramatic and caught the attention of everyone. I like to pick out lines that are politically incorrect, controversial or that conjure up images that people will remember.

This kind of approach is more for someone that likes to be bold and expressive.

2. Ask a Question

This is one of the best ways to get attention and if you have not used this approach before, then I suggest that you do it. There are some things to keep in mind though.

Do not ask a question that has a "yes" or "no" answer. You need to ask a question that provokes the people to think.

Using the example of "living by faith", you could ask a question such as, "Why are your prayers not being answered right now?"

This makes the hearer think. Do not ask, "Would you like to have more faith?" Boring! So do not use rhetorical questions.

Ask a question that makes them ponder and also gives them a promise that you are going to answer it by the end of your sermon. This is a quick and very effective attention getter. Use it the next time you have to preach or even present something at work.

3. Share a Story

This is the one I use the most. In fact, at the beginning of every chapter you will see that I share a story or illustration. I take my cue from Jesus who was the master at parables. The Word says that He did not open His mouth except by parables.

Have you ever thought why He did this? It is because we remember pictures. The Lord made us humans with a keen perception of imagery. We have no problem at all imagining something. You might remember some numbers and birth dates, but you will not forget a picture that a preacher painted.

If you want people to remember what you shared, then share a picture. Think about the story I just shared about of that 200-year-old bread. You have no problem remembering that picture do you? In fact, the next time that you prepare a sermon I hope you remember it and remember my point, "Fresh manna! Preach what you are living!"

Picking Out Your First Scriptures

Now that you have your opening line put together, decide if you want to share a scripture like Jesus did before your "bold statement" or if you want to leave it for after your illustration.

Pick up your notes and pick out no more than 3 scriptures that are relevant to your topic and paste them where you will need them. I suggest including the full scripture and not just the reference. This makes it a lot easier for you than flipping through pages.

You are set! The introduction part of your sermon note is now complete and you are ready to transition into the main part.

Main Part

Nothing gives you a greater sinking feeling in the pit of your belly than seeing a preacher stand up, with sermon notes that are 15 pages long. Even though he might be a good teacher, you cannot help but feel that you have you brace yourself for the long haul.

Here are some easy steps to follow that will keep your notes short and also allow for the Holy Spirit to add to them as you are speaking.

Main Points

Pick out no more than three main points for your notes. If you are speaking on faith, you might want to address specific points. In which case, your three main points could be:

> A. Faith for Healing
>
> B. Faith for Finances
>
> C. Faith for Spiritual Gifts

Of course that is just a guideline. You might want to preach on other aspects. When you pick out no more than three main "legs" of your sermon note, filling in the rest is quite easy.

So go ahead right now and using the topic you have chosen for your message, write down three main points for it.

Sub Points

This is where you will start to fill in the meat of your message. Under each of your main points begin to list the things you want to cover.

Let us take the C. "Faith for Spiritual Gifts" part of your sermon.

What do you want to teach about this point? I can think of a few:

    a. Gifts are for Every Believer

    b. Desire is Needed

    c. Faith and Love

Can you think of any other points I have left out? For now, let us look at these three principles and flesh them out a bit more shall we?

a. Gifts are for Every Believer

1 Cor 14:5 I want you all to speak with tongues, but I would prefer it if you prophesied: for he that prophesies is greater than he that speaks with tongues, unless he interprets, that the church might be built up.

- Paul is speaking to all believers
- God wants to grant your request
- God does not play favorites

b. Desire is Needed

1 Corinthians 14:39 Therefore, brothers, earnestly desire to prophesy, and do not forbid speaking with tongues.

- Earnest desire releases your faith
- Do you have desire?
- Then God wants to grant you your request!

c. Faith and Love

1 Corinthians 13:2 And though I have prophetic[insight], and understand all the hidden things, and all the known things; and though I have absolute faith, so that I could remove mountains, and do not have [agape] love, I am nothing.

- Why do you want to flow in the gifts?
- Unless it is for others, your prayer is useless
- Gifts are for the Body – not you
- Love unlocks the gifts
- The faith of God's people releases you
- Example – Moses sent when people prayed

It All Comes Together

Can you see how nicely the notes are coming together? I also want you to notice that I am not writing long paragraphs in my notes. I am just using short points to jog my memory. Because this is something you have lived, when you stand up, you will speak from experience.

Your notes are simply map to guide you - they are not the entire journey. If you put too much in your notes, you will end up reading them instead of speaking them.

Too many notes will also confuse you. So keep things in point form. They will act as a nice guideline to keep you on track, while giving the Holy Spirit leeway to change your direction at the same time.

Conclusion

If you have done your job correctly, then this is the quickest part of the process and your conclusion will go quickly. I find it very effective to conclude in two ways:

1. Give a project

2. Present a challenge

Either of these conclusions will make sure that your hearer leaves and applies what you have taught them. Because I am a trainer at heart, I often give a project and if I have a small group I like to do the project with them right away.

If you are speaking prophetically though, presenting a challenge is a better way to end. This will drive your point home and make it "their own." Do not be afraid to use the words, "you" and "yours" when preaching and presenting your challenge.

It is way more effective to say, "What are you asking God for right now? What are *you* prepared to do about it?"

If you had to say, "God is challenging us right now and we need to ask ourselves what He wants us to do about it."

It gives them too much room to say, "Ah yes, the preacher must be talking to the guy next to me."

So do not be afraid to put on some pressure. I will share with you a bit more on how to end your sermon correctly. For now, let us go over all the points that I have mentioned so far and put your notes together.

Step 3: How to Close

So, your message has come to an end. You have applied all of my principles. Fantastic! You even remembered all of my principles. I am impressed.

Now the meeting has come to an end and you are thinking, "Whew! Let me go sit down. Man I'm starved, are you hungry? Let's have lunch… what are we having for lunch?"

Apply the Word

I remember a powerful principle that my dad taught me and I never forgot it. He said, "Once you have preached the word is usually when the Holy Spirit moves the most, because now the word is in their heart."

He said to me, "Don't be too quick to end the meeting, because I have seen the Lord move mightily at this time, to prove the word that is in them."

So while their hearts are open, it is the time to let God move. It's the time to wait. This is a fantastic time for the prophetic ministry to flow, because as you have spoken, your word has hit different hearts. These are the times you will get decrees for people. You will get words of encouragement.

The evangelists can convict. These are the times you will see your signs and wonders. There's no point preaching on healing and then breaking for lunch. If you are speaking on healing, you make sure you apply it at the end of your message. They have received the word, you have built up their faith and now it is time to release the anointing. It is the time to pray for the sick.

Unfortunately, we often see it being done the other way around. Before you get up to speak on healing, you pray for healing.

You've got it the wrong way around. Let the word cut the hearts and then you step in with the anointing. Often this is the most powerful part of your meeting.

Only after the Holy Spirit has moved and everything settles down is it time to bring the meeting to a close.

Closing the Meeting

You close the meeting like you opened it. Get their attention, give them direction, and let them look forward to the next meeting.

Something that I like to do is to end with another upbeat song. It gets them motivated. It gets them ready for the next meeting, and everybody digests their food better!

Sermon Summary:

Choosing Your Topic

- What am I living right now?
- What is the goal of my message?

INTRODUCTION

Introduction – What is my opening line?

- Bold statement
- Question
- Illustration

Pick out Scriptures – 2 or 3

MAIN PART

What are my main points?

- Fill out my main points with sub points

- "Flesh out" my sub points with short notes

CONCLUSION

Will I challenge or give a project?

- What challenge will make an impact?
- Will I be doing this project with the group afterwards?

Some Do's and Don'ts in Preaching and Speaking

I have given you a couple of points above on putting your notes together. In fact, I have given you a fantastic recipe to use for baking some good spiritual bread again and again.

Any good recipe is more than a bunch of ingredients though. It also comes with instructions. So, taking the points above I am going to flesh them out with some personal experience and show you a step at a time what to do and especially what *not* to do when baking up your next sermon offering.

Let's Bake Bread Together!

1. DO: Share an Illustration

It can be a picture, story, parable or dream. Call it what you will, but don't start your message without it.

Think about what you have read so far in this book. What pictures come into your mind? It is possible that you are seeing a number of pictures.

You could be seeing a shepherd with his sheep or you see bread fresh out of the oven. Perhaps you just cannot shake that horrible stale 200-year-old bread from your mind. The point is, you see a picture, which means you will remember my message.

Pictures are the eggs and milk for your message. They hold everything together and they mean the difference between remembering your message or not.

2. DO: Use Pregnant Pauses.

We have a term in English called the "pregnant pause." Let me give you a picture of what a "pregnant pause" is.

There is this pregnant woman and she is carrying all out front. She is in her ninth month and she could "pop" at any minute. Her back aches and she is walking with that typical "preggy waddle" that only those who have "been there" can truly understand.

That big heavy baby could drop at any minute. That is a picture of a nice big pause. It is one of those pauses during speech… where… the speaker stops… to look you right in the eye. Standing still and taking a deep breath, allowing the point to sink in, with unwavering gaze.

Just before you think that baby is going to drop, he picks up his point again and continues.

You see, there is a reason they call it a "pregnant pause." It is not an athletic pause. It is not one of those "skinny little women that look like a stick" kind of pause. No, it's a big fat pregnant woman, shaking under the weight thinking, "Please Lord, let today be the day" kind of pause.

When you put... pregnant pauses in your message... it makes an... impact. It makes people want to hear what you have to say.

Now, if you are anything like me who speaks way too quickly, we need that pregnant pause just to breathe! You need to use this especially if you fumble over your words or if you are speaking in a foreign language.

The "Deep and Intelligent" Approach

If you speak too fast and trip over your words, people think you are stupid. However, if you take your time with the pregnant pause, they think you are deep and intelligent.

You can fool them all with one good pregnant pause. Use it!

3. DO: Use High Emotion

No monotones! Take your voice right up high, and take it right down low. Shout this out with me... "Keep! Their! Attention!"

Speak Loudly and Clearly!

If I am an emotive ball of fire you might be thinking "She's crazy" but you will be watching me. You might not even remember what I am saying, but you are entertained and I have your attention. It's an important key.

When you put emotion into what you are saying and you speak loudly and clearly, it is like opening a door in your soul and letting all that anointing out. You forget about thinking too hard and you tap into what is in your spirit.

When you use a lot of emotion, you can't be too controlled. Something just starts coming up from inside of you. The next thing you know, you are being emotional everywhere. This means that the Lord gets a chance to speak, because you are getting your mind out the way and your spirit can start to talk.

Now, I know you are going to feel stupid, especially when you have got a microphone. Even so, do not be too afraid to be loud and proud! When you take that approach then people don't just hear what you have to say, the people will *feel* what you have to say.

Jesus could do it. Did you ever wonder how He kept everyone's attention while standing on a boat preaching to the masses? You can bet he spoke pretty loudly and proudly to keep them from forgetting that they had not eaten lunch.

When you take this attitude on as your own, people may forget what you said sometimes, but they will never forget what they felt as you said it.

This goes together with speaking loudly and clearly. Don't speak too softly because it takes away your presence. It also makes you look insecure. When you mumble and speak softly it says to your audience, "I am not really sure of what I want to say and I don't really feel like being here. But I hope you want to listen to me."

When you come like that, they do not want to listen to you. If you look like you do not want to be there, they do not want to be there either.

So don't just make people listen to you, make them feel you and then they will remember you.

4. DO NOT: Read Long Passages of Scripture

This is especially important if you do not know how to pronounce the words in that passage. Trust me when I say as one having to sit through you fumbling... It hurts!

It's like me reading this passage here and saying,

"Even though I pass through the valley of death... oversh... shadowed by d...d... death..."

It hurts me and it hurts you! So don't do it okay? It would be like me trying to read a scripture in a foreign language and slaughtering it.

That would be crazy. Either you will be laughing at me, or you will be hurting with me.

You know you get these terrible passages sometimes where you've got Melchizedek, Methuselah and Ishbosheth in them. Who can even say Ishbosheth clearly!?

Either pick another passage or learn the correct pronunciation before standing up. If you are going to choose them, then stand in front of a mirror and go over it again and again so that you sound convincing.

If you are feeling uncomfortable when you are reading it wrong, what do you think everyone else feels? They know that you are feeling uncomfortable because they are also feeling uncomfortable.

Spare us all. Choose a different passage or refer to the passage as you speak like my husband Craig often does. In fact, he is a pro at this one. He hates to read long passages so he will often refer to them, allowing the audience to go and look them up later if they want.

So, if you have ever struggled with dyslexia or you battle to read in front of others, you could even just share about the passage.

Perhaps we are breaking some rules here. So what? They get the point. As long as you tell them where the passage is they can even go look it up for themselves. In all honesty, do you really pay attention to that full list of scriptures that are rattled off?

So unless the passage is really central to your message, do not read long passages. Keep it simple. The people will thank you and you will feel more comfortable when you next stand up to preach.

5. DO NOT: Talk Too Fast

This was my bad habit when I first went into ministry and a habit I have to keep working on. I would ramble on with my broad South African accent very, very fast. Nobody understood what I was saying! Go listen to my teaching on *Prophetic Child* - it is awful.

That message is proof that these principles work and that you can change… no matter how long you have been preaching!

This is especially true if you are speaking in a foreign land and have an accent. Rather take your time and speak clearly - the people will be happy to wait for you.

6. DO NOT: Be What You Are Not

We have some fantastic prophets in this ministry. They are powerful, they are anointed and they have a real relationship with Jesus. It always fascinates me however, when they stand up to speak and try to be teachers.

I can't figure it. They are anointed. They are powerful and then… they are in deception. They mess up because they think, "Everybody else is being a teacher and so I should be a teacher too".

So the bottom-line here? Unless the Lord is leading you into the teaching ministry, stick with what you know.

On the other hand, if you are a good teacher, be a good teacher!

Don't think, "It's not fair! The prophets get all the attention. They get to 'chase the rabbit' and run through their messages and I have to stick to my boring notes. That's it! No notes this week! I have decided I am going to be prophetic. I am going to stand up there and just talk."

Oh yeah, you will talk all right. You will talk in circles for an hour. By the end of your message you won't know what you spoke about and the people will not know what you spoke about.

They will be hurrying out the door at the end of the meeting, trying not to catch your eye so they don't have to lie and say something nice about your message.

The Church needs prophets and it needs teachers. It also needs evangelists and pastors. I've even heard that it even needs apostles. What it does not need is someone trying to be something they are not.

So be confident in what you are because the Church needs you. There is nothing better than the awesome feeling that comes from knowing you stood up and you delivered the word of God under the anointing. To see God move, and people touched by it, charges you.

By Colette Toach

You don't want to leave a meeting thinking, "I missed it" just because you were trying to be clever and act like everybody else. Just be what you are. Enjoy what you are doing.

7. DO: Have an Other-Orientation

Finally, stand up with an other-orientation to meet the needs of the people.

Get yourself out of the way and know that you are there to feed God's sheep. You are not there to have a lamb barbeque.

When you stand up to meet your own needs you are saying, "I am going to stand up and tell everyone how great I am. That's a nice little lamb there. I'm going to put him on a skewer. I'm going to stoke a nice fire here... yumm... lamb chops! I'm going to roast him nicely and have a good meal."

God's people are not there to meet your need for recognition or to make you feel good about yourself. You are there to feed them grass and to take them to the water, not the other way around.

If your motivation is to meet your need it doesn't matter how good your notes are, or even how good you speak. You haven't done what God sent you there to do.

I have given you a lot to think about and with every recipe you can feel free to tweak it to fit your personal taste. I have given you a structure, but what you put into it can only be what God has given to you.

Below are the sermon notes for a teaching I did on *How to Get People to Follow You* in fact it is part of what I based my book on with that title. Feel free to use the structure and to put your own points in.

Series: How to Get People To Follow You

Get Your Boat Into The Water.

INTRODUCTION

Illustration: The beauty of the sailing ship is seen when it is on the water (Not in dry docks).

> *Matthew 13:1 On the same day Jesus went out of the house and sat by the sea.*
>
> *2 And great multitudes were gathered together to Him, so that He got into a boat and sat; and the whole multitude stood on the shore.*
>
> *Matthew 28:19 Go therefore and make disciples of all the nations, baptizing them in the name of the Father and of the Son and of the Holy Spirit,*

MAIN PART

A. Plot the Course

By Colette Toach

a. Where Are You Going? Jesus knew the point of His birth and death.

- How will you know when you are there?
- Not enough to have a fire or a desire.
- You must have a direction from God.

b. What Are Your Goals? Jesus knew what He was born to do.

- What will it look like when you get there?
- Your ministry goal or vision.
- Your core desire.
- Your hopes for the future.
- How you want the church to look.

c. What Are Your Capabilities? Jesus knew what He had.

- What are you qualified to do?
- What anointing do you have?
- Do not imitate others.
- Know YOUR call and destination.

B. Plan the Trip

a. What Will You Need?

- Spiritual and natural things.
- Resources, materials
- A clear picture of the price.

b. What Do You Have to Offer That Others Do Not?
Woman at the well

> *Luke 2: 47 And all who heard Him were astonished at His understanding and answers.*

- Why SHOULD people follow?
- What do you have to impart to others?
- Natural abilities.
- Gained knowledge and wisdom.
- Strength of Character.
- The ability to handle rejection.
- The ability to see the needs others have.
- Spiritual strengths

- Received spiritual training if you have a fivefold calling.

C. Set Sail

a. Having Courage and Confidence

John 12:32 And I, if I am lifted up from the earth, will draw all peoples to Myself.

- Stand up and be noticed.//
- To step out ahead of others.
- To be the FIRST to step out
- No longer waiting.
- Take the first step.
- Jesus did not wait for others - He took the first step.

b. Catching the Wind.

- You are not waiting for God
- God is waiting for you
- Once your boat is in the water, God can direct it.
- GET MOVING!

CONCLUSION

- You cannot wait for others to follow before you lead.

- Lead first and others will follow.

- Joshua did not take a poll to see who wanted to cross the Jordan.

- He gave the order

- The others followed.

- If they did not – they lost out!

- Challenge: Set your Sights

- Prepare yourself

- Step out and launch!

By Colette Toach

CHAPTER 13

How to Lead Worship

Chapter 13 – How to Lead Worship

Forget about the Beetles or Elvis Presley. The man that could "bring down the house" in no uncertain terms was King David himself.

> *2 Samuel 6:14 Then David danced before the Lord with all his might; and David was wearing a linen ephod.*
>
> *15 So David and all the house of Israel brought up the ark of the Lord with shouting and with the sound of the trumpet.*

The Most Famous Praise Service Ever

This passage outlines the moment in history I am talking about. It brought the house down. It was the most outstanding moment of his career. In fact, he danced so hard that all of Israel followed him. He brought the presence of God into Israel.

This is a fantastic picture of what God has given you to do as a worship leader.

When you are leading a meeting you are not just trying to get past the first part so we can get onto the preaching.

Unfortunately, the problem is when you are really bad at leading worship is that you do it because you have to. When you have this attitude, you want to get it out of the way as quickly as possible so you can get onto the main part of the meeting.

That's not what it should be like at all. Praise and worship sets the stage for what the rest of the meeting will be like. It prepares the groundwork.

If you do not introduce the meeting correctly, then the rest of the meeting will fall flat.

Now, I'm not going to teach you how to play guitar. Instead, I want to show you how to take what you already know and to present it in praise and worship.

How to Get Started

All the announcements have been done and there's that little uncomfortable silence that we all know so well, where the speaker hands over to the worship leader.

Your heart is beating and your stomach is turning as you stand up in front of everybody.

It's up to you now. It's in your hands. The question is - what are you going to do about it?

1. Pull Out the Megaphone

The first picture I have for you is of a megaphone. Imagine that you are standing on one side of a soccer field and there is somebody else on the other side.

They try to get your attention by whispering really quietly to you. Do you think you will be able to hear what they are saying - never mind follow their orders?

They are trying to get your attention with a soft, mousy voice. They whisper, "We're going to worship the Lord now ladies and gentlemen. Please join me."

If I called to you like that, would you feel like joining me? Forget it! I don't feel like joining me!

No, you need to shout! So instead of whispering, pull out your megaphone and shout, "HEY YOU! WE'RE HAVING A WORSHIP MEETING HERE! ARE YOU GOING TO JOIN ME?" Now you have my attention.

You've got to have something to shout about! "Let's shout! Let's worship the Lord - ladies and gentlemen! We serve a wonderful God and I'm so full of joy this evening I cannot wait to share it with you! Tada! Here I am and in me is the living God. Look at me!"

How are you approaching your worship?

Do NOT Make This Mistake

Picture this with me if you will.

The worship leader stands up front. He has his notes neatly stacked in front of him. Not completely sure of himself and in a quiet monotone voice he says,

"Okay... we are going to begin now.... with the song..." in mid-sentence he stops to shuffle through his notes, because somehow the one he wanted to start with fell off the pile. Finally finding it, he continues, "It's called, 'Burn Fire Burn.'"

To prolong the suffering, he starts to look around at the rest of the team to make sure that they have their notes and that everyone is ready to get started.

Everyone looks ready and it is time to begin. The leader does a quick strum through each of the notes quickly, to check to see if his guitar is sounding good, thinking, "Ok, I think I have it now."

Clearing his throat, he begins to sing, keeping his eyes firmly fixed to the song sheet. Too afraid to come across overly loud through the sound system the melody comes out flat and un-emotive. "It is time to tap into the spirit," he thinks. So he closes his eyes and gets "swept away" in the moment.

He looks really spiritual at this point in time.

Some people think, wow, he is really in the spirit there.

And maybe our worship leader thinks that he is in the spirit there... unfortunately for him though, everybody else sitting on the other side of him, is bored out of their minds!

The Hard Truth

Let's go behind the scenes now and let me explain things to you as someone sitting and watching as you go through this process. As you are trying to find your notes, the people are starting to feel uncomfortable.

In fact, they are starting to feel embarrassed for you. Take charge! Get their attention. Pick up that microphone and it doesn't even matter what you say - it's really how you say it.

Never forget you are presenting the Lord to them. Be proud of that! Come already in the spirit. Don't come and think, "Well let's hope I get in the spirit by the first song."

If you do not come already in the spirit, instead of singing the melody of the first song effectively, at the back of your mind you will really be singing, "Oh Lord, please help me!"

He won't. You should have been in the spirit before you came. Newsflash! You didn't come to get your need met - you came to get *their* need met. So you come loud and you come proud and don't close your eyes.

Use Emotion

Look at the people. Talk to the people and when you are staring them right in the face, they have no choice but to stare right back at you. What are they going to see when they stare back at you?

Will they see a plain-faced, un-emotive, "Well I hope you want to praise God now?"

No, come on! I'm not inspired to praise!

Instead, let them see a smile and some joy! Let them see some wrinkles on your face. Let them see gums. I don't care how un-emotive you are, you and I both know that you have gums. Let's see them huh? How much effort does it take to smile?

Why don't we do it right now? Smile your biggest smile right now as you are reading this. Scare the guy who walks into the room with that smile. Did that feel so bad?

Now when that poor unsuspecting person walked in on you grinning like a Cheshire cat, could they ignore you? No, they could not. In fact, I bet that they smiled right on back. Even if they were having a bad day, you would have pulled at least a little twitch at the corners of their mouth out of them. You can't help yourself. When someone smiles at you, you just want to smile back.

If you want people to respond to you, you have to give them something to respond to. Emotion! Emotion will get attention.

Now I know you are going to feel stupid. I know I did. Just so you know, when I preached this message live I felt like a real idiot standing and grinning like that. But you know what? You'd be surprised how quickly you get used to feeling like an idiot.

In fact, you will even start to enjoy it and the emotion that you had to "put on" at the beginning, becomes natural to you.

When this happens, you will begin to feel the power, because when you let the emotion out, you open up a door in your soul that leads to your spirit. There is power inside of your spirit and when you open that door it all comes gushing out.

2. Keep Your Bait Handy

There is a fisherman at the side of a lake. He throws his fishing line into the water and it has a nice big lump of worms on it, all squirming on the hook.

So there they are, dangling in the water. One of the fat worms is throwing what looks like an electric shock kind of twitch. It is not long and a fish comes along gliding through the water with one thought in its mind, "Yum... dinner." As he is about to take a nice big bite the fisherman pulls on the line just a bit and the hook darts away from the fish.

"Huh? Where did it go?" The fish is looking for it again, willing to give it another try. There is no way he is giving up on that juicy worm doing the "electric shock" dance there.

The fisherman can keep the fish interested for a long time if he plays it right.

Can you see the worms dangling on that hook? This is a picture of what you need if you want to lead God's people into the Throne Room of God.

Keep the Attention

You have to keep their attention. Again, the best way to do it is to keep the emotions high.

If you are going to praise, praise hard. If you are going to worship, then worship hard. It might seem like overkill to you, but it will look just barely normal to everybody else.

Now as you have captured their attention for the first time, you need to keep it.

How to Lose Attention

Let us pick on our worship leader from before as he decides to sing a song that he usually struggles to play on the guitar. Picking out each chord carefully, he still ends up fumbling because for some reason B7 has just never been a chord that he could get right.

Trying to just get through the song, he presses through with the singing, even though the chord he is playing is in direct rebellion to the melody he is trying to whisper out.

You are feeling uncomfortable for him. It hurts you to watch him mess it up so bad.

But you know why he is messing it up? He is failing because he is thinking too much.

Do not fall into the trap of trying so hard to get the chords right that you are not thinking about the people. If you try to sing a song and play an instrument and you feel insecure about what you are playing, it will show.

Do not think that you can just hide it from people. They will pick it up.

Where to Look

So try to look at the chords as little as possible. Learn the chords properly, get your eyes off your fingers, get them off your notes and look at the people and pour out with your spirit.

If you are singing with emotive confidence and you do happen to mess up, as long as you feel secure, it will not matter. If you are singing with conviction and the anointing is there, a little bump in the road like that will not derail you.

It doesn't matter then if you play the wrong chord. Who cares? They are so busy joining you and having fun, that they don't care. Do your practicing at home. When you come to worship, you come to give.

In-Between the Songs

Now there's another thing that everybody does that makes things uncomfortable.

You come to the end of your song. You sang it with high emotion and everyone feels like jumping and praising God. You end the song dead and then look down as you flip through your notes searching for the next one.

You give everyone an insecure smile, "Hi, just trying to find my place."

Dead silence. The people were all built up and waiting to see what will happen next and guess what happens next… absolutely nothing!

It's like watching a movie and they build up the suspense with the music and then suddenly the music stops to reveal… absolutely nothing. Nobody jumps out and grabs the good guy. The scene just changes to something else. It leaves you thinking, "Hello? I was built up! I was ready and… I was dropped."

That's what you do every time you give long silences between songs.

Help is on the Way

Now there are two things that you can do to prevent this. If you've got a hundred pages to page through and you need your time and you are extremely analytical and you don't know how to page and talk at the same time, then get somebody else in the band to at least play music in between the songs.

This works especially well if it is going to be a very long pause. Don't give that sudden broken silence. It makes people feel uncomfortable. If they are uncomfortable, it breaks the spirit.

The best solution is what you will see us doing and that is to talk between the songs. You see, you've still got your bait dangling. "Come on guys, come on fishy. I am taking you to the next point here. See the little worm dangling there? There's more good stuff coming your way."

Oh that little fish is going to keep swimming.

If you suddenly pull the worms out of the water, that fish is gone. It's looking around and saying, "Where did the bait go?" You lost him - he is out of here.

Keep the bait. Take them from song to song.

3. You Are the One Driving

My husband gave me some wonderful advice when I first started learning to drive. (Yes, my husband taught me to drive, which is a sure testimony to the "longsuffering" fruit of the spirit that is evident in him.)

I got so stressed when there were cars behind me, especially if I was going too slowly. So I kept going faster and faster. Okay, later on that still continued as a deliberate habit, but at the time, it was because I was stressed. Craig said to me "You are in front of them. You are driving this car. You go as slow or as fast as you want. It is for them to change lanes or follow you."

It's the same thing with worship. I have given you these nice silver keys, can you hear them ringing? I have dropped them into your hand and you have slipped into the comfy bucket seat of a nice Ferrari.

You are in control. Don't feel that you have to rush through the songs and think, "Let's get to the next song as quickly as possible!"

By Colette Toach

Fifteen minutes later you have sung all the songs, you are out of breath and everybody else is out of breath with you.

You are exhausted. They are exhausted and everybody is thinking, "What just happened?"

The worst part is that you don't sense the flow of the Spirit that way. When you are rushing through it you are not going to sense what God is saying.

You wonder why you did not sense the Spirit of God or hear His voice through the service. Well you ran so fast, He couldn't keep up with you! Chill out. Imagine you are driving in that Ferrari and you are out on the open road, somewhere in the country, in a place that you have never been before.

Now for most of us (unlike all you crazy city drivers) we are going to slow down a little. We are going to look around a bit to take in the scenery.

Every now and then it's fun to put your foot to the accelerator and to go. I don't mean that you should drag through the meeting so much that people are looking at their watches. The point is to be in control.

You are the one driving here and if you want to sing that song three times, then sing it three times. If the Lord does not want you to sing any more songs, then don't sing any more songs. Don't feel pushed thinking that you have to do it the same way every week. The

Lord may want you to skip five songs and go straight to the worship.

Perhaps you have one of those songs that has a dreaded B7th in it. Now I know B7 isn't really a bad chord. It's quite a nice chord… for everyone else. For me however, B7th and I have never really been good friends. I can play every other chord, but the B7…

And so every now and again we will come to one of "those" songs. The problem is whoever chose the songs for this service obviously loves B7. I can only take B7 so much and then I've had it and now there's the 5th song with a B7 every second chord and I feel the stress rising up.

You singers out there can relate to what I am talking about as well. You know you get those songs that just hit your "break" perfectly. When you are in the flow you can sing through the break and it sounds great. Other times, when you have been pushing your voice, all that comes out is a nasty squeak.

Now I have a choice to make. I could struggle through that song, but everybody will have to struggle through it with me.

It is not fun! It is not comfortable. You spend a good part of the song dreading "that" part in the song where your voice usually rebels and does what it wants.

Let it go. Go past the song - don't sing it. It doesn't matter. You're getting so stressed about getting all the protocol right.

It's like driving that nice Ferrari. If you want to stop off at the side of the road and look at the lake - you can. If you want to overtake that horrible looking Fiat - you can. It's in your hands and it's better if you are relaxed.

In our ministry we write all of our own songs, so I know I have often had this problem myself. I start with all this great gusto on a song and then half way through the song, I catch the eye of the person who wrote it. This look passes between us and we both are thinking the same thing, "You are singing it all wrong!"

I look back at him apologetically and in that look I am saying to him, "I know I am singing it wrong, but I'm half way through the song – I can't stop now! I have to push through!"

Now, I'm not going to be stupid so that when I come to the end of the song… that I sing it all over again! I can only take so much punishment!

Unfortunately, I've seen song leaders do this, "Well we know this is a favorite song and usually we sing it twice and the chorus three times. So that is what we are going to do. We are going to suffer for a full 5 – 7 minutes together… "

So while you are suffering, the people are suffering with you.

The Minister's Handbook

That doesn't feel like a nice drive through the country. That feels like sitting in rush hour traffic for over an hour.

When you take control of the meeting and you rest, you put God in control of the meeting. This is where you let the Spirit of God lead. You will start feeling the Lord move the most as you transition from praise to worship usually.

4. Time for God to Move - Worship

Perhaps, you got up to lead worship feeling a little bit unprepared, but you smiled your smile, you showed your gums, everybody smiled back at you and as you started pumping out some of that emotion you started feeling the anointing come.

Through the praise everyone started to come into unity. Then, as everybody got into unity the corporate anointing began to flow. You see that is the purpose of praise and why all of that high emotion is so important. It gets the people into the same spirit and brings unity.

What you have done is you have actually led them into the presence of the Lord. They are no longer your audience. They are His audience now.

Just imagine that you are a beautiful thoroughbred horse. You have got this beautiful black shiny coat. Your head is held high and the sun is on your back. Your handler is nearby and he has his hands on the reins. He is leading you around as you walk.

You follow where he leads. He could climb on your back. You could take a nice walk through the country together. You are his legs. But it's him that controls the direction.

He nudges a little bit this way and you go to the right. He digs his heels in and you know that it's time to canter. It's for him to control the reigns and for you to follow. In the same way it is now for you to give God the control. Let Him be the handler and you just go to where He tells you. Be His vehicle in the meeting to lead God's people into His presence.

If you are rested in your leadership, you will know where to go. You should not be feeling pressured. You will be in a place where you can feel the nudging of the Holy Spirit now. The worship is the most important part of the meeting.

You could make it or break it right here.

Now don't do like I did the first time. I did great, built everybody up, and I thought, "You know I have already gone 35 minutes." I looked around at everybody in the band and I thought to myself, "I know what they are thinking. 'She is going to take another hour again. What is it with Colette? She goes on and on in the worship. In fact, her worship sessions are longer than anybody else's!'"

I felt sweat trickling down my back. I started to get nervous. I thought, "Alright, let's quickly get to the end."

So while everybody was all built up nicely - I sang one song of worship and, "Whew it's over! Bye guys!"

Everyone was brought out of the spirit with a bang thinking, "What just happened?" They were left hanging.

When this happens you feel, "Well, that was a great meal, but I only took one mouthful and the waiter whipped the plate out from under me. Where did it go? I was just starting to enjoy it."

Again, you are in control of the meeting. If you worship for another hour, it's up to you and the Lord. If they don't like it, they can go to another church. If my team doesn't like it, they can kick me out of the band. I don't care, but this is what God wants me to do.

Don't stop until you have finished the job. Don't feel uncomfortable as you come to the worship because you see things quiet down a lot. Do not think, "Well the Lord didn't' give a prophetic word in the last 15 seconds, so let's end."

There are people with problems attending that meeting. They have had a bad week. Sometimes the best part of the meeting is the ten minutes you spend quietly in the Lord's presence. Once you have come to the end of your songs it's all right to just play some music for a little while.

Leading Through Worship

There are a couple of things that I enjoy doing during worship. Either, I will go into free worship in the spirit, or if I feel the Lord wants to say something, it's nice if you can get somebody else in the band just to play a bit of music on the piano or the guitar.

It doesn't even matter if you don't say anything. Wait on the Lord. This is the most important part of the meeting. Let the Lord speak. You shouted off your mouth for 40 minutes, let Him have His two minutes. If you will just allow yourself to wait, the Lord might give you a word to share.

Some thoughts may come to you that you want to share, but this is also an opportunity for the Fivefold Ministry to share and particularly the prophets may have a word from the Lord and you should give the Lord the opportunity to talk.

Flowing in Prophetic Ministry

It's common in many churches that nobody stands up to speak.

Now I know you think it's the other way around, but it's not always true. More often than not there is a silence that leads to just more silence. Again you are in control of the meeting. It's for you to say, "If you have got something to share, please share it."

Often the Lord is speaking, but the person is not sure if it is the right time, so it is good to give a bit of encouragement if you feel there is a word.

Now if you feel that there is a word and no one brings it, you don't just pack up and walk away. You bring the word. You are in charge of the meeting and if you put yourself in that position, God will give you the word.

5. Handing Over the Baton

Everything has gone well so far. You've had your praise. You announced yourself with a loudspeaker – let's worship.

Then you cast your fishing rod with your worms on the hook and the little fish have followed you all the way to worship.

Then you felt the move of the spirit. You were that beautiful stallion that the Lord led so perfectly and now you have come to the end. This again is such an important phase. Because it is time now to hand over.

You are like a runner and you look good. Come on, dream with me a little. You are nice and firm and buff. You are running and you feel the wind in your face. You are running a relay race and you have got the baton in your hand.

You see the next runner just ahead of you and he's sitting waiting for you to hand him the baton so that he can finish the race.

You don't run until you are ten meters away, stop, and throw the baton at him! There goes the poor runner... and there goes the whole meeting.

The other runner has to find where the baton is and try to get up and start running again with a big lump on his head.

No, you need to hand it over nicely. Like anyone knows, you prepare to hand that baton over way before you get to him. You don't slow down to a jog. In fact, you run the hardest to get there. You run as fast as you can and you reach over and you hand it to him. For a short moment the two of you run together, until he has it in his hand.

This is the mistake that some worship leaders make. The worship is over and a sweet silence hangs in the room. Not even the dogs are barking in the property next door like they usually do. The Lord has said His piece and it is time to get into the Word.

You need to bring the people up again. You can't stop ten meters too short and throw the baton. This is the time for your second wind. You take a deep breath and you run hard with full emotion. That is why we often end on an upbeat song.

You don't want to leave the meeting on a low note. You want to end it on a high. Even if you don't sing an upbeat song at the very end, you can at least relay some of that emotion using speech.

But you know what some people do? They come to the end of the meeting. There has been a beautiful move of the Spirit. They open their eyes and think, "Okay, what do I do now?"

So you look over to the preacher. You give him "the eye." Hopefully he knows what "the eye" is. Usually "the eye" means, "get over here and take the microphone."

Once again there is this uncomfortable silence as the preacher tries to find his notes. And so our poor speaker gets up there with a bump on his head as the meeting is landed on him just like that.

Everybody starts fidgeting and a hum of noise starts to rise. And so he has to pick up the pieces and try to bring it all back together.

I had this once at a seminar and it was a terrible experience. The worship ended on a beautiful note and there was a sweet presence of the Lord. Instead of handing over to me with boldness, the worship leader whispered very quietly into the microphone, "That was a beautiful time with the Lord and as we get into the Word now I know you will be blessed."

Him and the worship team quietly took their seats as I stood up. Once up front I saw that many of the congregation still had their heads bowed. Some were looking around and others were fidgeting. An uncomfortable silence hung in the air. I felt like every noise I made walking in my clunky high heels reverberated through the room.

I felt almost bad having to break everyone out of the silence to begin my message.

Give preachers all over the world like me a break! Hand it to us nicely. Be Polite. Get the emotions up again. When your song ends, and the Lord has spoken the time has long past for pregnant pauses.

You can say something like, "Well let's end off in another one of our favorite songs. We've had a wonderful time in the presence of the Lord this evening, but let's shout one more time and then we are going to hand over to our speaker for the Word."

Then get in there and sing your song until everybody feels nice and full of life again. Get their hearts pumping, some oxygen through to their brain so that they wake up and then you can hand over.

If you don't have a song, you can still end with a little bit of emotion.

You don't want to talk in spiritual whispered tones, "Well, we've come to an end now. It's been a good time in the presence of the Lord!" And then try to walk away quietly only to trip over something and scare everybody half to death.

Instead say something with high emotion along the lines of, "Thank you for a wonderful time together! I've been so blessed by what God has done today and I look forward to our next meeting. Now we have Apostle "so and so" speaking today. I know he was up late last night still preparing his notes but I know that you feel like me. You cannot wait to hear what he has got to share. So I'm going to hand over now, and I want you all to be prepared and ready to receive. Apostle, the microphone is yours."

You hand it over. You give him the microphone. He picks up the microphone and probably says something like, "Thank you for the introduction."

Then you can take your seat. You feel good. The speaker feels good. The people feel good. And you've completed a successful worship session.

Now I know that this seems like a lot of principles. You probably have to go through this a few times but try to just remember the pictures.

Remember, you are in charge of the meeting. God has you in His hand. This should be your time to shine just like King David did. Dance with all of your might. Sing with all of your might and you will bring the power of the Lord.

CHAPTER 14

Prophesying Publically

Chapter 14 – Prophesying Publically

The Rules of Engagement

It is one thing to get an order and another thing to carry it out. If you look at a typical battlefield there are the generals who lay out the plan and then pass down the orders. However, it is the job of the rest of the officers to take those orders and to make them work.

It is for them to train the men and to give them direction. In the same way, the Lord has a plan for His Church and He will pass down His orders to you. It is then for you to implement them. Now as one having been in ministry, I know that receiving God's orders and carrying them out can be two different things.

This rings true especially of public ministry. You might have the anointing and even receive a word for the Lord's people, but the question here is how to make that word as effective as possible.

There are many good principles that you can use when it comes to public ministry and I want to begin by laying this out clearly for you. It is one thing to flow in the Gifts of the Spirit, but it is another all together to take what God is giving to you and to feed it to the people.

You see, the best lessons for ministry are the ones you have learned through living them along the way. So I will be taking some of my own experiences and lessons and sharing them with you in this chapter. My hope is that as you learn from some of my experiences that you will avoid some of the pitfalls awaiting you.

Step 1: Receive the Vision

Think back on the last time you heard a prophetic word brought in a public meeting. In a day and age when the prophetic ministry is being embraced more and more, it is easy to find a church that allows the prophets to stand up and speak.

However, no matter how exciting it might be to stand up and give such a prophetic word, think back a little. What exactly do you remember from the words you heard over the years? Perhaps, you remember how they made you feel.

You might remember the main concept or the picture that the person shared. In fact, I guarantee that if you remember anything at all, it is the picture that they painted with their words.

This brings me to my point right away. You see, people will remember pictures.

So I want you to have a clear picture of how you can minister publically in a way that is simple and that brings rest. Let's be honest if the Lord has ever used you to bring a prophetic word publically, the first time you feel so nervous!

You hope that you do not mess up. That is why starting by sharing a vision is the best first step in flowing in public ministry.

This is simple and you do not need to be a prophet for years to flow in this way. You can simply receive a vision from the Lord and share the interpretation. By doing this, you will be ministering to God's people. I think that with so much hype over the prophetic ministry that everyone is seeking all of the Gifts of the Spirit at once.

We forget the basics of why we are flowing in the gifts in the first place and that is to just minister to God's people.

Visions minister! When you are going through a difficult time in your life, all you need is that word of encouragement.

Step 2: Share Interpretation

In previous chapters, I shared that when you receive a vision that you can just share it as you received it with a person. This rule does not apply to the public meeting.

Before you stand up and share a vision or an impression in a public meeting, you need to have an understanding of its interpretation first. You see, no one can jump up and say, "Well I identify with that!" And so add to the interpretation.

This does not edify the Body. It would be like standing up and speaking in tongues and not following through with the interpretation. Apostle Paul says,

> **1 Corinthians 14:5** *I wish you all spoke with tongues, but even more that you prophesied; for he who prophesies is greater than he who speaks with tongues, unless indeed he interprets, that the church may receive edification.*

Now it is one thing to receive a vision in personal ministry, but another publically. In personal ministry, you will receive a vision that you might not know the interpretation to right away. However, as you share it, it makes perfect sense to the person.

When the Lord gives a message to His Body in a public meeting, He is going to give it with an interpretation. The reason is that the vision will mean different things to different people. And so you must focus that revelation and apply it to the hearts of the people.

Just sharing the vision is not good enough. If you receive a vision to share during the praise and worship of the public meeting, you should also have an impression of what that vision means.

If you don't, do you know what that means? It means that you do not have a good knowledge of the Word! Do you know why? It is because all of the symbols in your visions can be found in Scripture. So if you are struggling to interpret any visions that the Lord is giving to you, then it is a good time to get into the

Word. Without the Word as your foundation, you will flounder.

The problem is that a lot of people stand up and try to share their vision without having a clue of the interpretation and so just make something up. They start adding what they feel and think, but it has absolutely nothing to do with what God is trying to say at all.

Be Clear on This Point

When the Lord gives you a vision in a public meeting, it is for the purpose of edifying and maturing of the saints. It is a message to the church to produce faith, hope and love so that when they leave the meeting, they do so with an image of what God wanted to tell them.

Imagine that you are in a public meeting and you are in praise and worship. As you are worshiping the Lord, you see a waterfall. In the spirit you see some people running towards the waterfall, splashing around in it. On the other side, you see some people shying away from the water. What would you say this vision means?

Well, what does water speak of in Scripture? It speaks of the outpouring of the spirit. It is a picture of the rivers of living water that flow out of our spirits! This water that you are seeing in the spirit is speaking of the anointing of the Lord.

When you know this, then the interpretation is clear. There are some that are thirsty for God and run towards Him. However, there are others that are afraid. It is easy to then apply the vision. You can say, "Do not be afraid! You can come into His presence and He will wash away all the dirt."

Isn't that simple? From there as you start sharing your vision, you can break out into prophecy.

Progression to Prophecy

I flow like this all of the time. In fact, it was the way I started to prophesy in the public meeting. I stood up to share a vision and then as I started to share the interpretation and what I felt the Lord was saying, it just bubbled up out of my spirit.

The next thing I knew, I was prophesying! So if you are not used to bringing prophetic words in the public meeting, then this is the best place to begin. Start by sharing the vision and then follow on to share the interpretation.

No Interpretation?

What happens if you do not receive an interpretation to a vision? If you are in a public meeting, then you need to sit down and wait until you do. The best you can do is to ask the Holy Spirit for a confirmation.

Often someone else in the meeting will share something that will line up perfectly with what you are seeing - opening the way for you to stand up and share.

Step 3: Minister

There is no use standing up in a public meeting and saying something like, "The Lord gives me a vision of dry bones."

And so…?

What does that mean exactly? Well, let us take a look at the Word. We have the illustration of Ezekiel and the dry bones. The bones were brought together and brought back to life. Perhaps the Lord is saying that there is death and that He wants to bring life to those that feel dead.

So what will you stand up and share? Will you say, "The Lord says that everyone here is dry and that you are like dry bones."

Well, I guess that is a start. You shared your vision, you shared your interpretation, but what is the next step? The next step is to minister! What is the solution if you are dry and thirsty?

According to the Word, there is only one solution and His name is Jesus Christ! He stood up and said to the crowds, "I am the water of life, whoever drinks of me will never thirst again."

Unfortunately, though we have two extremes:

1. We have those that do not know the interpretation and so make up the biggest load of garbage.

2. There are those that do in fact have the interpretation to the vision, but do not apply the ministry afterwards that brings the revelation to life. Using my illustration of the waterfall, if you share the vision and the interpretation that there are some who are afraid to enter in, will you leave it there?

Instead you must encourage the people and motivate them to come into His presence. Follow the vision through and minister.

It is when you follow through with this step that you will receive further revelation, prophetic words, decrees and function in many of the other Gifts of the Spirit. It will depend on what God wants to tell His people at that time.

Draw the people into the presence of the Lord. Perhaps your revelation is a lovely one of the Lord Jesus walking through the church and putting His hands on people. You can share that you see the Lord Jesus and that He is there to meet every need.

You can encourage the people by saying, "Just reach out and allow the Lord to meet your need, no matter what it is. He loves you and is here to touch you right now. You do not need to be afraid or feel that He will pass you over. No, He is there for you right now."

You see, by starting with the vision and then moving onto the interpretation, it is like getting a ball rolling. You start getting a bit more comfortable with standing up there. By the time you are into sharing the interpretation the anointing has kicked in and you do not feel as nervous any longer.

Unless the revelation is applied, you would only have put on a show and not been effective. So here are three steps for you to remember regarding public ministry.

> **Step 1:** Receive the Vision
>
> **Step 2:** Share Interpretation
>
> **Step 3:** Minister

A Personal Tip

Now here is a personal tip to keep in mind. You know prophets have a terrible flaw when it comes to ministry. We tend to babble. We can talk and talk and talk. We can go on for hours. **So my tip here is:**

Learn to know when to shut up!

So when you feel the flow of anointing stop, even if you are in the middle of a sentence - shut up. Do not labor your point and go on after the anointing has left, because you will end up stealing what you just gave the people.

By Colette Toach

So learn when to share and when not to share.

Understanding Revelation Given Publically

It is important to remember that not every revelation given in the public meeting is for everyone. Perhaps you are in a public meeting and during praise and worship you are seeking the Lord for yourself. You are giving the Lord your cares when you see a vision.

That vision is not for the entire church. Remember, you will see visions according to what you are praying for. So that vision is clearly for you. Do not jump and share that personal vision with the entire congregation.

On the other hand, if you are the one leading the praise and worship and you are focused on leading the people into the presence of the Lord. As you receive a vision, it is going to be for the church as a whole.

General Prophecy in Public Meeting

It is a modern trend during this time for prophets to jump up and give prophetic words to specific individuals in public. In my opinion, this is something that should be done in private. Otherwise, how can those prophetic words be followed through with real ministry?

I am not ashamed to say that I am a bit old fashioned when it comes to giving prophecy to the church. I believe that general prophecy should be given to a group in a public meeting, while personal prophecy, should be reserved for one on one ministry.

I cover this in complete detail in the *Prophetic Functions* book. (The Prophet Field Guide Series)

There is just something very powerful and unifying in giving a general prophecy that is for an entire group. This is something that we function in as a group every time we get together for a meeting or to just worship the Lord.

When the Lord gives us a general prophetic word as a team, it feels good for the Lord to say, "This is what I am doing with you as a team or as a church." It brings such unity! It is a powerful way as a prophet to bring unity in the Church.

However, if you are in the habit of singling people out all of the time, what bothers me the most is that there are so many there that desire a touch from God and are not spoken over. They go away from that meeting saying, "That's great, he got a word. God loves him and not me."

I would hate to leave a meeting where I ministered knowing that there were people thinking that in their hearts.

Bringing Maturity

That is why general prophesy in a public meeting is so important. You as a prophet hold in your hands the power to bring unity in the Body of Christ.

There is no better way to do that than in the public meeting under the inspiration of the Holy Spirit.

When you share just the simple vision that you received, everyone can walk away saying, "I heard from God today! That word was just for me." Even though you gave it as a general prophecy, each one there can reach out and say, "That is God speaking to me." You edify the Body as a whole.

You mature the body of Christ and bring them that much closer to the Lord. Do not get hung up on trying to flow in all of the Gifts of the Spirit at once and trying to give out prophetic words left, right and center.

Just minister to God's people; whether you do that by sharing a vision or by giving a prophetic word or just by sharing something you sense in your spirit, do it with all of your might. In all things, let your motivation be to bring maturity and unity.

Have it in your heart at all times to bless God's people. When your motivation is right, the Lord will anoint you and your words will go out like a double-edged sword that will accomplish that for which it was sent!

When your heart is right before the Lord, the visions and your understanding of them will flow. You will experience things in a way that you never have before.

Breaking The Rules – Group Intercession

Now there is a time when you will break the rule of always sharing an interpretation. A good example of this is if you have got together with a group for the purpose of intercession. It is quite common to get just a piece of the picture of what God wants to say.

What we always find when we pray as a group is that the Lord will give us each a piece of a picture. One of us will get a vision or just an impression in our spirits. Then the Lord will give someone else the other half. Between all of us we will get the full interpretation.

Then together we will pray it through. You see that is learning to work as a team and just like in personal ministry - you might not have the full interpretation when you receive the vision.

CHAPTER 15

Practical Ministry Guidelines

Chapter 15 – Practical Ministry Guidelines

Following on from our last chapter I am going to lay things out clearly on how you should be approaching public ministry – especially as it relates to flowing in all of the Gifts of the Spirit.

So pick up your pen and paper and make some notes. Compare your past experiences with what I share now and notch down any mistakes you made as an opportunity for maturity!

1. You Should Produce Faith, Hope and Love

You will hear that often from me. Ask yourself, "Does this ministry produce faith, hope and love? Does it bring unity and does it exhort?" If not, then do not speak and wait for confirmation.

Anything that you share should bring about positive action.

2. Do Not Guess What Your Vision Might Mean

Do not try to figure out the interpretation logically. Get into the Word and find out what God is saying. Do not try to guess according to your culture, because that will always change. Having worked with many different cultures, I am so grateful for the Word!

There are many pictures that evoke a different meaning to people, depending on where they are from. However, the Word is universal and you can apply it to any culture. Whether I receive a vision in South Africa, Germany or the United States, the Word means the same thing.

I have met believers from all over the world and do you know what? Their visions had the same symbols as mine. It is because the Word of God is our standard. The visions that the Lord gives to other cultures are the same as He gives to you. We are after all, one Body.

The Lord speaks in types and shadows and He will take them from His Word.

3. Do Not Read Your Own Ideas Into the Revelation

As you are in praise and worship, you look over to this guy in the congregation and he looks plain bored. He is not even making an effort and then later on you receive the nice vision of that waterfall I shared about earlier.

You think to yourself, "Yeah, that word is for you!"

And so you start blurting out, "You are not getting into the presence of the Lord and as a result the Lord is not going to bless you. You are not going to feel His presence and you will go away feeling dry."

That is not what the Lord is saying, is it? No, He is not shouting at those who are not experiencing His presence. He is trying to woo those who are afraid to come into His presence. Not only that, but you could not be more wrong.

That man might just have more of a hunger for the Word and does not really get excited about praise and worship as much as you do. Trust me, I come across different people all the time. Do not be so quick to judge, because the prophet that was dancing a hole in the floor during worship is the one nodding off during your sermon.

One thing I learned early in ministry is that you cannot judge by what you see. It takes the Lord to look into the heart and without revelation you have no clue what is really going on inside of anyone.

So do not think that public ministry is a fantastic opportunity to get your message across. Revelation is something that is the Lord's origination and not your own. That is why it is called "revelation." So when you receive a vision and your first impression is, "Yes! That is exactly what I thought God would say." I would hold off on sharing that.

It could just be that you are speaking what is in your mind and not the true revelation of what God wants to say. Revelation is something you did not know or "get" before. If your revelation feels obvious and logical, I would suggest waiting for confirmation.

If a pastor has been going a way that you do not approve of and the Lord gives you a vision during a meeting, do not think that this is the perfect time to get your message across to him. That is not the heart of the Lord.

4. Visions do Not Always Need to be Shared in a Public Meeting.

Be sensitive when you receive a revelation. If the Lord has given you a personal revelation, you do not need to share that. The same applies if the Lord gives you something to share with an individual in a public meeting.

The last thing you want to do is stand up in that meeting, point to that poor, unsuspecting churchgoer hidden in the corner and to tell them what God is saying right now. Wait until after the meeting and share with them in love. Of course, using tact will also take you a long way!

Know what is for the group, what is for an individual and what is for you. Now this takes a little bit of trial and error and you will learn the difference through experience. Again, the best rule of thumb to determine whom the vision is for, is to consider what you were doing or praying for at the time.

If you are the one leading the meeting, then it is clear that you will get revelation for the group. However, the Lord could also give you something for an individual. Rather wait until the end of the meeting to share.

A True Story

There was an incident where a prophet was leading the meeting and received a revelation for someone in the congregation regarding their marriage. So right in the middle of the service she pointed them out from the back of the room and said that there was division in their marriage and that the Lord wanted to fix it.

Now her revelation might have been spot on, but I do not need to tell you how that couple reacted! They were new to the group and did not know anyone there. Not only did they feel humiliated, but they also refused the vision outright!

A true ministry opportunity was lost right there and the Lord never got to do what he had planned for that couple. How many others have suffered in the same way at the hands of prophets who simply do not know the simple art of diplomacy?

Instead that prophet should have approached that couple after the meeting and stuck up a conversation. It would have been a good time to introduce herself and to find out a little bit about them.

Then when they had let down their guard a little, she could have shared that while she was leading worship that the Lord showed her a division that the enemy was trying to bring in their relationship.

If they were open to receive that, she could proceed and minister by the spirit and then follow them up with counsel.

It is clear why many would rather just stand up front and share revelations. It takes a lot less effort than stepping forward and following through with real ministry. What you have to decide is if you want to look good "up front" or if you want to see real change in the lives of God's people.

Prophetic Preaching

I could not stand to preach without the use of visions! Although preaching prophetically is really a lot of fun, because you tend to "chase the rabbit" quite a bit, you can get a bit long winded.

In personal experience, I think that the most important thing to do here is to be aware of the visions that you are receiving. I guarantee that you are receiving a lot of visions when you minister or when you preach, but that you are just not identifying it.

The most practical thing to do to make your prophetic preaching come to life is just to be aware of those visions. Whether you are standing behind the pulpit at your local church or getting together in a home for a home church meeting - be aware of the visions God is giving to you.

They will not only come when you minister personally or publically, but will come when you are preaching as well.

Being Aware of Visions

Now you do not need to stop in the middle of your message and say, "Oh! I had this vision!" That is a bit cheesy don't you think? (Especially if you are in a home church meeting.) Rather jump straight to the point. Consider Jesus and how He shared parables.

Did He have to stop and say, "And I saw a vision of the sower and he was walking along…"

He just shared. He was so chilled out. He could walk along and share so easily. I function this way all of the time. I will be sharing with someone and I will get a vision and instead of saying, "I see this vision…" I would simply go straight to the picture.

Say for example I see new seeds being planted into the soil as I am chatting with someone. Should I stop and say, "I see this seed and it is being planted…" No, it is not always necessary when you are in casual conversation and it is definitely not necessary when you are preaching!

There might be times when you want to share a specific vision with them, but if you stop and do that for every vision you receive, you will bore your hearers to death.

Rather say it like Jesus said it. "Your life is like this... it is like planting a seed into the soil. Just like it takes a seed, time to be planted and germinate, it is the same in your spiritual life. It takes time to develop new things in your life, so if you will be diligent to water the good things that God has given to you, you will see the fruit of it."

Just be natural and use the visions that God gives you as illustrations for your preaching. You do not need to be super spiritual. Just be normal and allow people to relate to you. Say rather, "You know your situation reminds me of this..."

As you learn to develop using visions in preaching you will come to a point where you cannot live without them! How else do you think I can share the illustrations I do here? I receive them in vision. The Lord gives them to me in my spirit all of the time.

I do not need to stop after every paragraph and say, "The Lord gave me a vision there!"

For people to respect you and to want to receive from you, they need to be able to relate to you. Jesus was certainly like that. He came across as a normal man that spoke about the normal things of life. However, when they touched His garment, they discovered that He was anything but normal!

The people loved Jesus. Sure the odd Pharisee wanted to crucify him, but for the most part, the crowds flocked to him. Even though they knew He was a Master, He did not go around acting super spiritual.

In the same way, be real in your ministry and in your preaching. Let the same be said of you. Rather come across as normal and approachable and then when people come to receive, they will see that you are anything but normal. They will come and truly be touched by God.

Conclusion

When you first stand to minister, the revelation starts with an initial impression or vision. Then as you share that you feel, the anointing and more words and visions start to flow.

After that everything will suddenly become quiet in your spirit. You feel yourself having to "find the next word." Now, this does not mean that you are being told of God to push through to second wind! It means that it is time to shut up and to give someone else a chance to talk.

Visions are like signposts along the highway. They are sets of directions leading you towards what God wants to do in His church. All you need to do is follow them one at a time. It is as simple as looking up and seeing an exit or an onramp and taking it.

Just follow the billboards - that is what visions are. Whether you are giving a prophetic word or you are standing up and sharing or preaching, follow the signboards. Then when they stop, you have arrived at your destination.

CHAPTER 16

A Note on Handling Rejection

Chapter 16 – A Note on Handling Rejection

It is tough when you have the truth, but the person you are sharing with just does not want to hear it. You have shared your vision or given your interpretation and they refuse it outright.

You shared what you received from the Lord and they responded with an outright, "No. I cannot relate at all. I do not believe that is what the vision or dream means".

What Not to Do

Do not make the same mistake as many arrogant ministers and grab the poor guy by the scruff of the neck and say, "If you do not receive this revelation you are going to burn in hell! You will lose everything and God will prove to you that *my* word is true!"

We are told that Jesus attended a little party at the house of a Pharisee and there proceeded to insult them by saying that they put on a good face for others to see but that their hearts were black with sin. They were like cups, clean on the outside, but dirty on the inside. (Luke 11:39)

This was not exactly a message that was well received. Jesus made His point, got up and went home. You do not read of Him flying across the table, grabbing His host by the neck and saying, "You better believe what I say or you will die!"

No, those Pharisees made the choice for themselves. Jesus had no interest in justifying Himself. He knew what He said was the truth and He did not need them to accept Him or that truth.

Jesus spoke the truth - it was for them to receive it. They did not. He went home. They condemned themselves.

What to Do

If you used wisdom in the first place when sharing a revelation, then you can say, "Perhaps, the vision I had is symbolic or a picture of how you feel right now."

Or "Perhaps, the Lord will give you further clarification on the dream at another time."

You can perhaps press your point just once more, but if they refuse outright, there is no point in forcing it. Jesus said Himself that a prophet was not welcome in his own hometown.

If the Son of God Himself could not do miracles in a place where the people would not receive Him, then what chance do you have of getting someone to receive from you? The Lord never forces His will or His love on us. He offers it freely. If your ministry is rejected, accept it graciously like Jesus did.

He wept over Jerusalem and said how much He desired to gather it as a hen under His wings, but how they had refused and sealed their own doom. Jesus did not walk through the streets and beg them to reconsider. He made His offer and when they rejected it, He went on to die for them, offering salvation to those that took advantage of that offer.

Ministers sometimes get the idea that if they got a revelation that it is for them to deliver it and to make sure that it brings conviction and change. If this is what you think, then you are in for a rough ride in ministry. The Word says that the watchman on the wall is meant to announce the oncoming enemy. It is for the people to receive that word and to act on it.

It is for you to give out what God has given to you, but it is not for you to force them to receive it. You present the truth with tact and under the anointing. Be bold in sharing the truth in love and then it is in the hearer's hands. You cannot force them to like you.

You cannot force them to have faith. You cannot force them to accept your revelation. You can only play your part and then wait for the Holy Spirit to do His.

I do not think that you ever get used to rejection or people turning their backs on you. However, I promise that if you are diligent to do this God's way and to show grace and love, that things will turn around.

Perhaps this person rejected your counsel or ministry outright this time, but because you handled it with grace, they will be open for it next time. Where before they turned their back on you, the next time they will open their arms to receive what you have.

The Final Word

The Final Word

There was a season when all the Lord had me do was learn. However, that season came to an end and I had to apply what I had learned. When a demon manifested in front of me for the first time, I did not stop to think about principles. There was just no time. I did what poured out of my spirit.

You see that is the best part about being a blood bought child of God. You have the Holy Spirit inside of you. You will read how the Scripture often says how the Holy Spirit quickened everything Jesus had said to the Disciples later on.

There was so much that Jesus taught them in those three years He was on the earth. In fact, He accomplished and taught so much that all the books of the world could not have contained it. Do you think that the Disciples had incredible memories?

No, before Jesus left them, He said that He was sending the Holy Spirit to remind them and to teach them of all things. It is good to take a season to learn, but in the heat of the moment it is the Holy Spirit who will burn these principles into your heart.

If you really want these principles to stick, it will take a lot more than just reading them. It will take some good mentorship and pressure from your circumstances. Like I have said many times… you have to live it.

By Colette Toach

So if the Lord has put you under a mentor or a spiritual parent, combine that with what you have learned here and these principles will not just be "principles" any longer. They will become a way of life for you.

In our ministry, Craig and I teach what I have given you here to all of our team and spiritual children. We give them the opportunity to lead and to step out and minister. Do you know when the most change comes though?

The change comes when we step back and have the courage to let them fail. It is when you fail that you learn the greatest lessons of all. Could you experience conviction if you had no sin? Could you rejoice in God's grace if you were never lost?

Could you know real love If you had not suffered hurt at one time or another? It is when we face tough times and even failure that we realize how dependent we are on God and how much we need to change.

So in amongst learning what to do, I hope that you have taken time to look at your mistakes as well and turned them around for good. It is never fun to fail, but you do not need to fail at the same thing again. Take your mistakes. Confront your weaknesses and allow the Lord to "work all things together for good."

After I have allowed one of my team to fail, I walk them through the principles and show them their weakness. Then I give them a chance to try again to succeed. The Lord does the same with you. The reason is, because He trusts the Holy Spirit inside of you!

You should learn to trust the Holy Spirit as well, because at the end of the day, He is the ultimate spiritual parent and mentor. Allow Him to challenge you and to make you live each principle. Then as you have overcome and as you rise up higher in your ministry, take the time to pass these principles on to those that God sends you.

If you can do that, then together we will equip the body of Christ. Together we will be fulfilling the full purpose of what the fivefold ministry has been called to do in the Church.

About the Author

Born in Bulawayo, Zimbabwe and raised in South Africa, Colette had a zeal to serve the Lord from a young age. Coming from a long line of Christian leaders and having grown up as a pastor's kid she is no stranger to the realities of ministry. Despite having to endure many hardships such as her parent's divorce, rejection, and poverty, she continues to follow after the Lord passionately. Overcoming these obstacles early in her life has built a foundation of compassion and desire to help others gain victory in their lives.

Since then, the Lord has led Colette, with her husband Craig Toach, to establish *Apostolic Movement International,* a ministry to train and minister to Christian leaders all over the world, where they share all the wisdom that the Lord has given them through each and every time they chose to walk through the refining fire in their personal lives, as well as in ministry.

In addition, Colette is a fantastic cook, an amazing mom to not only her 4 natural children, but to her numerous spiritual children all over the world. Colette is also a renowned author, mentor, trainer and a woman that has great taste in shoes! The scripture to "be all things to all men" definitely applies here, and the Lord keeps adding to that list of things each and every day.

How does she do it all? Experience through every book and teaching the life of an apostle firsthand, and get the insight into how the call of God can make every aspect of your life an incredible adventure.

Read more at www.colette-toach.com

Connect with Colette Toach on Facebook!
www.facebook.com/ColetteToach

Check Colette out on Amazon.com at:
www.amazon.com/author/colettetoach

By Colette Toach

Recommendations by the Author

Note: All reference of AMI refers to Apostolic Movement International.

If you enjoyed this book, we know you will also love the following books.

How to Get People to Follow You

By Colette Toach

"You have the potential for something magnificent, but until you can get your boat into the water and unfurl those sails... you are not going anywhere." - Colette Toach

Colette pours out leadership secrets straight from the Throne Room that will make you the kind of leader others want to follow. No more hitting your head on the wall. No more being the only one excited about your vision.

Sharing from her own failures and triumphs, Colette hands you the keys to your success as a leader.

Just like Gideon, David, Peter and Moses who weren't born leaders, but were forged into leaders - so you can have the kind of crowd that will follow you anywhere. There is a strong leader inside of you yet. One who is admired, loved and sought out! Learn how to get people to follow you and fulfill the vision that God has given you.

Mentorship 101

By Colette Toach

Mentorship! What picture comes into your mind? It is a very hot topic in the church today, but clear teaching is lacking. In this series, you will not only find out what the role and purpose of a mentor is, but you will see the heart that is required!

God is raising up His Mighty Warrior, and if you want to be on the front lines of equipping God's people, this series will show you how!

Strategies of War

By Colette Toach

Warfare is a very important part of our Christian lives. Whether we know it or not, the enemy is always looking for a way to take down the children of God. Now it is time that you learned how to stop taking the hits and take the fight to him instead.

No more allowing the enemy to have his way. Take back your land and remove him from your life for good.

Your victory is at hand. So, take hold and allow Colette Toach to guide and teach you the strategy to tearing down the kingdom of darkness

By Colette Toach

Everything is Awesome When You are Part of the Team

By Colette Toach

Ladies and gentlemen, God has a new plan and a new idea for us - He is creating teams. He is raising up teams that can take down the enemy, teams that can stand with one another and teams that will follow through with all that He has asked of them.

Now, how does this pertain to you exactly? Well, that is what this book is here for - to help you find your team and to train you into being a part of that team.

The Apostolic Handbook

By Colette Toach

This book has the potential to not only confirm your calling, but launch you headfirst into the training that will take you to apostolic office.

If you have the suspicion or the strong conviction that you have been called to be an apostle, then you are on for the adventure of a lifetime. In fact, you hold in your hands a treasure map that gives you clear directions.

Pastor Teacher School

www.pastorteacherschool.com

The Lord had not called me to simply educate. He called me to train. To shape and equip His mighty warriors. I was not allowed any shortcuts. So my training never ended. To this day, He continues to shape and change me. With each lesson I learn, I pass it on to those He sends me.

This is the core of what you will find in the Pastor Teacher School - **Education by means of training**. An interactive experience that causes you to live and walk out the call that God has given to you.

Every lesson is practical, direct, and it... equips! Along with the knowledge, you gain experience and the steps to fulfilling your ministry right now.

There are many who are willing to sell you a book in the Church today, but not many who are willing to *train* you. This is what burns in us and if the Lord has sent you to our ministry, then that is what you can expect from us. A no-nonsense, boot camp that is designed to train you for your calling.

You bring your passion for God to the table and we will bring the anointing and skill to train you into what God has intended. **Together... we will change the world!**

- Colette Toach

Contact Information

To check out our wide selection of materials, go to: www.ami-bookshop.com

Do you have any questions about any products?

Contact us at: +1 (760) 466 - 7679
(8am to 5pm California Time, Weekdays Only)

E-mail Address: admin@ami-bookshop.com

Postal Address:

>   A.M.I.
>   5663 Balboa Ave #416
>   San Diego, CA 92111, USA

Facebook Page:
http://www.facebook.com/ApostolicMovementInternational

YouTube Page:
https://www.youtube.com/c/ApostolicMovementInternational

Twitter Page: https://twitter.com/apmoveint

Amazon.com Page: www.amazon.com/author/colettetoach

AMI Bookshop – It's not Just Knowledge, It's **Living Knowledge**

www.ingramcontent.com/pod-product-compliance
Lightning Source LLC
Chambersburg PA
CBHW072003150426
43194CB00008B/977